A HISTORY OF A
AMERICAN PO

African American poetry is as old as America itself, yet this touch-stone of American identity is often overlooked. In this critical history of African American poetry, from its origins in the transatlantic slave trade, to present day hip-hop, Lauri Ramey traces African American poetry from slave songs to today's award-winning poets. Covering a wide range of styles and forms, canonical figures like Phillis Wheatley (1753–84) and Paul Laurence Dunbar (1872–1906) are brought side by side with lesser known poets who explored diverse paths of bold originality. Calling for a revised and expanded canon, Ramey shows how some poems were suppressed while others were lauded, while also examining the role of music, women, innovation, and art as political action in African American poetry. Conceiving of a new canon reveals the influential role of African American poetry in defining and reflecting the United States at all points in the nation's history.

LAURI RAMEY is Xiaoxiang Scholars Program Distinguished Professor at Hunan Normal University. Her previous publications include *Slave Songs and the Birth of African American Poetry* (2010), *The Heritage Series of Black Poetry, 1962–1975* (2008), *Black British Writing* (with R. Victoria Arana, 2009), and a two-volume anthology set (with Aldon Lynn Nielsen) *Every Goodbye Ain't Gone: Innovative Poetry by African Americans* (2006) and *What I Say: Innovative Poetry by Black Writers in America* (2015).

A HISTORY OF AFRICAN AMERICAN POETRY

LAURI RAMEY

Hunan Normal University

CAMBRIDGE
UNIVERSITY PRESS

CAMBRIDGE
UNIVERSITY PRESS

University Printing House, Cambridge CB2 8BS, United Kingdom

One Liberty Plaza, 20th Floor, New York, NY 10006, USA

477 Williamstown Road, Port Melbourne, VIC 3207, Australia

314-321, 3rd Floor, Plot 3, Splendor Forum, Jasola District Centre, New Delhi - 110025, India

103 Penang Road, #05-06/07, Visioncrest Commercial, Singapore 238467

Cambridge University Press is part of the University of Cambridge.

It furthers the University's mission by disseminating knowledge in the pursuit of
education, learning and research at the highest international levels of excellence.

www.cambridge.org
Information on this title: www.cambridge.org/9781108995559
DOI: 10.1017/9781139548939

First published 2019
First paperback edition 2021

A catalogue record for this publication is available from the British Library

ISBN 978-1-107-03547-8 Hardback
ISBN 978-1-108-99555-9 Paperback

Contents

Illustrations

Acknowledgments

I am indebted to many individuals and institutions for their kindness and enthusiasm in helping me complete this book. My research was greatly aided by a Security Pacific Fellowship from the Huntington Library, Art Collections, and Botanical Gardens, and two Visiting Fellowships from Goldsmiths College, University of London.

My sincere thanks to California State University, Los Angeles for invaluable support through course release and funding for travel and research. I am grateful to have been awarded a Creative Leave Grant, two Sabbatical Leaves, Barry Munitz Fellowship, NEH American Communities Program/Joseph A. Bailey II, MD Fellowship, and two Katherine Carter Fund grants. Encouragement for my research – as well as its application to my teaching – from Cal State LA administrators, staff, faculty, and students played a significant and profoundly appreciated role in this book's development and progress.

Materials from special collections greatly added to my understanding of this field, and the support of curators and staff members was of inestimable value. For their outstanding help and knowledge I would like to thank Curator Scott Krafft, Sigrid Pohl Perry, Kathleen Battle, and the staff of the Charles Deering McCormick Library of Special Collections in the Northwestern University Library; Executive Director Lloyd L. Clayton and Librarian Herb Cobbs of the Mayme A. Clayton Library and Museum; Sarah Bernstein and the National Library of Scotland; Julie Ramwell, Special Collections Librarian of the John Rylands Library at the University of Manchester; Ken Grossi, College Archivist at Oberlin College Archives, Sophie Davis in the Oberlin College Reference Department, and Jeremy Smith, Special Collections Librarian in the Oberlin Conservatory Library; Special Collections Research Center staff at the University of Chicago Library; the staff of Special Collections and Archives, Goldsmiths College, University of London; the staff of the Huntington Library; the staff of the Vivian G. Harsh Research Collection of Afro-American History and Literature at the Chicago Public Library; the Brown University Library staff; Curator of Manuscripts Joellen ElBashir and the staff of the Moorland-Spingarn Research Center at Howard University; the staff of Special Collections in the Fisk University Library; Colonel Rob Burrows, Curator of the Ivanhoe Wheelhouse Museum and Art Gallery; the University Archives and Harvey Library at Hampton University; and the reference staff of the John F. Kennedy Memorial Library at California State University, Los Angeles.

For creating such a supportive environment for my scholarship and research at Hunan Normal University, I am deeply grateful to Executive President Li Min, President Jiang Hongxin, Dean Zeng Yanyu, students and faculty in the Foreign Studies College, and colleagues at the British and American Poetry Research Center and *Journal of Foreign Languages and Cultures*.

It is humbling to look back at my correspondence for this project and realize how much it has benefited from information, advice, and encouragement from so many colleagues and friends. I am particularly grateful to Charles Bernstein, Tony Bolden, Connie Corley, David Crittendon, Rita Dove, Ron Fair, Shelley Fisher Fishkin, Sesshu Foster, Sarah Frankland, Joanne V. Gabbin, Wendy Garen, Maryemma Graham, Arthur Greenwald, Doug Hales, William J. Harris, David Henderson, Juan Felipe Herrera, Anthony Joseph, Douglas Kearney, Hank Lazer, Luo Lianggong, Nathaniel Mackey, Jean-Philippe Marcoux, Lenard D. Moore, Harryette Mullen, Nie Zhenzhao, Aldon Lynn Nielsen, Eugene B. Redmond, Ishmael Reed, Hollis Robbins, Susan M. Schultz, giovanni singleton, Mike Soldatenko, Mike Sonksen, A. B. Spellman, Fred Viebahn, Jerry W. Ward, Jr., Tyrone Williams, and Jon Woodson. I also remember with deepest respect and affection those who have passed on but whose formative impact remains: Paul Breman, Dieter Georgi, Michael S. Harper, Calvin C. Hernton, F. Abiola Irele, Clara Smith, Lorenzo Thomas, and Tom Weatherly.

I am grateful to the conferences and universities that invited me to give lectures on the contents of this book as it progressed; I greatly benefited from the thoughtful feedback. Early versions of materials revised for this volume appeared in *The Fight and the Fiddle*, edited by Lauren K. Alleyne, *Wasafiri*, *Foreign Literature Studies*, *American Poetry Since 1945*, edited by Eleanor Spencer, *Diasporic Avant-Gardes: Experimental Poetics and Cultural Displacement*, edited by Carrie Noland and Barrett Watten, and *Black Music, Black Poetry: Blues and Jazz's Impact on African American Versification*, edited by Gordon E. Thompson. Grateful acknowledgment is expressed to the editors for enabling me to share and develop my ideas at crucial stages.

This book would not have been completed without the trust and involvement of Brigitte Shull. It is an honor that this is my third book that has benefited from her participation. Others at Cambridge University Press who have been instrumental in the editing and production process are Linda Bree, Chris Harrison, Tim Mason, Sharon McCann, and Bethany Thomas. I am grateful for the insightful advice and enthusiasm for this project from the anonymous readers. Thank you to Mike Leach for his care and skill in producing the index, and to Caroline Drake for brilliant copy-editing. Finally, I am grateful for the love and support of my family within and beyond this book: Lois and Stuart Scheyer, Marit, Max, my brothers Eric, Jim, and Steven and their families, Pamela, Anita, and Rustin in memory.

All reasonable efforts have been made to contact poets or their heirs for permission to publish poems in this volume.

"Floodsong 2: Water Moccasin's Spiritual" appears by permission of Douglas Kearney and Fence Books.

"Spyrytual" appears by permission of Russell Atkins. This poem was published in a letterpress and mimeographed pamphlet titled *Spyrytual*, published in 1966 by 7 Flowers Press in Cleveland, Ohio, the successor to d.a. levy's Renegade Press. It was released in an edition of 200 as stapled sheets in printed wrappers. © Russell Atkins. Special thanks to Russell Atkins, and to Kevin Prufer, Diane Kendig, and Robert McDonough for facilitating permission to reprint this poem.

Gregory Pardlo, "Written by Himself" from *Digest*. © 2014 by Gregory Pardlo. Reprinted with permission of the Permissions Company, Inc. on behalf of Four Way Books. www.fourwaybooks.com. All rights reserved. Special thanks to Gregory Pardlo, Vaughan Fielder, Fred Courtright, and Martha Rhodes.

"D Blues" and "Fall Down" by Calvin C. Hernton appear by gracious permission of Antone Hernton, and by courtesy of Tyler Kerington Hernton, Calvin Spencer Hernton, and Antone Christopher Hernton, who are heirs to the legacy of their grandfather.

"Song of the Decanter" by Alfred Gibbs Campbell was provided courtesy of the Hay Harris Broadside Collection in the Brown University Library.

All poems by Conrad Kent Rivers appear in *The Wright Poems* (London: Paul Breman, 1972): "Postscript to a Poem" and "Postscript" on pages 8–14, "Night Letter from Paris" on pages 16–17, and "A Mourning Letter from Paris for Richard Wright" on pages 18–19.

"Fig. 1" by giovanni singleton from *AMERICAN LETTERS: works on paper* (Marfa, TX: Canarium Books, 2018) was provided courtesy of giovanni singleton.

The images were created for this book by Andy Luo Hui and Bernard Kane.

CHAPTER I

Introduction to a Genre

Speak this because I exist.
This is my voice
These words are my words, my mouth
Speaks them, my hand writes.
I am a poet.
Calvin C. Hernton, "The Distant Drum"

African American poetry pre-dates the nation that became the United States of America and is a central part of its identity and expression. It is a major touchstone of the American literary tradition and deserves recognition for its aesthetic quality and influence on world culture. Yet this extraordinary body of writing remains under-explored as a topic of research, study, understanding, and appreciation. *A History of African American Poetry* seeks to provide critical and historical insight into this genre from its origins to the present with the hope of stimulating new ideas. As a critical study, this book does not aim to replicate or synthesize existing scholarship. It is "a" history, not "the" history. There is no pretense or possibility of being exhaustive in such an immense field, or of implying that there is a uniform perspective on issues about this diverse body of writing. Questions and controversies will be neither avoided nor resolved: they will, and should, remain alive and vital by the end of this book. My publications often have addressed formal innovation in poetry of the black diaspora. I will bring that interest to bear here in sharing the insights that I have gained through the process of researching and writing this book. A wealth of excellent critical, bibliographical, and biographical resources is readily available in this field. Most cover the poets and poems that are viewed as canonical, but a rising number address the writers and writings that have been deliberately or inadvertently excluded or forgotten. Often, these overlooked texts display qualities that affiliate them with new forms and concepts, features that would categorize texts in other forums as avant-garde, experimental, oppositional, innovative, or difficult. A central motive is to examine the theoretical and practical implications of why these texts are "missing" or invisible, and how their inclusion might impact the existing canon. This book is designed to offer a summative and illustrative overview of the genre from its origins to the present, but it has a strong mission towards revision and recuperation. Readers will be directed to many materials on commonly accepted and respected information and interpretations, as well as figures and trends that have been unjustly disregarded and which often reveal hidden continuities and progressions.

A major goal of this book is to raise questions about how and why we have inherited a fundamentally conservative canon and to think about how it might be imagined differently. I was originally drawn to the field of African American literature because it provided examples, ideas, perspectives, and encounters which struck me as essential American voices that were excluded from my education. As I looked more deeply into this rich body of writing, the texts that often seemed most compelling and revelatory were not part of the African American canon as it had evolved. This book invites attention to valuable poets and poems that have been marginalized or forgotten from the African American, American, diasporic, and Anglophone literary corpus. Since many of these writings were well known in the past, we gain important insight into which texts became alternately validated and excluded in varying iterations, which provokes speculation about the reasons.

The foundations of the African American literary tradition are in its poetry. Although this body of poetry is as diverse and varied as its individual creators, some common themes and threads appear which justify its consideration as a literary tradition: attention to both orality and print culture; themes and impacts of migration, diaspora, and transnationalism; the location and meaning of home and family; African survivals and the role of Africa; imagery of enslavement and freedom; the purpose of art as social and political action; art as defining a relationship between the individual and the community; music and musicality; art as a bridge between the present and the past; the deep and spiritual significance of land and place; play with multiple audiences and levels of address; creative and hybrid senses of diction; concerns with assimilation and authenticity; a clear pattern from the time of its origins of self-referencing, citationality, and allusion, even as it is in dialogue with the Anglo-American canon; and concern with the best critical tools to evaluate and appreciate African American poetry, including the question of whether a special theoretical lens should be developed and applied to this writing, which reflects its features, goals, and identity. This book is organized chronologically to discuss a range of poetic styles and critical perspectives, representing both oral and literary traditions, from the arrival of the first Africans in America to the current moment. Key ideas – for example, politics, race, religion, duality, identity, performance, oratory, slavery, freedom, music, Africa, America, and discrimination – recur in the chapters to demonstrate traits that define this field as cohesive and special, yet also part of larger traditions of literariness.

Two of the most important critical texts in this field are now more than forty years old: *Understanding the New Black Poetry* by Stephen Henderson and *Drumvoices: The Mission of Afro-American Poetry: A Critical History* by Eugene B. Redmond, both written during one of the most active periods of production of African American poetry and scholarship. Redmond and Henderson invited increased attention to be paid to the connections and advances in this field that reveal its fundamental cohesiveness while recognizing its tremendous diversity. Both critics call for the reconciliation of various critical commonplaces about this genre, which are sometimes perceived as schisms or parallel paths, such as its relationship to oral and English literary traditions, and its address of dual audiences. According to Henderson, "an attempt should be made in which the continuity and the wholeness of the black poetic tradition in the United States are suggested. That tradition exists on two main levels, the written and the oral, which sometimes converge."[1] Redmond writes, "From the ditties, blues, spirituals, dozens, sermons, and jokes, the poet fashioned an endless stream of poetic forms and fusions."[2] The statements by Henderson and Redmond articulate some of the fundamental premises of this book: sound, performance, visuality, and inscription are integrally connected in this tradition, which is characterized by wholeness and continuity. The wholeness indicates its central core of values and identity, and the continuity reflects its capacity to navigate change and continuously refresh itself for new times and conditions.

It is impossible to mark the precise genesis of African American poetry, but its history of documentation must begin no later than the poetic expressions of the first kidnapped Africans landing on American soil, which is often dated to 1619. Although it can only be hypothesized and

---

[1] Stephen Henderson, *Understanding the New Black Poetry: Black Speech and Black Music as Poetic References* (New York: William Morrow, 1973), p. 3.
[2] Eugene B. Redmond, *Drumvoices: The Mission of Afro-American Poetry: A Critical History* (New York: Anchor Books/Doubleday, 1976), p. 420.

imagined, as discussed in Chapter 2, I consider the African American poetic tradition to have started with the slave songs forged from African survivals, synthesized with the trauma of the Middle Passage, and radically impacted by the experience of enslavement in American plantation culture. This body of oral poetry was not transcribed until the nineteenth century – probably two hundred years or more after it was first created – but its rhythms, dictions, perspectives, rhetorical strategies, and themes initiate a context for an authentic canon to which future generations of readers and writers could refer and allude from the seventeenth to the twenty-first century. Starting with slave songs as its roots – as I have discussed in *Slave Songs and the Birth of African American Poetry* – the poetry of African Americans has been viewed as something "unique" and with a distinctive capacity to impact audiences.[3] This level of "difference" has been a significant factor in both the valuation and the depreciation of this body of poetry, which is reflected in the intertwined development of the canon and curriculum. It has generated a history of contention and claims about how best to respond to and critically evaluate this body of poetry – how and what it signifies. It has long been debated whether it should be regarded as original, authentic, and apart, or as reactive, conventional, and imitative, as only two – but abiding – perspectives. Is it a central and essential part of the larger American cultural panorama, or does it represent voices of "outsiders" coming from "the margins" to speak truth and independence to a perceived national mainstream? In the earliest eras of its critical evaluation, the enthusiasms and skepticisms in judgment reflected the fears, values, and prejudices of now distant and different times. External commentators wondered whether African American poetry and its original sources were primitive or sophisticated, high or low art, American or "foreign," random or structured, tricky or sincere, wily or childish, true "poetry" or meaningless noise. As we will see, the kernel of these lingering questions can remain implicitly buried in the discourse.

Early auditors described the slave songs as "weird," "wild," "unique," "strange," and "different" in ways that were hard to define.[4] Even

---

[3] See Lauri Ramey, *The Heritage Series of Black Poetry: A Research Compendium* (London: Routledge, 2008) and *Slave Songs and the Birth of African American Poetry* (New York: Palgrave Macmillan, 2010).

[4] Some of the early important collections and commentaries expressing this perspective on the poetry known as Negro spirituals, slave songs, or plantation verse are William Francis Allen, Charles Pickard Ware, and Lucy McKim Garrison, eds., *Slave Songs of the United States* (1867), William E. Barton, ed., *Old Plantation Hymns* (1899), E. P. Christy, ed., *Christy's Plantation Melodies* (1851), and Thomas Wentworth Higginson, *Army Life in a Black Regiment and Other Writings* (1870).

W. E. B. Du Bois, who called them "the most beautiful expression of human experience born this side of the seas" also referred to them as "weird old songs" containing "strange word[s]."[5] Though these slave songs were considered curiosities, critics disregarded their quality and originality. Some attributed their strangeness to being poor imitations of white hymns or verse. Others raised suspicions about the "foreignness" of their unknown words, sounds, and phrases. Efforts were made to "translate" these unfamiliar expressions into "comprehensible" messages. Observers were baffled by their semi-improvisatory, performative, and physical style of oral delivery and communal participation. These features contrasted with contemporaneous ideas of poems as fixed printed texts by sole authors.[6]

From its origins, African American poetry had to be inventive and cleverly subversive. Communication was an immediate challenge for kidnapped Africans, brought together on slave ships from multiple cultures, who needed to establish linguistic and social common ground. When they arrived on plantations in America, many of the enslaved people were legally deprived of literacy. Slave songs needed to be transmitted orally and serve diverse purposes efficiently. The oral tradition of Africa would have served as a strength. These sung lyrics offered the enslaved peoples a means of expressing their own theology, preserving African survivals, building community, keeping hope alive, communicating during work, relaxing with entertainment, sending messages of resistance to oppression, sharing local and political news, and carrying practical information. It is rare for a body of art to be called upon to mean so much for so many.

The perception of African American poetry as being unlike mainstream Anglo-American verse has been a double-edged sword that has followed the genre from its roots and into the present. It is expected to be "different" but only in particular ways. The peculiar criterion of "authenticity" has gone hand in hand with "otherness." The more African American poetry is viewed as "odd," the more it has seemed to be considered an "authentic" expression of the language, ideas, and experiences of its creators. As we will see with the poets who are often credited with originating this tradition, such as Phillis Wheatley, the ability to work

---

[5] Quoted in Patricia Liggins Hill, gen. ed., *Call & Response: The Riverside Anthology of the African American Literary Tradition* (Boston and New York: Houghton Mifflin, 1998), p. 749. The text is widely available in multiple whole editions and excerpted.

[6] See, for example, *Methodist Error Or, Friendly, Christian Advice to those Methodists, who indulge in extravagant religious emotions and bodily exercises* (1819), authored anonymously by "A Methodist," and later attributed to John F. Watson.

within English poetry's conventions has generated negative comparisons. Yet, ironically, when African American poetry is the most original and distinctive, it has been criticized as primitive, unsophisticated, or strange. It seems as if African American poetry has been judged by two sets of standards and it cannot gain respect from either of these alternative views. As a result, this body of poetry has had a long history of exclusion from the lyric poetry and literary canons, until very recently. Critically speaking, African American poetry has long been framed as the marked term, reflecting the circumstances of a population that has fought for equality for more than four centuries. Inevitably, the issue of racial discrimination in America is integrally related to perceptions of African American poetry. As Paul Robeson wrote in "The Negro Artist Looks Ahead" (1951), "America is a nation based upon oppression, where black artists in all fields have suffered discrimination, exploitation, and limited opportunities for success and recognition." Despite the vast influence of African American artists on world culture, Robeson offered numerous examples to show how "the fruits have been taken from us."[7]

Canons are not eternal verities of quality, but mutable and competitive, and change to reflect the current values of times, places, institutions, and sociopolitical forces. In *Kinds of Literature: An Introduction to the Theory of Genres and Modes*, Alastair Fowler identifies three primary kinds of literary canon: potential, accessible, and selective. Potential refers to all works in existence, accessible means that a reader can discover it, and selective is the authoritative choice of texts with some special value to preserve and revere. As Fowler describes it, canon formation is a somewhat unruly and changing power struggle to control the official version of literary esteem. He writes, "The official canon is institutionalized through education, patronage, and journalism ... Someone must be first to see merit in an experimental work."[8] That is true, but those seeing merit are not necessarily those with the power of institutions behind them. Before the 1997 appearance of the first edition of *The Norton Anthology of African American Literature*, edited by Henry Louis Gates, Jr. and Nellie Y. McKay, which was a long-awaited signal event of canon-establishment for educators, few African American and black

---

[7] Paul Robeson, "The Negro Artist Looks Ahead," in Manning Marable and Leith Mullings, eds., *Let Nobody Turn Us Round: Voices of Resistance, Reform, and Renewal* (Lanham, Boulder, New York, and Oxford: Rowman & Littlefield, 2000), p. 353.
[8] Alastair Fowler, *Kinds of Literature: An Introduction to the Theory of Genres and Modes* (Cambridge, MA: Harvard University Press, 1982), pp. 213–16.

diasporic poems entered the canon. Those few that were included tended to reinforce the mainstream national narrative in style and content, or to serve as an acceptable version of alterity which also reinforced the dominant culture's vision. To give an idea of the momentousness of the preparation and publication of the Norton anthology, in *Drumvoices* in 1976, Redmond specifically decried the absence of the imprimatur of a Norton anthology for African American literature. In the Preface to his 1922 *Book of American Negro Poetry*, James Weldon Johnson wrote that no group that produced great art had been disrespected. Was the Norton meant to be such a display of respectability? Did its birth perpetuate the idea that there might be a separate and equal canon of African American literature that was somehow different and tangential from "American literature?" Yet it was an important and necessary move because it sought, in the esteemed academic venue of a Norton anthology, to establish the bona fides of the literature of African Americans. That it followed firmly in the conventional tradition of Norton anthologies also perpetuated the problems of how restrictively this canon came to be defined.

A parallel signal event in its own way was the re-release in 1999 of *The New American Poetry, 1945–1960*, edited by Donald Allen. Originally published in 1960 with its iconic four red waving lines evoking the bent stripes of the American flag, the anthology was indeed a counter-cultural bombshell or breath of fresh air, as has been thoroughly documented and discussed. Its re-release by new publisher University of California Press almost forty years after its original publication by Grove Press coincided with the publication of the first edition of the *Norton Anthology of African American Literature*. University of California Press's website states:

> With more than 100,000 copies sold, *The New American Poetry* has become one of the most influential anthologies published in the United States since World War II. As one of the first counter-cultural collections of American verse, this volume fits in Robert Lowell's famous definition of the raw in American poetry. Many of the contributors once derided in the mainstream press of the period are now part of the postmodern canon: Olson, Duncan, Creeley, Guest, Ashbery, Ginsberg, Kerouac, Levertov, O'Hara, Snyder, Schuyler, and others.[9]

One problem with this anthology, described as representing the "counter-cultural," "the raw," and others "derided in the mainstream press" was its inclusion of only one African American among forty-four poets: LeRoi Jones

---

[9] www.ucpress.edu/book/9780520209534/the-new-american-poetry-1945-1960 (last accessed August 19, 2018).

(later to become Amiri Baraka). In the history of American literature, it appears that only certain kinds of counter-culturalism and difference have been acceptable or even visible where issues of race are involved.

Until late in the twentieth century, few African American poets entered the canon, and the token representation of the Allen anthology had become the norm. When a few black poets were included in anthologies used in the classroom, the selections were typically formally and conceptually accessible, written in either urban slang or conversational diction and free verse, and depicted African Americans' alienation and struggles to surmount oppression, such as "Theme for English B" by Langston Hughes and "Still I Rise" by Maya Angelou. Since the beginning of the twenty-first century, African American poetry appears in much greater quantity and variety, which proves the point that potential and access – existence and presence – are the paths to selection, but that also depends on the terms of selection. Things have come a long way, especially in quantity, towards including more African American poets in the canon, but not necessarily in range and diversity.

Published in 2006, the *Wadsworth Anthology of Poetry*, edited by Jay Parini, presents a substantial representation of African American and black diasporic poetry: "The Bars Fight" by Lucy Terry, "On the Death of Rev. Mr. George M. Whitefield 1770" by Phillis Wheatley, "The Slave Mother" by Frances Ellen Watkins Harper, "Douglass" by Paul Laurence Dunbar, "Paul Laurence Dunbar" by James David Corrothers, "O Black and Unknown Bards" by James Weldon Johnson, "I Sit and Sew" by Alice Moore Dunbar Nelson, "America" by Claude McKay, "Yet Do I Marvel" by Countee Cullen, "For My People" by Margaret Walker, "For Mack C. Parker" by Pauli Murray, "A Poem for Black Hearts" and "A New Reality is Better Than a New Movie!" by Amiri Baraka, "malcolm" by Lucille Clifton, "Double Elegy" by Michael S. Harper, "Parsley" and "David Walker" by Rita Dove, "The Black Clown," "Harlem," "The Negro Speaks of Rivers," "Esthete in Harlem," and "Theme for English B" by Langston Hughes, "Middle Passage" and "A Plague of Starlings" by Robert Hayden, "Telephone Conversation" and "Night" by Wole Soyinka, "Beautiful Black Men" and "Poetry" by Nikki Giovanni, "For Black Poets Who Think of Suicide" by Etheridge Knight, "Negro Hero" and "my dreams, my works, must wait till after hell" by Gwendolyn Brooks, "Poetics" by Yusef Komunyakaa, "Ballad of Birmingham" by Dudley Randall, "Ballad from Childhood" by Audre Lorde, "In the Mountains of the Moon, Uganda" by Lorna Goodison, "homage to my hips" by Lucille Clifton, "As from a

Quiver of Arrows" by Carl Phillips, "Twenty-Year Marriage" and "Killing Floor" by Ai, "Prelude" by Kamau Brathwaite, "Come Thunder" by Christopher Okigbo, "Stowaway" by Olive Senior, and "African Sleeping Sickness" by Wanda Coleman.

In this massive anthology of 712 pages, covering all poetry in English or influencing the English tradition, the percentage of African American and black diasporic poets may be slim, yet I list all poems and poets canonized by Parini because it is a legitimately thoughtful and well-chosen selection that does reinforce the international links. It appears to indicate progress. Yet of all the choices available, a conventional cultural ideology abides with the accompanying exclusions and oversights. Unsurprisingly, the largest selection given to any black poet belongs to Langston Hughes, who is represented by five poems. Considering the wealth of possibilities, this anthology selects Charles Simic but not Ed Roberson, Jorie Graham but not Harryette Mullen, Walt Whitman but not James Monroe Whitfield, William Carlos Williams but not Jean Toomer, Ezra Pound but not Melvin B. Tolson, Robert Service but not James Edwin Campbell, Anne Carson but not Russell Atkins. Of course, the list of choices and absences could go on and on, but even with a good-hearted and relatively generous taste of the black poetry genre, the issue of style appears to be less important than who is using it based on who they are. As written in the same year by Aldon Lynn Nielsen and Lauri Ramey in the Introduction to *Every Goodbye Ain't Gone: An Anthology of Innovative Poetry by African Americans*, "Despite what you've been reading, there's more and better reading."[10]

Mostly locked out of the canon until recently, African American poems existed mainly as "potential" literature, occasionally as "accessible," and very rarely as "selective." When poems do enter the "selective" category by way of volumes like the *Wadsworth Anthology of Poetry*, *Norton Anthology of Poetry*, *Longmans Anthology of Poetry* and others, they typically do not represent the boldest, or the most innovative, self-possessed, experimental, oppositional, disruptive, or interventionist choices. In short, the ignored or marginalized poetries and poetics are precisely those that may be of greatest threat to the literary and cultural status quo and power center of taste. A very partial listing of some formally, thematically, and conceptually innovative poets who were actively publishing in the 1960s and 1970s includes Lloyd Addison, Russell Atkins, Jayne Cortez,

[10] Aldon Lynn Nielsen and Lauri Ramey, eds., *Every Goodbye Ain't Gone: An Anthology of Innovative Poetry by African Americans* (Tuscaloosa: University of Alabama Press, 2006), p. xix.

Julia Fields, De Leon Harrison, David Henderson, Calvin C. Hernton, Ted Joans, Percy Johnston, Stephen Jonas, Jones/Baraka, Bob Kaufman, Clarence Major, Oliver Pitcher, Norman H. Pritchard, Ishmael Reed, Ed Roberson, A. B. Spellman, Lorenzo Thomas, Melvin B. Tolson, Tom Weatherly, and Jay Wright.

The next generations of progressive and visionary African American poets followed in the footsteps of these predecessors, who were in turn examining and extending the legacies of their own predecessors. Some of the most innovative and challenging poets of the last two decades include Will Alexander, Ron Allen, T. J. Anderson III, Tisa Bryant, Pia Deas, Latasha N. Nevada Diggs, Tonya Foster, C. S. Giscombe, Renee Gladman, Duriel E. Harris, Harmony Holiday, Erica Hunt, Kim D. Hunter, Geoffrey Jacques, Douglas Kearney, John Keene, Nathaniel Mackey, Dawn Lundy Martin, Mark McMorris, Tracie Morris, Fred Moten, Harryette Mullen, Mendi Lewis Obadike (often working with her husband Keith Obadike as keith+mendi obadike), Julie Ezelle Patton, Claudia Rankine, Deborah Richards, Evie Shockley, giovanni singleton, Tyrone Williams, and Ronaldo V. Wilson. What have they been modeling, representing, and voicing when compared with the group that has been taken as exemplary of the mainstream practices and conventions of the genre?

White experimental writing has been a subject of production and scholarly attention since the early modernist works of the historical avant-garde movements of Dada, futurism, and surrealism. An academic industry has been devoted to the innovations of long-canonical figures such as T. S. Eliot, Hart Crane, Ezra Pound, Wallace Stevens, and William Carlos Williams. Two even earlier figures often viewed as the founders of the American poetry tradition – Emily Dickinson and Walt Whitman – displayed (now) well-accepted inventive practices that convey an "American" voice and spirit of independence, individuality, and freedom. The issue of acceptance does not appear related to the oppositional, challenging, or unfamiliar poetic modes themselves. It appears to be based on ideas about who the author is, and specifically the author's race. One of this book's major threads is to reveal the continuing and integral presence of avant-garde practices in the African American poetry tradition, such as formal innovation, deliberately placed obstacles of production and reception, and resistance to – not ignorance of – conventions. This tradition has always been "experimental" and original.

Experimental poetry and African American poetry have historically been viewed as unrelated fields – meaning that truly original poetry, ironically, has been considered the domain of the poets with the greatest access to centers of cultural power which they have the authority to challenge and disrupt with eventual acceptance. Those factors include race, class, education, sex, and other signifiers of conventional control. The limited quantity of African American poetry that has entered the canon has too often been considered "predictable" in specific ways which will be addressed. In the 1980s and 1990s, most anthologies and scholarship on experimental writing focused almost exclusively on white poets. Anthologies of and scholarship on African American poetry have rarely discussed innovative and avant-garde practices. Why has so little attention been paid to the skillful originality and purposeful innovativeness of African American poetry? If this diverse body of poetry were more available and better known, how might it change the African American poetry canon – and even the canons of American and Anglophone poetry? Connected to its stylistic diversity, which includes a long lineage of formal innovation, many African American poems address a body of recurring themes, figures, events, and experiences that still provide cohesion as a canon. This history of direct references and allusions reveals an African American literary identity that is inextricably connected to the imaginary of "America" – including themes, people, and events that have fought to rise to visibility in the national consciousness, beginning with slavery and progressing through the fight for human rights even in the present. African American poems to and about America from all chronological periods include well-known but also less famed poems deserving of recognition. Some examples are "Bury Me in a Free Land" by Frances Ellen Watkins Harper, "America" by Claude McKay, "Pilate in Modern America" by George Leonard Allen, "An Anniversary Poem Entitled the Progress of Liberty" by James Madison Bell, "To the White People of America" by Joshua McCarter Simpson, "I, Too" by Hughes, "America" by Henry Dumas, "Can I Write You an Anthem" by William J. Harris, "right on: white america" by Sonia Sanchez, "American" by Nayo Barbara Malcolm Watkins, "Blue Ruth: America" by Michael S. Harper, "Junglegrave" by S. E. Anderson, "Belly of America" by Lisa Tarrer-Lacy, "September 11th" by Kevin Powell, "AMERICAN LETTERS" by giovanni singleton, "National Song" by Alfred Gibbs Campbell, "Blue Magic" from Jay Z's *American Gangster* album, "Homestead, USA" by D. L. Crockett-Smith, "My Blackness is the Beauty of this Land" by Lance Jeffers, Wanda Coleman's American Sonnets, "Thanksgiving" by Patricia Spears Jones, and perhaps the most famous of them all, "Let America Be America Again" by Hughes. Poetic tributes to African American literary precursors and role models offer an alternative pantheon to those usually revered in the Anglo-American tradition, such as Malcolm X, W. E. B. Du Bois, Phillis Wheatley, Paul Laurence Dunbar, John Coltrane, Frederick Douglass, Emmett Till, Bobby Seale, Nat Turner, Booker T. Washington, and Martin Luther King, Jr. Examples are replete and discussed in each chapter.

Most studies of African American poetry start with a "literary tradition" as the launching point, but I suggest that we start a full century earlier based on the premise that slave songs – encompassing religious songs or "spirituals," "folk seculars," and "field songs" – are the founding documents. By considering slave songs to be the roots of the African American – and American – poetry tradition, we can appropriately consider African American poetry and culture in national, transnational, and diasporic contexts from the time of its origins. Slave songs – the verses created by enslaved African Americans on Southern plantations – are rarely categorized as lyric poetry, and often overlooked as foundational sources of the African American lyric poetry genre. Yet their influence on modern and contemporary African American poetry is pervasive, which calls for a reexamination of their place in African American poetry, and the scope of the African American poetry canon itself. Based on the pattern of allusions and citations of slave songs, this focus also offers an opportunity to recognize that the poems created by enslaved African Americans are more diverse and original than is often acknowledged. Their national and international impact has been hidden but omnipresent. They have been suppressed as part of a pattern of ignoring or rejecting messages seen as different or uncontrollable. This book hopes to show that the origins of African American poetry are rooted in a body of diasporic literature integrally connected to methods and motives associated with innovative practices.

Slave songs, created and performed by anonymous enslaved African Americans, are essential to the foundation of the African American poetry tradition, and among the most original artistic products created in America. Combining African survivals with the experiences of enslavement in the American South, they very probably date to the early seventeenth century as oral texts but were not transcribed until the early nineteenth century. This brilliant body of sung verse, encompassing some 6,000 or more examples, has not been fully credited for its influence on American or African American literature and culture, or its rightful place in the lyric poetry tradition. Wrote John Lovell, Jr., the brilliant and impassioned Howard University Professor of English and ardent literary defender of slave songs,

> And so we still have 800 to 1,000 original songs, comprising an epic tra-
> dition in the class of the Iliad, the Songs of Roland, or the Lays of the
> Nibelungs, with no clear analysis of the soil from which they sprung or
> the process of their growth. In other epic traditions, patient scholars have
> found seeds of racial and national culture. They look there first. And yet
> for how many years have the dabblers in American "Negroitis" ignored or
> treated with disgraceful cavalierness the heart of the Negro spirituals![11]

This volume pays respect to the epic monument of slave songs as the seeds and creative progenitors of African American poetry. It is a common practice for African American poetry of the last hundred years to cite and allude to slave songs, but these foundational poems are not typically regarded as part of the canon. Many modern and contemporary African American poems are infused with phrases, forms, themes, techniques, and rhetorical strategies of slave songs. Through greater awareness of their presence, function, and influence, readers can better understand both the continuities and progressions in African American poetry, including its most innovative manifestations. This pattern of marginalizing slave songs as lyric art and a major source of textual appropriations also shows how an exclusionary and ideological canon has developed that misrepresents and limits the scope of African American poetry.

Since they first were discussed in print by musicologists, critics, scholars, clergy, slavers, seafarers, and other auditors, there have been curiosity and debate about the messages and creators of these unique songs, and what to call them. Eileen Southern explains that they were originally called "hymns," but it quickly became clear that they differed significantly from conventional Protestant church music.[12] Reflecting the dilemma of how to describe these unusual lyrics, *Slave Songs of the United States*, one of the earliest compilations, uses the term "slave songs" in its title and "sper-ichils" in its introduction.[13] Nineteenth-century abolitionists commonly

---

[11] John Lovell, Jr., *Black Song: The Forge and the Flame: The Story of How the Spiritual Got Hammered Out* (New York: Macmillan, 1972), p. 130. When Lovell made this statement in 1972, the figure of 800 to 1,000 was believed to be accurate, though it now appears that there are some 6,000 slave songs.

[12] Eileen Southern, *The Music of Black Americans: A History*, 3rd edn. (New York: Norton, 1997), p. 180.

[13] William Francis Allen, Charles Pickard Ware, and Lucy McKim Garrison, eds., *Slave Songs of the United States* [1867] (New Bedford: Applewood Books, n.d.), p. ii.

portrayed the enslaved African Americans as free of any malice or resentment about their status, and solely concerned with Christian patience and piety. By popularizing the term "spirituals," abolitionists reinforced the message that the enslaved people were innocent and compliant, and former slaves, after Emancipation, would bear no anger and pose no threat towards their former oppressors.[14] But the word "spirituals" fails to reflect the critique and mockery in these lyrics, which rebuked slaveholders who considered themselves to be Christians. Slave songs were not exclusively Christian hymns of praise, politeness, patience, forgiveness, and sanctity. Examples in the Moorland-Spingarn Research Center at Howard University, which remain uncollected even today in compilations of slave songs, display a normal human variety of desires, passions, and emotions, which are especially suitable and understandable for the circumstances of enslaved people. A small sampling of "work songs" sometimes appears in anthologies in separate categories from "spirituals" rather than placed together in a single category of authorship, as we would expect with other esteemed bodies of writing. There is no indication that the enslaved people maintained such rigid barriers between their sacred and terrestrial lives or reserved certain songs for specific contexts. They would sing "spirituals" while working in the fields, and "work songs" interspersed with religious songs during "ring shouts" while in relatively private space.

The term "spirituals" covers up the full humanity of the enslaved African Americans by presenting them as emotionally partial human beings, and childlike followers in the practice of their obedient faith. Extending the griot function into the New World, these verses encompassed a range of topics, purposes, and attitudes, many of which were not religious in content or tone or meant for devotional purposes. Even those songs that conveyed messages of Christian piety did not express the same interpretation of Christianity as Southern slaveholders. Slave songs most typically conveyed dual messages directed towards black and white audiences and expressed coded ironic commentaries on the hypocrisy of slaveholders who claimed to be pious.

Although the best known and most commonly reprinted slave songs are religious in nature, at least tangentially, this situation results from the systematic exclusion of counter-examples. The "slave songs" that convey protest, resistance, anger, impatience, social and political critique, sexuality, and social interactions have largely been omitted from compilations of

---

[14] Ramey, *Slave Songs and the Birth of African American Poetry*, pp. 10–11.

the songs created by the enslaved African Americans.[15] If such examples had been included in nineteenth-century collections, they would have undermined characterizations like those of Colonel Thomas Wentworth Higginson: "Almost all their songs were thoroughly religious in their tone ... The attitude is always the same, and, as a commentary on the life of the race, is infinitely pathetic. Nothing but patience for this life, – nothing but triumph in the next."[16] Comments by Higginson and others that the tone of slave songs is "always the same" and that they are "monotonous" contrasts with descriptions by others in the nineteenth century, such as Fredrika Bremer and John F. Watson, stressing their "difference."[17] The history of critically evaluating African American poetry is full of such contradictory and conflicting expectations from the origins of this genre.

An additional critical dilemma raised by slave songs is the correspondence of these poems with the perceived identities of their creators. The issue of authorship inevitably would be problematical for an enslaved and oppressed population that was legally deprived of literacy in many states during slavery. Curiosity about the origins of slave songs was coupled with a belief that an important part of their significance was as an anonymous and communal oral expression of a homogeneous population, rather than as the voices of distinctive individual authors. In reviews of public performances following Emancipation, commentators noted their anonymous and collaborative composition as a central part of their meaning. As a result, slave songs have been consistently marginalized from poetry canons, which give cultural esteem to printed texts, authorial individualism, and pride of ownership. James Weldon Johnson's famous poem "O Black and Unknown Bards" makes a common claim that the bards of slave songs "sang a race," implying that they were the voice of a unitary population. It is often overlooked that Johnson also expressed a more nuanced assessment in the preface to *The Books of American Negro Spirituals*: "Some of them may be the spontaneous creation of the group,

---

[15] For further background on spirituals and slave songs, useful resources include Lovell, *Black Song*, Dena J. Epstein, *Sinful Tunes and Spirituals: Black Folk Music to the Civil War* (Urbana: University of Illinois Press, 1977), John W. Work, *American Negro Songs: 230 Folk Songs and Spirituals, Religious and Secular* (Mineola: Dover Press Reprint, 1998), and Ramey, *Slave Songs and the Birth of African American Poetry*.

[16] Thomas Wentworth Higginson, *Army Life in a Black Regiment, and Other Writings* (New York: Penguin, 1997), p. 154.

[17] See, for example, Fredrika Bremer, *The Homes of the New World: Impressions of America*, trans. Mary Howitt (New York: Harper & Brothers, 1853) and John F. Watson, *Methodist Error, Or, Friendly, Christian Advice, to those Methodists, who indulge in extravagant emotions and bodily exercises* (Trenton: D. & E. Fenton, 1819).

but my opinion is that the far greater part of them is the work of talented individuals influenced by the pressure and reaction of the group."[18]

This focus on slave songs' romantic and irretrievable origins – and the misperception that they are anonymous folk or cultural products, and not works of art created by talented individuals – has generated patronizing, objectification, depreciation, exoticization, and sentimentality. Nineteenth-century auditors and observers commented on their peculiarity compared to white Christian hymns even when they noted similar phrases and concepts. "Wild and strangely fascinating," were the words of Allen, Ware, and Garrison in 1867.[19] In his conflicted assessment, author George McDonald described the "rude hymns" as a "mingling of the pathetic with the unconscious comic ... shot here and there with a genuine thread of poetry."[20] Commentators found them consummately "other," and called them both childish and mesmerizing, weird and poetic, cheery and mournful, and pious and blasphemous. Firsthand reports often referred negatively to the exuberant physicality of their performance, and their oddly mystifying turns of phrase and diction. A major debate hinged on the issue of whether slave songs were original and authentic, or poor imitations of white religious and cultural products. They were embraced by some as the only true flower of American culture, and by others as meaningless and alien nonsense. A letter by Theodore Ledyard Cuyler in *The New York Tribune* reported that, when hearing slave songs at the Jubilee Singers' performance at his church during their December 1871–January 1872 New York tour, "grey-haired men wept like little children" because they were so moved.[21] In trying to make sense of the disparities among these responses, it is useful to draw on F. Abiola Irele's contention in *The African Imagination: Literature in Africa and the Black Diaspora* that difference or distinctiveness, on several grounds, is an inherent feature in the production and reception of African and African diasporic literature.[22] Here we have a case study

---

[18] James Weldon Johnson, ed., *The Book of American Negro Poetry* (New York: Harcourt, Brace and Co., 1922), p. 21.

[19] Allen, Ware, and Garrison, eds., *Slave Songs of the United States*, p. viii.

[20] Rev. Gustavus D. Pike, *The Singing Campaign for Ten Thousand Pounds: Jubilee Singers in Great Britain*, rev. edn. (New York: American Missionary Association, 1875), p. 71.

[21] Quoted in J. B. T. Marsh, *The Story of the Jubilee Singers; with their Songs*, 4th edn. (London: Hodder and Stoughton, 1875), p. 32.

[22] F. Abiola Irele, *The African Imagination: Literature in Africa and the Black Diaspora* (Oxford: Oxford University Press, 2001). See especially chapter 2, "Orality, Literacy, and African Literature," pp. 23–38, which addresses the sources of inevitable distinctiveness, including the predominance of orality.

in the literature that forms the roots of the African American poetry tradition.

Recent developments in conceptual poetry, and critical reexaminations of the conventional bifurcation of ethnicity and avant-garde practices, now open the way to reimagine the African American poetry canon, starting with slave songs at the foundation. From the late nineteenth century to today, slave songs have been alluded to and cited in diverse forms and styles of African American poetry, including some of the most formally challenging. They have been an irresistible resource for postmodern experimentation from the mid-twentieth century onwards because of their identity as a gnostic source, amenability to deconstruction, double voicing, metaphysical and ethical questioning, linguistic and conceptual ambiguity, use of language as an inherently creative material, semiotic ontology, signifier of Pan-African identity and community, and symbol of the African American experience. The complexities of their role as the expression of an individual, as well as the universalized and anonymized voice of a group, remain central to their power and critical interest.

How does one speak for one's people and still speak in the voice of an individual poet? This dilemma was exemplified by Paul Laurence Dunbar (1872–1906), widely regarded as America's first black man of letters, whose poems are replete with both veiled and explicit references to slave songs. In his pivotal role as a bridge to modernism, Dunbar both uses and progressively constructs an authentic African American poetry tradition from the roots of these early verses. It might seem likely that slave songs' influence would emerge during the Black Arts Movement of the 1960s and 1970s. This was an era when the identity of the individual black poet often was fused with social awareness, when poetry was determinedly affiliated with music, performance, populism, political action, and human rights. African American poetry was looked on to express the key issues of contemporary politics, serve as a vehicle of political action, reach a large black audience, call for art to effect social change, and use stylized representations of black speech as an aestheticized simulacrum of poetic diction. In fact, there was recognition at that time of the influence of slave songs as cultural touchstones and rallying cries for civil rights, but not of their determinative role as the foundational body of lyric poetry, despite their active use by figures including Margaret Walker (1915–98), Gwendolyn Brooks (1917–2000), Baraka (1934–2014), Nikki Giovanni (born in 1943), Alice Walker (born in 1944), and the Last Poets, among many others.

The pattern of erasure continues into the present: the influence of slave songs on African American poetry since the 1970s remains a fruitful topic that is drastically underexplored. Slave songs play a particularly determining role in breaking down perceptions of African American poetry as homogeneous, aesthetically conservative, and the product of diasporic but not avant-garde influences. They are bold in structure, tone, function, and concept. In bringing together orality and textuality, Redmond and Henderson both called for increased awareness of the essential role of speech and song in African American poetry. Slave songs resist being reduced to either and only the voice of an individual or the voice of a people. By integrally entailing both identities and impulses, a major source of the power and impact of this individualized and universal poetry is revealed. In this way, one of the most abiding and unique features of African American poetry is shown, with slave songs as the bedrock of this genre.

Russell Atkins (born in 1926) is a member of the older generation of post-World War II avant-garde poets whose long and productive life spans the modern and postmodern eras conceptually, stylistically, and chronologically. Following in the footsteps of predecessors including Dunbar, Melvin B. Tolson (1898–1966), Sterling A. Brown (1901–89), Langston Hughes (1902–67), and countless others, Atkins often uses folk materials to link current practices to African American origins, including a series of musical as well as literary spirituals. Since the earliest recorded African American writing, in the eighteenth century, there has been a critical split – the repercussions of which are still felt today – between the diasporic "oral" or "folk art" and "literary" or "high art" verse. This perspective of dualism was exemplified at the turn of the twentieth century by Dunbar, who famously produced two styles of verse: standard diction and dialect poetry. While this perspective of dualism has been perpetuated – Ishmael Reed (born in 1938) has even produced a poem by this name, "Dualism in ralph ellison's invisible man" – there are greater benefits in recognizing that most poets have integrated these traditions. Figures such as Atkins, Reed, Hughes, Harryette Mullen (born in 1953), Douglas Kearney (born in 1974), Evie Shockley, Tracie Morris, and Baraka/Jones, among many others, have worked in the interstices joining oral and written language.

The avant-garde poetry of the 1960s and 1970s often is regarded as following a separate path from literature that is perceived as "diasporic" in its focus – which is to say Pan-African, concerned with issues such as racism and oppression, politically engaged, populist, performing resistance and race, viewing art as a mechanism of progressive politics, and privileging oral modes of expression over textuality. By looking at their common foundations in slave songs, we see that formally innovative poetry and Black Arts activist products are generated by the same roots and need not be considered mutually exclusive. The historical avant-garde movements, certainly, were motivated by a strong principle of political action through formal means. Kearney, a younger generation inter-media experimentalist, also shows the continuing presence of the oral and folk traditions in postmodern avant-garde African American poetry. Kearney frequently incorporates folk materials in his writing, often positioning them, both rhetorically and spatially, as alternately familiar and precarious.

A 1997 poetry anthology edited by Jerry W. Ward, Jr. is titled *Trouble the Water*, an allusion to the slave song called "Wade in the Water," one of the most frequently cited slave songs in modern and postmodern African American poetry. In Ward's volume, once we are alerted to look for them, we find numerous poems – typical of virtually all collections of African American poetry – where slave songs play a dominant role in establishing the central themes, prosody, formal structures, imagery, characterizations, diction, and rhetorical modes. *Trouble the Water* is replete with direct references and allusions to slave songs. Examples of poems that use them directly and/or indirectly – from a wide range of chronological periods and literary styles – include "O Black and Unknown Bards" by James Weldon Johnson, "On Listening to the Spirituals" by Lance Jeffers, "Song of the Son" by Jean Toomer, "Calvary Way" by May Miller, "'Go Down Moses!'" by Marcus B. Christian, "Runagate Runagate" and "O Daedalus, Fly Away Home" by Robert Hayden, "For My People" and "Harriet Tubman" by Margaret Walker, "Harriet Tubman aka Moses" by Samuel Allen, "Gabriel" by George Barlow, and "Medicine Man" by Calvin C. Hernton.

A similar pattern of influence and presence occurs throughout modern and contemporary African American poetry – but, if slave songs have not been valued as poetry, they will be illegible and invisible as an influential body of writing with the capacity to create an authentic canon and to forge allusions and direct references, which too often go unseen. Understanding that slave songs are both highly innovative and the founding body of the African American poetry tradition enables us to do nothing less than clearly recognize the full diversity, innovations, and lineage of African American poetry as a self-determined body of writing based on a past and present of sparkling originality. From its origins to the present, a continuous feature of African American poetry – derived from slave songs – has been a tendency to forge and negotiate a set of bold, diverse, and individualistic styles and forms that bear witness to the circumstances of the community. We see it echoed in the performative communal presentation, and in the call-and-response structure. We see it in the exhortations to others to survive and move ahead while, simultaneously, such encouragement is poignantly offered to the self. We can't even dream of asking the question "What was African American poetry?"[23] without understanding what it has been all along.

African survivals are clearly present in slave songs' structure, style, rhetoric, themes, and presentational modes. After Emancipation, slave songs were favorably received internationally in formal concerts by choirs from Historically Black Colleges and Universities (HBCUs), notably the choir of Hampton Institute (later Hampton University) and the Jubilee Singers of Fisk University, who used performance proceeds to "sing up" buildings on their campuses. Slave songs were spread internationally by black American troops stationed abroad during both world wars. They have maintained a role of high impact for cultures throughout the world, especially those dealing with issues of ethnic and racial oppression. For example, slave songs are greatly treasured as part of the repertoire of the Armenian National Philharmonic Orchestra. For decades, they have been sung in American and global places of religious worship, community organizations for children and adults, and schools, often without the singers realizing that these songs were created by black Americans in a state of enslavement. "Kumbaya," "This Little Light of Mine," "Michael, Row the Boat Ashore," "Go Down, Moses," "Nobody Knows the Trouble I've Seen," "Sometimes I Feel Like a Motherless Child," "Go Tell It on the Mountain," "Let Us Break Bread Together," "When the Saints Go Marching In," and countless other examples of the 6,000 or more slave songs have become staples of the world's songbook.

Since it first began four hundred years ago with slave songs, the poetry of African Americans has been evaluated both positively and negatively – but always with a sense of "other" – as "unique," "curious," and "amusing," and with a distinctive and unusual capacity to reach audiences. In one of the earliest descriptions, published in *Atlantic Monthly* and *Army Life in a Black Regiment and Other Writings* (1870), Colonel Thomas Wentworth Higginson used the metaphor of "strange plants" for the songs sung by black soldiers under his command. Even the black collector of early African American music, John Wesley Work, described slave

---

[23] This reference paraphrases the question in Kenneth Warren's book, *What Was African American Literature?* (Cambridge, MA: Harvard University Press, 2011), which claims that "African American literature is not a transhistorical entity" (p. 9) and now appears to be over "as a distinct entity" (p. 8).

songs as "exotic" and "at all time weird," in a possible appeal to popular perceptions.[24] In 1875, J. B. T. Marsh wrote that the slave songs, "furnished a refined and wholesome entertainment, which Christian people who did not care to visit the theatre and other kindred places of amusement could attend and enjoy." Quoted in the same book, Henry Ward Beecher provided this endorsement: "They will charm any audience … They make their mark by giving the 'spirituals' and plantation hymns as only they can sing them who know how to keep time to a master's whip. Our people have been delighted."[25] This postbellum appreciation is uncanny in its echo of the attitudes of plantation culture. The positive responses during both the antebellum and postbellum eras were based on theatricalizing the experience. Distance was maintained between the performers and auditors: auditors, including Higginson, transcribed the lyrics while hiding themselves and overhearing in secret. On plantations, enslaved singers, dancers, and musicians performed for entertainment at social events, or were overheard by watching overseers when they were performing their work. Formal performances, of course, reinforced the divided relationship between performers and audiences. Many of the positive responses were motivated by feelings of sentimentality, dramatization, and pity for the painful suffering of the singers. A literary example of this external gaze is found in Henry Wadsworth Longfellow's poem, "The Slave Singing at Midnight," in which "a Negro and enslaved" sings both "sweetly" and "wildly" with the semantically opposed rhyming pair of "glad" and "sad" to fill the auditor with "strange emotion:"

> He, a Negro and enslaved,
> Sang of Israel's victory,
> Sang of Zion, bright and free.
>
> And the voice of his devotion
> Filled my soul with strange emotion;
> For its tones by turns were glad,
> Sweetly solemn, wildly sad.

This pattern of white society looking to black culture for "strange entertainment" continues into the twentieth century and beyond, including the popularity of the minstrel tradition and white visitors to exotic Harlem during the Negro Renaissance. This level of aesthetic and

---

[24] Higginson, *Army Life*, p. 160; Work, *American Negro Songs*, p. 9.
[25] Marsh, *Story of the Jubilee Singers*, pp. 38–9 and p. 32.

experiential "difference" has generated a history of critical debate about whether this body of poetry is naïve or cunning, original or imitative, folk product or art, American or alien, profane or pious, and many other elusive categories where this writing refuses to be easily placed.

African American poetry is a major touchstone of the American literary tradition, and deserves recognition for its aesthetic quality, exceptional diversity which is only increasing, and influence on Anglophone literature and culture. This body of literature unquestionably has played a unique role in identifiable moments in American history in chronicling specific types of American experience. For example, the slave songs had an indelible impact on the American character during slavery and after Emancipation, and the poetry of protest of the Black Arts Movement radically shaped the political texture of America during a time of general national turmoil. Slave songs have provided a clarion call for the cause of abolition and human rights in the United States and internationally, and community-building sustenance to enslaved and other oppressed populations. They always have been an internal medium of self-definition, self-respect, and self-determinacy, and an external mechanism of resistance, protest, and critique. Their theology of liberation questioned a formal policy separating Church and State by calling out hypocritical white slave owners who used the Bible to justify slavery. Slave songs were an important manifestation in the development of the African American Christianity that historically has revealed the evils of racism. They also established a tradition of African American poetry that criticizes America's failure to live up to its founding principles and fulfill its promise to all people because it upheld political policies and social practices that allowed oppression, racial violence, and discrimination. Dunbar, Joshua McCarter Simpson (1820?–76), James Monroe Whitfield (1822–71), Frances Ellen Watkins Harper (1824–1911), Albery A. Whitman (1851–1901), Joseph Seamon Cotter, Sr. (1861–1949), James Weldon Johnson (1871–1938), Fenton Johnson (1888–1958), Jean Toomer (1893–1967), Joseph Seamon Cotter, Jr. (1895–1919), Melvin B. Tolson (1898–1966), Marcus B. Christian (1900–1976), Robert Hayden (1913–80), Margaret Walker (1915–1998), Lance Jeffers (1919–85), Raymond R. Patterson (1929–2001), Carole Gregory Clemons (born in 1945), Mullen, Baraka, Atkins, and Kearney are only a sample of countless African American poets – not to mention black and minority ethnic British and poets from throughout the black diaspora – who allude to or signify on aspects of slave songs. Slave songs, themselves the product of extraordinary creativity, have provided the inspiration, form, and content to generate creative material throughout the history of African American poetry in all periods and styles. Tracing and analyzing their appearances, operations, and purposes will form one of this book's major emphases.

After Emancipation, the position of slave songs became more equivocal for black and white society, which viewed them as negative reminders of plantation culture, the world of slavery, the Civil War, and the failures of Reconstruction. But perpetuated by organizations such as African Methodist Episcopal Churches (AME) and the newly established HBCUs, slave songs continued to be an important articulation of the creativity, assertiveness, resistance, humor, intellect, and survival of the voices of African Americans. They became an emblem and a constant reminder that slavery did occur as an indelible mark on American history, and African Americans surmounted these terrible conditions to produce independent works of art. In fact, slave songs are the first African American protest songs. They are justified to be considered the foundation of this tradition in terms of their chronological primacy, the enormity of this canon, and their technical operations, which originate the principle of the central duality which abides throughout the genre. Slave songs helped generate such uniquely American art forms as ragtime, gospel, blues, jazz, rhythm and blues, soul, funk, and hip-hop. In addition to their central role in musical history, they have maintained a prominent place in religious services of varied faiths, and remained potent during later eras of cultural change and turmoil, including the supposed "rediscovery" of black folk products during the Negro Renaissance, and the perceived "protest era" of the 1960s and 1970s during the Civil Rights Movement, Black Power Movement, and Vietnam War, where we even find Bob Dylan singing one of the oldest slave songs, "No More Auction Block for Me."[26] Today, slave songs continue to be routinely performed and recited as symbols of such virtues as the human spirit's tenacity, the value of community, and the eventual conquest of evil by good.

This book is organized chronologically, by which I mean sequentially and progressively, rather than being locked into rigid dates and eras. It addresses a range of poetic styles and critical perspectives – representing both oral and print traditions – from the arrival of the first Africans in America to the current moment. Some traditional ideas about periodicity will be questioned where artificial boundaries uphold interpretations

---

[26] Bob Dylan, born Robert Zimmerman, is an American Jew and therefore a member of a diasporic population. Dylan's affinity for this song is another example of the relevance of slave songs for other exilic and oppressed groups of people.

that may be misleading, bear rethinking, or obscure connections among time frames that sometimes are presented as separate and self-contained. How do we justify starting the tradition with figures like Phillis Wheatley when we know the oral tradition of slave songs came first, and had greater allusive utility and influence? Later, the question of periodization occurs with the eras often referred to as the Harlem Renaissance and the Black Arts Movement, and the gap in scholarship between them. Where do we position figures like Atkins, Du Bois, and Baraka who lived in and impacted multiple eras? As a result of such complications, periods and categories have been rationalized but construed with the maximum latitude to allow links and patterns to emerge rather than arbitrarily disrupt them.

It is a special concern in this book to examine the issues of chronology and periodization as they impact canonization, and, in turn, perceptions, stereotypes, and discrimination. People of black diasporic origin had been in America since colonial times, so it is illuminating to compare survey courses in "American" and "African American" literature. The originating point of American literature courses typically is placed far earlier than African American literature, which is logically difficult to defend, particularly if it is understood that oral products, such as song lyrics, are literature. Survey courses in American literature sometimes start in 1492 with Columbus but certainly no later than the seventeenth century. The periods that are typically covered are colonialism/settlers/Puritans, Romanticism, transcendentalism, and realism, followed by two twentieth and twenty-first century periods, modernism and postmodernism.

University classes in African American literature most often start at the twentieth century. Occasionally, brief preliminary attention is paid to an "early" document, such as a nineteenth-century "slave narrative," David Walker's Appeal, and/or a Phillis Wheatley poem, which reinforces erroneous impressions that African Americans were not generally literate, artists, or contributors to American culture until the twentieth century. African American literature survey courses typically open with "the Harlem Renaissance," skip over the middle decades of the twentieth century, move ahead to a period referred to as "the Black Arts Movement," and close with a view of "today," the contemporary moment. Survey courses in American literature have covered a massive swath of periods and styles before arriving at the point where African American literature courses usually begin. Then the American literature courses do a tidy two-part glide through the twentieth century while the African American twentieth century is typically chopped into at least three periods with a literary desert in the middle. How can this structure not have an impact on perceptions? A strong argument is presented throughout this book that African American poetry is best analyzed by theories designed to interpret these texts, so "difference" is not an inherent concern: it is the type of and motivation for the difference that matters in this comparison. In the teaching of American literature, the division of the twentieth century into "modern" and "postmodern" periods, following at least three or more prior periods (and attendant media and styles), suggests a linear path of steadily forward progress for the relatively unified and orderly American literature canon. The contrasting treatment in African American canon formation tends to suggest a legacy that is late, disrupted, and comprises a series of discrete slow steps moving indeterminately (where?) rather than the "continuity and wholeness" so accurately emphasized by Henderson.

The history of African American poetry has been preserved through a distinguished legacy of anthologies, many of which contain selections of poems and critical essays discussing major figures, moments, movements, and themes. The earliest antebellum volumes mainly address slave songs, which have been primarily collected as "folk products," and have been wrongly excluded from the African and American poetry canons from the origin of the genre to the twenty-first century. The early anthologies explicitly correlate lyrics with music, performance, and Christian worship, such as Richard Allen's *A Collection of Spiritual Songs and Hymns* (1801), Edwin F. Hatfield's *Freedom's Lyre: or, Psalms, Hymns and Sacred Songs, for the Slave and his Friends* (1840), and E. P. Christy's *Christy's Plantation Melodies: Originators of Ethiopian Minstrelsy and the First to Harmonize Negro Melodies* (1851). The postbellum fascination was reflected in and built by compilations and commentaries such as William Francis Allen, Charles Pickard Ware, and Lucy McKim Garrison's *Slave Songs of the United States* (1867), Higginson's *Army Life in a Black Regiment* (1869) and *Atlantic Essays* (1871), Theo. F. Seward's *Jubilee Songs As Sung by the Jubilee Singers of Fisk University* (1872), J. B. T. Marsh's *The Story of the Jubilee Singers with their Songs* (1875), Rev. Gustavus D. Pike's *The Singing Campaign for Ten Thousand Pounds: Jubilee Singers in Great Britain* (1875), Rev. M. Taylor's *Plantation Melodies* (1882), and William E. Barton's *Old Plantation Hymns: a collection of hitherto unpublished melodies of the slave and the freeman, with historical and descriptive notes* (1899), as well as magazines such as *Dwight's Journal of Music.*

These collections were followed by others that extended and expanded the attention paid to plantation culture and its verse, including adding sophisticated musical arrangements. Many segments of black and white society, for differing reasons, shared ambivalence and hostility towards slave songs in the post-Civil War years and at the turn of the twentieth century. For some African Americans, they represented the degradations of slavery and were best left in the past. In the context of America's abiding racial divides during Reconstruction and entering the twentieth century, these songs were often considered primitive ditties beneath the level of serious attention that reinforced pernicious stereotypes of African Americans. Yet important collections continued to preserve these treasures, including Thomas P. Fenner, Frederic G. Rathbun, and Miss Bessie Cleaveland's *Cabin and Plantation Songs as Sung by the Hampton Students* (1901), W. H. Thomas's *Some Current Folk-Songs of the Negro and their Economic Interpretation* (1912), Henry Edward Krehbiel's *Afro-American Folksongs: A Study in Racial and National Music* (1913), John Wesley Work's *Folk Songs of the American Negro* (1915), Howard Odum and Guy B. Johnson's *The Negro and His Songs: A Study of Typical Negro Songs in the South* (1925), the classic two-volume *Book of American Negro Spirituals* edited by James Weldon Johnson and J. Rosamond Johnson (1925, 1926), R. Nathaniel Dett's *Religious Folk-Songs of the Negro as Sung at Hampton Institute* (1927), selections in V. F. Calverton's *An Anthology of American Negro Literature* (1929), and Augustine T. Smythe et al.'s *The Carolina Low-Country* (1931). Their perspectives and motives ranged from generally well intended though historically conditioned curiosity (such as Thomas and Krehbiel), to cultural and educational preservation (such as Fenner and Work), and to supercilious racism (such as Odum and Johnson). HBCUs, black literary societies, and churches were instrumental in maintaining interest in the slave songs, especially with the development of the concert tradition that removed them – or that was thought to elevate them – from their original styles and performative roots. Another generation of song selections followed to help respectfully preserve and perpetuate the tradition through the twentieth century, such as John W. Work's *American Negro Songs: 230 Folk Songs and Spirituals, Religious and Secular* (1940) and Moses Hogan's *The Oxford Book of Spirituals* (2002).

Early works of critical analysis such as *The Negro in Literature and Art in the United States* by Benjamin Brawley (1918) and *To Make a Poet Black* by J. Saunders Redding (1939) established African American poetry and poetics as a worthy subject of study early in the twentieth century. Subsequent important critical studies have aimed to identify what makes African American poetry distinctive and/or part of the

Anglophone or American lyric poetry traditions. Landmark works by anyone's measure are Henderson's *Understanding the New Black Poetry* (1972) and the extended treatment of poetry in *Negro Poetry and Drama and The Negro in American Fiction* by Sterling A. Brown (1972). Several important early collections do not address poetry exclusively but consider it in the larger context of African American literature, cultural expression, and history. Such seminal volumes now out of print include the legendary *The Negro Caravan*, edited by Sterling A. Brown, Arthur P. Davis, and Ulysses Lee (1941), and *Cavalcade: Negro American Writing from 1760 to the Present*, edited by Arthur P. Davis and J. Saunders Redding (1971), later followed by the two volumes of *The New Cavalcade*, edited by Davis, Redding, and Joyce Ann Joyce (1991).

The field was progressively augmented by landmark poetry anthologies – many with critical essays or introductions – including James Weldon Johnson's *The Book of American Negro Poetry* (1922), Countee Cullen's *Caroling Dusk* (1927), selections in Calverton's *An Anthology of American Negro Literature* (1929), Robert Thomas Kerlin's *Negro Poets and Their Poems* (1935), and Arna Bontemps and Langston Hughes's *The Poetry of the Negro 1746–1949* (1949). A bumper crop was published in the 1960s and 1970s, including *American Negro Poetry*, edited by Bontemps (1963), *New Negro Poets, USA*, edited by Hughes (1964), *Kaleidoscope: Poems by American Negro Poets*, edited by Robert Hayden (1968), *Black Fire: An Anthology of Afro-American Writing*, edited by Amiri Baraka and Larry Neal (1968), *We Speak as Liberators: Young Black Poets*, edited by Orde Coombs (1970), *Dices or Black Bones: Black Voices of the Seventies*, edited by Adam David Miller (1970), *Soulscript: A Collection of African American Poetry*, edited by June Jordan (1970), *Natural Process: An Anthology of New Black Poetry*, edited by Ted Wilentz and Tom Weatherly (1970), *The Black Poets*, edited by Dudley Randall (1971), and *The Poetry of Black America: Anthology of the 20th Century*, edited by Arnold Adoff (1973). Two 1970s collections display consciousness of African American poetry in the international context of the African diaspora: *You Better Believe It: Black Verse in English*, edited by Paul Breman (1973), and *3000 Years of Black Poetry*, edited by Alan Lomax and Raoul Abdul (1970). Breman's editorial perspective was unusual, especially for its era. This prescient volume was early to connect the origins of the African American poetry tradition, including some of its most innovative practitioners, to poets from Africa, the United Kingdom, and the Caribbean. Containing a brief preface and editorial introductions to each poet, this book opens with one of the first African American poets, George Moses Horton, and ends by expanding this potential canon with the inclusion of figures such as Kamau Brathwaite, locating African American poetry in a transnational, transcultural, and migratory context.

Since the late 1990s countless important critical studies and anthologies have been produced that have aimed to identify what makes African American poetry distinctive and/or part of the Anglophone or American lyric poetry traditions. Some of the later anthologies of African American poetry have specific topics of focus, demonstrating the increasing levels of knowledge and interest in this genre. *African-American Poetry: An Anthology, 1773–1927*, edited by Joan R. Sherman (1997), is a Dover Thrift Edition which covers a wide swathe of the field but ends at the Harlem Renaissance. Similarly, *Selected African American Writing from 1760 to 1910*, edited by Arthur P. Davis, J. Saunders Redding, and Joyce Ann Joyce (1995), is another substantial and inexpensive anthology that omits most of the twentieth century. Twentieth-century poetry is the exclusive focus of Clarence Major's *The Garden Thrives: Twentieth-Century African American Poetry* (1996), *I am the Darker Brother: An Anthology of Modern Poems by African Americans*, edited by Arnold Adoff (1997), *Every Shut Eye Ain't Asleep: An Anthology of Poetry by African Americans Since 1945*, edited by Michael S. Harper and Anthony Walton (1994), and Bontemps's *American Negro Poetry*, which focuses on twentieth-century poetry (last revised in 1974). Joan R. Sherman has edited two magnificent collections which shed important light on African American poetry of the nineteenth century: *Invisible Poets: Afro-Americans of the Nineteenth Century* (1974, and republished in a 1989 second edition), and *African-American Poetry of the Nineteenth Century: An Anthology* (1992). Adoff's 500-page *Poetry of Black America* offers in-depth coverage but is restricted to a seventy-five-year period. As indicated by the publication dates, many of these excellent collections do not represent either the oldest or the most current African American poetry, or the full range of the genre, nor is it their intention to do so.

Several recent poetry anthologies are in print and readily available which cover a full chronological spectrum of the genre. These volumes include *The Oxford Anthology of African-American Poetry*, edited by Arnold Rampersad (2005), *Trouble the Water: 250 Years of African-American Poetry*, edited by Jerry Ward, Jr. (1997), and *The Vintage Book of African American Poetry*, edited by Michael S. Harper and Anthony Walton (2000). Other superb African American poetry anthologies that focus on specific styles or themes include *Black Nature: Four Centuries of African American Nature Poetry*, edited by Camille Dungy (2009) and

One Window's Light: A Collection of Haiku, edited by Lenard D. Moore (2018). *Double-Take: A Revisionist Harlem Renaissance Anthology,* edited by Venetria K. Patton and Maureen Honey (2001), provides a valuable perspective of the contribution of women writers during the Harlem Renaissance. *Every Goodbye Ain't Gone: An Anthology of Innovative Poetry by African Americans* (2006) and *What I Say: Innovative Poetry by Black Writers in America* (2015), edited by Aldon Lynn Nielsen and Lauri Ramey, concentrate on formally innovative African American poetry from the middle of the twentieth century to 2015. *Angles of Ascent: A Norton Anthology of Contemporary African American Poetry,* edited by Charles Henry Rowell (2013), provides a stylistically diverse selection of the contemporary period. Increasingly from the second half of the twentieth century to the first two decades of the twenty-first, a distinguished roster of varied new critical writings has grown in tandem with the dramatic increase in the quantity and diversity of African American poetry. These include single author studies, texts driven by varied themes or theories, and works of historical recuperation. Reflecting the historically marginalized status of African American writers, mainstream publications have hardly provided an open venue for these poets. Many poems throughout the genre's history appeared in publications sponsored by churches, such as the Quakers, and in the critically important forums of black owned, edited, or oriented newspapers, journals, little magazines, and broadsides, including *Frederick Douglass' Paper, The Anglo-African Magazine, Voice of the Negro, The Crisis, Champion Magazine, The Favorite Magazine, The Crusader, Journal of Black Poetry, Messenger, Fire!!, Phylon, Negro Digest/Black World, Opportunity, Yugen, Yardbird Reader, Umbra,* and *The Southern Workman.* Equally important has been the development since the early nineteenth century of black owned, operated, or focused presses, such as Dudley Randall's Broadside Press, Naomi Long Madgett's Lotus Press, Breman's Heritage Series, Don L. Lee/Haki Madhubuti's Third World Press, and Renee Gladman's Leon Works. The great majority of poetry chapbooks published before and even into the twentieth century were privately printed limited editions. A plethora of literary journals has traditionally been published by black literary societies and HBCUs. Unpublished manuscripts that were hand-circulated or privately held can be found in private and special collections, such as the Schomburg Center for Research in Black Culture in New York and the Mayme A. Clayton Library and Museum in Culver City, California.

In addition to material in special collections and archives, relevant poetry and essays also appear in a number of anthologies produced for academic purposes, including *Call & Response*, edited by Patricia Liggins Hill (1998), three editions of *The Norton Anthology of African American Literature*, edited by Henry Louis Gates, Jr. and Nellie Y. McKay – and most recently Valerie Smith (the third edition was published in 2014), the classic volume *Black Writers of America*, edited by Richard Barksdale and Keneth Kinnamon (1972), and *The Prentice Hall Anthology of African American Literature*, edited by Rochelle Smith and Sharon L. Jones (2000). This book respectfully builds on the foundation of these and other materials, suggests the wealth of past and current resources, and provides an analytical map to interested readers at both the introductory and advanced levels. In fulfilling its mission to provide a history of both African American poetry and critical ideas about the field, it also draws on numerous scholarly studies on individual authors and relevant topics, specialized anthologies and essay collections, and resources of poetry and poetics that are out of print or difficult to access. These materials span the major periods of African American literary history, starting with early compilations and unpublished manuscripts of oral poetry and plantation verse, and encompassing some of the more recent forums such as publications produced by or related to *Callaloo*, Cave Canem, The Dark Room Collective, the Black Took Collective, the Carolina African American Writers Collective, and the Affrilachian Poets.

In recent years, the spectrum of new critical writings has paralleled the dramatic increase in the quantity and variety of African American poetry. In the late twentieth and early twenty-first centuries, the many influential studies have included *Black Song: The Forge and the Flame: The Story of How the Afro-American Spiritual was Hammered Out* by John Lovell, Jr. (1972), *Afro-American Poetics* (1988) and *Modernism and the Harlem Renaissance* (1987) by Houston A. Baker, Jr., *Black Chant: Languages of African-American Postmodernism* by Aldon Lynn Nielsen (1997), *Extraordinary Measures: Afrocentric Modernism and Twentieth-Century American Poetry* by Lorenzo Thomas (2000), *In the Break: The Aesthetics of the Black Radical Tradition* by Fred Moten (2003), and *Discrepant Engagement: Dissonance, Cross-Culturality, and Experimental Writing* by Nathaniel Mackey (1993). Two valuable collections of African American critical theory that include key essays on poetry and poetics are *Within the Circle: An Anthology of African American Literary Criticism from the Harlem Renaissance to the Present*, edited by Angelyn Mitchell (1994), and *African American Literary Theory: A Reader*, edited by Winston Napier (2000). It is significant that both volumes are restricted to essays written from the Harlem Renaissance to the present, which offers telling insight into the main eras of research and attention in African American literature. These compilations have been supplemented by *The Cambridge History of African American Literature*, edited by Maryemma Graham and Jerry W. Ward, Jr. (2011), an essay collection that aims to cover four centuries and offers an enhanced scope that incorporates recent perspectives in this tradition. These and many other important works have generated an increasingly interested and varied readership and appreciation for this genre.

The focus and goals of these studies demonstrate the diversity that has always existed in this field and continues to grow. In his exhaustive 684-page study, Lovell's primary focus is the poetics of the slave songs, or spirituals, as he identified these "black songs" as the progenitors of the African American poetry tradition, with the key themes of African survivals, diasporic syncretism, and international influences. A distinguished body of critical writing is available on the Harlem Renaissance, with such notable volumes as *The Cambridge Companion to the Harlem Renaissance*, edited by George Hutchinson (2007), and the marvelous work done by David Levering Lewis in the anthology *The Portable Harlem Renaissance Reader* (1994) and his revelatory critical-historical study *When Harlem Was in Vogue* (1981). Another burst of attention has been paid in recent years to the larger period that subsumes the Civil Rights and Black Arts Movements, and the transition into the contemporary period. Nielsen, Mackey, and Lorenzo Thomas share interests in avant-garde, marginalized, and formally innovative movements and practices, with Thomas addressing modernism and postmodernism, Mackey connecting African American poetry and poetics to interracial and diasporic poets and practices, and Nielsen illuminating the existence of a marginalized tradition of innovation reflected in postmodern African American poetry. Baker's studies have been justly lauded for his transformative address of issues of the black aesthetic, especially, but hardly limited to, applications to modernism and the Harlem Renaissance.

With exceptions such as Keith Leonard's *Fettered Genius: The African American Bardic Poet from Slavery to Civil Rights* (2006), many of the excellent recent studies that have opened the field to closer scrutiny have attended largely to modernism and postmodernism. Some of the highly recommended titles that have progressed the attention to this period – and that, not coincidentally, emphasize the integral connection between poetry and music – include Evie Shockley's *Renegade Poetics: Black Aesthetics and Formal Innovation in African American Poetry* (2011), Meta DuEwa Jones's *The Muse is Music: Jazz Poetry from the Harlem Renaissance to Spoken Word* (2011), Gordon E. Thompson's edited essay collection *Black Music, Black Poetry: Blues and Jazz's Impact on African American Versification* (2015), Howard Rambsy's *The Black Arts Enterprise and the Production of African American Poetry* (2011), Anthony Reed's *Freedom Time: The Poetics and Politics of Black Experimental Writing* (2014), Jean-Philippe Marcoux's *Jazz Griots: Music as History in the 1960s African American Poem* (2012), Adam Bradley's *Book of Rhymes: The Poetics of Hip Hop* (2009), Tony Bolden's *Afro-Blue: Improvisations in African American Poetry and Culture* (2004), and Harryette Mullen's *The Cracks Between What We Are and What We Are Supposed to Be* (2012), which contextualizes her own literary practices within the larger tradition. Even Thompson's collection, which aims to cover the full scope of African American poetry, opens with Paul Laurence Dunbar presented as an early modern figure.

Understanding the relationship between African American poetry and performance has been progressed by signal works which have become critical classics, such as *Performing Blackness: Enactments of African American Modernism*, by Kimberly W. Benston (2000) and *Performing the Word: African American Poetry as Vernacular Culture*, by Fahamisha Patricia Brown (1999). Numerous major critical studies have been produced on individual figures, such as Arnold Rampersad's magisterial two-volume biography of Langston Hughes (1986, 1988), and biography of Ralph Ellison (2007). African American poetry also has escalated in prominence in the context of postcolonial, transatlantic, and global studies. Landmark work in theory and application appears in *The Practice of Diaspora: Literature, Translation, and the Rise of Black Internationalism* by Brent Hayes Edwards (2003), which also focuses on modern and postmodern writing. The international influence of the genre is reflected in a comprehensive anthology of "black" British poetry, *Red*, edited by the diasporically oriented poet Kwame Dawes (2010), whose preface opens by citing Hughes. The influence of African American women poets similarly is unmistakable in *Bittersweet*, edited by Karen McCarthy (1998), an expansive anthology of contemporary black diasporic women's poetry, which prominently features African American figures such as Maya Angelou (1928–2014), Jayne Cortez (1934–2012), Nikki Giovanni (born in 1943), Alice Walker (born in 1944), Ntozake Shange (1948–2018), Rita Dove (born in 1952), and bell hooks (born in 1952). The focus on the contribution of women to the African American poetry tradition from its origins is represented in numerous critical studies and volumes, such as *The Cambridge Companion to African American Women's Literature*, edited by Angelyn Mitchell and Danille K. Taylor (2009), and an excellent anthology with expansive historical range, *The Prentice Hall Anthology of African American Women's Literature*, edited by Valerie Lee (2006).

It is astonishing that the book regarded by scholars as the definitive critical history of African American poetry appeared more than four decades ago: Redmond's ground-breaking *Drumvoices: The Mission of Afro-American Poetry: A Critical History* (1976), which covers slightly more than a century, the period from 1865 to 1975. Its singular position is a testimonial to the magnificent quality of care and detail in this book. For any reader interested in African American literature, and certainly poetry, it is an essential resource. Especially considering when it was written, long before digital methods of access and research were routine, the book truly is a wonder of preservation of the century of black poetry that it meticulously addresses. From the major to the most minor figures and texts, there is hardly one that is not mentioned, and Redmond's knowledge, opinions, and wit infuse each page. The only existing "complete" history of African American poetry ends in the mid-1970s. A superb volume, naturally it does not cover the full flourishing of postmodernism and, additionally, it necessarily omits the future directions of parallel critical scholarship and the cultural and historical developments in the following era. Times and methods have changed, and those changing insights can beneficially update the information in Redmond's foundational text. To put it in context, Redmond's book was published in the same year as Alex Haley's *Roots: The Saga of an American Family* and the first production of Ntozake Shange's choreopoem *For Colored Girls Who Have Considered Suicide/When the Rainbow is Enuf.*

Since *Drumvoices* was published, a large quantity of valuable poetry and scholarship has been produced reflecting creative modes and technological developments that did not exist in the middle of the twentieth century, from digital poetics to the future impact of the period in which this book was written. A massive quantity of important historical and literary material has been discovered, recuperated, and made accessible. Substantial new critical and cultural writing has been generated that explains why African American poetry deserves special focus and preservation. Academic fields have shifted and reconfigured in an age of true interdisciplinarity. Of compelling interest is this genre's place in the contexts of critical paradigms of border, multicultural, ethnic, transnational, class, race, diaspora, gender, ethnomusicology, and minority studies – growing fields, as indicated by educational and employment statistics, conferences, and publications. The world in which African American poetry exists and is published also has changed dramatically since the 1970s. Even Kenneth Warren's provocative study *What Was African American Literature?* (2011), which was the subject of a special session at the 2012 Modern Language Association annual convention, has drawn dynamic questions about the necessity and ontology of this field, generating spirited dialogue to determine its scope and role in the present and future. Today we inherit and build on this field, which differs in significant ways from the one so brilliantly encompassed by Redmond, though his work will remain a permanent cornerstone.

A key issue in this book is the relationship between African American poetry and American poetry – to what extent the latter has shaped the former, and to what extent the latter is an integral part of the former. Another dominant theme is music and musicality, which has long been considered one of the hallmarks of African American poetry. Imaginaries of Africa, migration, diaspora, trans- and multi-nationalism, and race slavery are historical themes with ongoing ramifications that are addressed as touchstones of identity formation, sociopolitical influence, and aesthetics. An additional topic throughout this book is the question of canonicity itself: how has a body of African American poetry developed over time? How has its allusive dialogue functioned? How have certain poets and poems come to be considered essential? How has the American poetry canon evolved to either marginalize or embrace certain voices in different periods of time? This book discusses the recognized canon of African American poetry; but considering the general disregard and neglect of this genre, it also stresses the recuperation of lost and overlooked poetries and poetics demonstrably worthy of attention. This motive is consistent with the current reconsideration and re-envisioning of American literature owing to increased recognition of minority writing and viewpoints in recent decades. An integral part of this book is to address the current composition of the genre, and to consider which poems and poetics may have been more and less acceptable to wider audiences based on the political and social conditions in which they were created. In examining these and other issues, the ideas of brilliant poet-critics Tyrone Williams, Mark McMorris, Fred Moten, Harryette Mullen, Nathaniel Mackey, Lorenzo Thomas, Claudia Rankine, and Evie Shockley have been invaluable in building a substantial body of criticism about experimental poetics to speculate on how and why the current canon has developed and consider some alternatives. I mention additional original and skilled poet-critics who are less well known. Their inclusion could spin the canon on its axis for a more expansive, diverse, bold, original, and demanding portrait of the full range of African American poetry – more self-determined, self-aware, authentically revolutionary, and challenging than the tradition that has been accepted.

A related goal in a comprehensive history of this nature is the careful contemplation of lesser known works that can beneficially be joined or rejoined to the canon. Poetry often is acknowledged to be on the margins of literature, and poetry associated with ethnicity, exclusion, and other forms of political and cultural "outsider" status – including African American – is generally neglected. African American poetry historically has been a voice of critique and, as such, an especially marginalized genre.

As a history of the genre, this book addresses the span of African American poetry from at least the early seventeenth century to the present. It identifies the origins of the genre in oral modes evolving into performative and spoken poetics, and early typographical experiments developing into contemporary conceptual practices. A selection of poets is highlighted in relevant chapters, with several figures spanning more than one period in their lifetime and impact. Each chapter presents literary analysis, combined with biographical and bibliographical information on poets and background on their major works, and draws on published and archival materials from a range of periods and approaches. This field contains landmark texts by towering scholars and poet-critics, many of which have been named in this chapter, whose ideas and approaches are discussed where relevant. This book seeks to identify earlier roots than 1760, the date used by Arthur P. Davis, J. Saunders Redding, and Joyce Ann Joyce – among many others – to reference the "Pioneer Writers" of the genre. As such, I address many writers who have been determined over time to be considered canonical for each major period. This designation refers to poets whose writing can be defended as being of the first order of quality or having been highly influential. In conjunction with critical commentaries on poetry, this book addresses the historical and cultural circumstances in which it was produced and its record of critical evaluation. It also discusses figures who previously were better known, or deserve fuller attention than they later received, and invites readers to reintegrate them with more familiar contemporaneous poets. Deliberate attention is paid to the range of styles and purposes for which African American poetry has been used over time to highlight the diversity and expansiveness of this field in a stimulating way to prompt further research and study at all levels.

By these criteria, there are certain poets that inarguably must be incorporated. These include Phillis Wheatley, Jupiter Hammon, George Moses

Horton, the anonymous poets of the slave songs, Frances Ellen Watkins Harper, Paul Laurence Dunbar, James Weldon Johnson, Claude McKay, Langston Hughes, Countee Cullen, Robert Hayden, Margaret Walker, Jean Toomer, Melvin B. Tolson, Frank Marshall Davis, Fenton Johnson, and Gwendolyn Brooks. The picture becomes more complex as we near the present for reasons that are proposed and discussed. Some of these figures must be included based on recognized measures of literary merit and influence, others through their cultural or historical significance, and, for some, these categories coincide. There are additional poets who may readily be included with little expectation of challenge. Full inclusivity is beyond the scope or possibility of this book, and many worthy and important figures must necessarily be omitted. Many other sets of figures could have been chosen, and the limitations of space are regretful. Thrilling research by many scholars on a variety of poets is underway and to be produced in the future.

In the current climate, with strong and increasing interest nationally and internationally, this book aims to respectfully broaden and update Redmond's magisterial study, while there is no need or aim to duplicate its phenomenal and meticulously reliable attention to encyclopedic biographical and bibliographic detail. The wealth of new poetry that has appeared in the interim is coupled with seismic cultural and political shifts, not least of which has been the appointment of African Americans to key political posts, including the appointment of the first black President of the United States, Barack Obama, whose inauguration was launched by a black poet's writing, Elizabeth Alexander's "Praise Song for the Day" (2009). In 2003, the idea was approved for an African American museum in the nation's capital. Thirteen years later, in 2016, the National Museum of African American History and Culture officially opened its doors, auspiciously at the end of the Obama administration. Robert Hayden was the first African American to serve as Consultant in Poetry to the Library of Congress – the role that pre-dated the Poet Laureate of the United States – from 1976 to 1978, the period of the United States' deeply symbolic Bicentennial. It took a decade for his appointment to be followed by another African American poet, Gwendolyn Brooks, who served in 1985–6. Appointments to this politically prominent position now have rapidly accelerated, building on the foundations of these esteemed predecessors. From 1993 to 1995, Rita Dove was the first African American to hold the official post and title of Poet Laureate, succeeded by Natasha Tretheway from 2012 to 2014, and Tracy K. Smith starting in 2017. These figures and their positions reinforce the centrality of women to the history of African American poetry.

There is frequent mention of the many texts and figures that previously were better known, and to compare them to canonical texts. Certain poets are acknowledged as essential to the canon in each period. Diverse media and forms are considered, from the origins of the genre in oral practices to today's spoken word, and from early typographical experiments to twentieth and twenty-first century formal innovations.

Chapter 2 addresses the earliest period of African American literature, which is presented here as the era extending from the first arrival of Africans – including their capture and journey to enslavement – until the end of slavery in 1865. In addition to slave songs, key figures and texts of this period include ephemera, notes, messages, diaries, hymnals, oratory, sayings, stories, folktales, proverbs, lore, political statements, and autobiographies and memoirs by authors, auditors, and transcribers, representing both oral and print-based culture. The history of critical evaluation has artificially perpetuated a split between a black "folk" tradition and a print "literary" tradition that emulates learned models, a dual perspective that I acknowledge but vehemently argue against in favor of a holistic reality. Examples of this split are easy to find if we consider the treatment of slave songs, which have generally been relegated to the "folk" category. As I discuss elsewhere, "folk literature" has usually been considered more primitive, less sophisticated, and not truly canon-worthy as "literature," even if such judgments are enacted but not directly stated. In the resoundingly influential *The Negro Caravan*, editors Brown, Davis, and Lee have a section called "Poetry," and relegate slave songs to a separate section called "Folk Literature," where they are divided into "Spirituals" and "Slave Seculars." Similarly, Dudley Randall, in another popular anthology, *The Black Poets*, has a section called "Literary Poetry," and places slave songs in a separate (but not equal?) section called "Spirituals."

The "literary" texts of the earliest period tend to include poems and other writings by Hammon, Wheatley, Harper, Horton, and Lucy Terry Prince, all of whom have received well-justified critical attention with new and important studies emerging. The founding role of women in African American poetry is present from the outset, very clearly through the positions of Prince, Wheatley, and Harper, followed by successive generations of women who display a tradition within a tradition, as Joanne M. Braxton has suggested in relation to African American women's autobiography. In Chapter 2 and throughout this book, readers are encouraged to consult the wealth of available material on canonical figures, which does not need to be duplicated here. One of the major purposes of Chapter 2 and this book is to look closely at the development of the canon, raise questions about the inclusions and exclusions, draw attention to lesser known figures of great interest, and propose a redrawn and expanded canon that reveals continuities and features that have been previously hidden.

Of the so-called "slave poets," Hammon typically gets the harshest treatment, Horton the most consistent respect, and judgments on Wheatley vacillate the most. Terry is a special case since she has left only one known poem instead of a larger body of writing to evaluate. Jean Wagner found the historical importance of Hammon to be more significant than the quality of his writing, but also acknowledged that his poem "An Evening Thought: Salvation by Christ with Penitential Cries" (1760) "represents a halfway stage between the guileless art of the unknown composers of spirituals and the already much wordier manner of the black popular preacher."[27] Redmond also stated that such "literary poetry" should be examined in the context of other contemporaneous products like slave songs. *The Negro Caravan* calls Hammon "a curiosity to his age, and he remains a curiosity. His religious doggerel and pious platitudes have no significance other than historical."[28] The editors of that important volume explain the failure of these early poets: "They had to be living proofs that the race was capable of culture ... It was therefore only natural that they should imitate too closely the approved American and English writers" (p. 275). Why do we have a canon that is based on figures whose quality has been judged with such ambivalence? And what are the explanations for those mixed reviews? These questions are asked in Chapter 2 and throughout the book. Chapter 2 discusses slave songs, as well as Alfred Gibbs Campbell, creator of what is probably the first concrete poem written in America, and Dr. Joshua McCarter Simpson, who produced an incendiary body of abolitionist protest poetry that – along with slave songs – helps locate the origins of revolutionary poetry far earlier than is typically recognized, and establishes a more visible lineage for the twentieth century "era of movements" in the poetry of modernism, the mid-Wars period, and the Civil Rights and Black Arts Movements.

---

[27] Jean Wagner, *Black Poets of the United States: From Paul Laurence Dunbar to Langston Hughes*, tr. Kenneth Douglas (Urbana and Chicago: University of Illinois Press, 1973), p. 17.

[28] Sterling A. Brown, Arthur P. Davis, and Ulysses Lee, eds., *The Negro Caravan* (New York: Arno Press and *The New York Times*, 1970), p. 274.

Chapter 3 focuses on the difficult closing decades of the nineteenth century and addresses the pivotal time from Emancipation through Reconstruction to the advent of the early twentieth-century era variously known as the Harlem Renaissance, African American modernism, or New Negro Renaissance, among other appellations. This challenging post-Emancipation pre-modern era laid the foundation for the famous and prescient prediction to follow of W. E. B. Du Bois: the problem of the twentieth century would be the problem of the color line. Equally renowned is the claim by historian Rayford W. Logan that this period encompasses "the Nadir" of racial relations in America, though recent scholarship argues persuasively that the period defies that stereotype in some respects by having generated an impressive record of creative and literary products. However, the reality still proved to be ironic considering the high expectations for racial harmony and equality brought about by Emancipation and national reunification after four long and bloody years of war.

Important poets of this era include some who are marginally well known, such as W. S. Braithwaite, Alice Moore Dunbar Nelson, Joseph Seamon Cotter, Sr., James Edwin Campbell, and Albery Allson (sometimes referred to as Alston) Whitman. The period also includes many poets who deserve to be far better known for their individual literary contributions, as the generation to inherit and use the legacy of the tradition's originators, and as significant precursors to the first generations of poets in the twentieth century. As Joan R. Sherman has written, there is a perception that no African American poets existed between Wheatley and Dunbar, and we can see that this false view is another pitfall in the existing canon. Sherman has done superb work in collecting and calling attention to African American poets of the nineteenth century, and some of the fine poets that she has written about include Alfred Islay Walden, George Marion McClellan, and Josephine Delphine Henderson Heard. These poets often addressed such topics as minstrelsy, post-slavery racial oppression, and the horrific status of human rights. Close attention is paid to figures on the cusp of the Negro Renaissance, such as Walter Everette Hawkins, and Fenton Johnson, addressed in Chapters 3 and 4, whose life was long, but whose known brilliant poetic output took place early in his life. Information also is offered in Chapter 3 that hopes to rectify erroneous preconceptions about early African American literacy and interest in poetry by discussing the journals and newspapers that often served as the means of expression.

Only one figure of this era is a truly renowned poet, Dunbar, who remains in the eyes of many as the greatest poet of the African American poetry tradition. This is an especially crucial period in the progressive development of an African American critical tradition side by side with its impressively expanding body of poetry. The publication in 1918 of the bellwether study *The Negro in Literature and Art* by Benjamin Brawley arguably establishes the presence of an aesthetic tradition and its founding figures. This era sees the self-defining presence of an African American poetry canon through patterns of inter-referencing and allusion. Themes that were pronounced in the earliest period emerge with increasing urgency in postbellum poetry: separatism versus integration, an authentic recording of African American experience and history, the proper educational and cultural standards appropriate for African American culture, African return and the symbolic meaning of Africa, ways to enforce legal rights and freedoms for African Americans, and the role – and the best means to achieve it – for African Americans in the American national imaginary and operation. Specific issues that also are seen to retain their importance from earlier periods include the relative values placed on speech-based versus print-based poetry and poetics, the pros and cons of writing for dual race-determined audiences, the use of vernacular diction versus ornate poetic language, and the relationship between African American poetry and music, as exemplified in this early period by slave songs, with ragtime, gospel, blues, and jazz soon to follow on the horizon. The presence of slave songs in African American poetry of all eras is demonstrated here in numerous examples as a continuous theme in this book. Allusions appear in the work of poets using many different forms and styles, and their uses and appearances are especially interesting among poets associated with experimentalism, subterfuge, indirection, and layers of multiple meaning, which slave songs achieve so adeptly.

Chapter 4 brings together the two periods often called the first and second "Renaissances." African American modernism is embedded in the pivotal era referred to most often as the Harlem or New Negro Renaissance, which is usually dated from the teens to the Depression. This period, which is also described as Afro-modernism, Afro-centric modernism, and other designations, produced indisputably significant poetry by well-known poets such as Hughes, Cullen (1903–46), James Weldon Johnson (1871–1938), Sterling A. Brown (1901–89), Claude McKay (1889–1948), and Jean Toomer (1894–1867), as well as lesser known figures. More recent critical terminology such as the New Negro

Renaissance (which harkens back to earlier usages) and African American modernism more appropriately broadens this literary period geographically and conceptually, removes this poetry from perceptions of ghettoization or isolation from the literary mainstream – as has been the case throughout the history of this genre – and places it more accurately and revealingly in dialogue with the British, American, and international Anglophone canons as they have developed. The self-confident voices and perspectives, and levels of verbal dexterity and formal innovation, are tied closely to the past of the genre instead of being presented, as is often the case, as unprecedented and anomalous. Rather than the first flowering of African American artistic originality, as it is often perceived, the New Negro Renaissance follows in a long tradition of self-possessed and self-assured originality, as demonstrated at the outset and throughout this book. From the roots that were already established, this era sees the further growth of African American poetics and criticism with towering critics such as J. Saunders Redding (1906–88), Brown, Alain Locke (1885–1954), and Johnson. Although the long life and monumental impact of Du Bois (1868–1963) resulted in multiple decades of lasting influence, his voice enters the tradition as early as 1903 with *The Souls of Black Folk* and its timeless chapter on "The Sorrow Songs," as he called the slave songs, the implications of his concept of "double consciousness," his bold statement about the color line, and his own under-appreciated poetry.

Typically characterized as a relatively brief era of spectacular literary production, this period also displays more diversity and a closer connection to national and international modernism than typically is recognized. As the product of a diaspora, the international dimension of African American poetry throughout its history is another under-examined feature that becomes especially prominent in this era of travel and expatriation. Surrealism and Negritude, and the ideas of Darwin and Marx, influenced many poets of this era. We again find little-known, forgotten, and under-appreciated poets who were working in highly original terrain, such as Will Sexton, Jonathan Henderson Brooks, Marcus B. Christian, Helene Johnson, and the full range of poetry by Bontemps and Waring Cuney, who often are viewed mistakenly as "single poem poets" – Bontemps for "Nocturne at Bethesda" and Cuney for "No Images." Other themes of the era are the literary impacts of cosmopolitanism, urbanization, Northern migration, and reactions against agrarian Southern society.

Just a few of the landmark publications that illustrate the new aesthetic directions of this period are Toomer's *Cane* (1923), James Weldon

Johnson's *American Negro Poetry* (1922) and *Books of American Negro Spirituals* (1925, 1926), Locke's *The New Negro* (1925), Hughes's *The Weary Blues* (1926), and two important single magazine issues, *Harlem: A Forum of Negro Life* (1928) and *Fire!!* (1926), both edited by Wallace Thurman (1902–34), which place the New Negro Renaissance in the tradition of modern little magazines that were publishing avant-garde manifestos. In the New Negro Renaissance, and through the mid-century transition to postmodernism, we also see the evolution – and traceable lineage – of African American poetry into disparate threads that are still perceptible today, and whose origins date back to the start of the genre.

By viewing modernism as extending from approximately 1910 to the era of World War II, we see the "New Negro" and "Black Arts" poets as part of an extended dialogue rather than separated by the middle of the century. In their essay "Foundations of African American Modernism, 1910–1950," Craig H. Werner and Sandra G. Shannon argue persuasively for this inclusive and expansive view of periodization based on similar motives and continuities in the earlier and later figures.[29] Other critics claim that the modern era ended in the 1960s, and still others agree with Mark A. Sanders that the early twentieth-century flowering of African American creativity continues today and has never ended. We may also call on Jean-Michel Rabaté, who considers the earliest wave of postmodernism to be a fulfillment of the need and desire to resolve the incomplete creative project begun in the first waves of modernism and interrupted by two world wars.

It is a common belief that African American protest poetry is a product of the Civil Rights Movement in the 1960s, but if we look at the full range of foundational literature in the African American tradition, we see protest, self-articulation, self-empowerment, and originality from the start. Thereby we have the foundation of a culture that prizes music and language in combination as a central social activity, and, in ironic tandem, white images of Africans as paid entertainers in exploitation of this trait. From the moment of their capture, the prominence of music, physical expression, and language in communication has been used both by and against African American poets. The 1950s and 1960s – contrary to stereotypes – reflected substantial social and political transformation and foment within the black literary community, including heightened empathy between African American writers such as Hayden and Dodson,

---

[29] Craig H. Werner and Sandra G. Shannon, "Foundations of African American Modernism, 1910–1950," in Maryemma Graham and Jerry W. Ward, Jr., eds., *The Cambridge History of African American Literature* (Cambridge: Cambridge University Press, 2011), pp. 241–67.

and European Jewish World War II survivors such as Rosey Pool, who engaged in a speaking tour of the HBCUs after the war. The 1960s and 1970s displayed tendencies that were formalist and accommodationist, as well as internationalist and formally innovative in their associations with Negritude, setting the scene for the surrealist experimentation to follow in figures such as Will Alexander (born in 1948) and Nathaniel Mackey (born in 1947). Such a readjusted perspective amplifies the fact that a fully operational and original African American literary canon was in active existence well before twentieth century writers came on the scene.

Issues of the oral tradition and performativity, introduced at the start of this book as part of the roots of the African American poetic tradition in the slave songs, become reinforced during the 1960s and 1970s, as black theatre and poetry became more aligned. From Dunbar to Margaret Walker, the performative component of this genre has been a recognizable trait. Don L. Lee's *Dynamite Voices: Black Poets of the 1960's* (1971) and Henderson's *Understanding the New Black Poetry* are shown to be touch-stones that articulate the aesthetic traits not only of this era, but also of its lineage within a black poetry tradition. Shange's "choreopoem," *For Colored Girls Who Have Considered Suicide / When the Rainbow is Enuf* (1975), reinforces the defining force of African American women poets during this period as much as any other, although questions have been raised about discrimination against women during the Black Arts Movement. With the full-blown emergence of performance poetry, hip-hop, spoken word, rap, and poetry slams, we see performance and orality reach a pinnacle of importance in the 1980s, and become organically reconnected to the genre.

This era may reflect the drama and power of the Black Arts Movement, but it also contains great diversity. In addition to creating poems during this period that are some of the centerpieces of the African American poetry canon, Hayden achieved two political milestones by winning the grand prize at the First World Festival of Negro Arts in Dakar (1966) and being named the first African American Consultant in Poetry to the Library of Congress (1976). This period still afforded relatively few publication and review opportunities in mainstream venues for African American poets. According to Melba Joyce Boyd's calculations, "From 1945 to 1965, only thirty-five poetry books by African Americans were published in the United States, and only nine of those were published by presses with national distribution."[30] For lack of other options, Hayden's

---

[30] Melba Joyce Boyd, *Wrestling with the Muse: Dudley Randall and the Broadside Press* (New York: Columbia University Press, 2004), p. 21.

first full-length collection was published in Breman's Heritage Series of Black Poetry, which was founded to publish Hayden. Dudley Randall (1914–2000), the US distributor of Heritage Press, was able to publish a collection of his own love poems, *Love You* (1971) with the Heritage Series rather than with his own more militant Broadside Press. Other publishing opportunities and venues, though limited, did exist. Jones/ Baraka's resounding *Preface to a Twenty Volume Suicide Note* was published in 1961 by Eli and Ted Wilentz's Beat-oriented Corinth Books. Ishmael Reed (born in 1938), Audre Lorde (1934–92), and Clarence Major (born in 1936) are examples of three African American poets during this era who exhibited sustained ingenuity, originality, and a nuanced approach to individual literary artistry and dissemination of their work during a time of perceived ideological dogmatism.

The lives, literary production, and influence of many poets in this tradition spanned several eras. For example, the aesthetic sensibilities of poets born around the time of World War I were heavily influenced by the New Negro Renaissance. The momentous project of Breman's Heritage Series provides a helpful case in point by demonstrating the hidden links between these two high profile generations. The series includes a number of poets who are worthy of far greater attention, including Atkins, Lloyd Addison (1931–2014), Fenton Johnson (1888–1958), Conrad Kent Rivers (1933–68), Ray Durem (1915–63), Calvin C. Hernton (1932–2001), Allen Polite (1932–93, whose personal papers were donated by his widow to Special Collections in the University of Connecticut Library), Cuney (1906–76), Ellease Southerland/Ebele Oseye (born in 1943), and others. The Press also exemplifies the international framework for African American poetry, which provided a more welcome environment than within America. Breman's project demonstrates the international dialogue that continues to be a prominent theme, partly as a result of the massive representation of African American soldiers serving in World War II. As disenfranchisement and alienation reached boiling points – in delicate tension with pressures to assimilate and accommodate – the anthemic poetry of Durem and Raymond Patterson (1929–2001) shows how the tone was set for the Black Arts and Black Power Movements. We also encounter two particularly important female voices during this era in Margaret Walker (1915–98) and Gwendolyn Brooks (1917–2000), and experience a perhaps unprecedented expansion of formal variety, from prose poems to sonnets to late modernist innovations signaling the coming explosion of postmodern experimentalism. In addition to the Black Arts Movement as the aesthetic wing – so perceived – of the Black Power Movement, key issues of that era include the relationships of both of those movements to the Civil Rights Movement, other literary/artistic organizations including Umbra, Free Lance, and Dasein, and themes of American nationalism/ self-empowerment and Pan-African internationalism, separatism, and diasporic consciousness. Little magazines and presses – many black-owned – rose to special prominence during this era, notably the literary magazines of HBCUs, and journals such as *Negro Digest/Black World, Journal of Black Poetry, Phylon, Umbra,* and *Black Dialogue,* along with the advent of four noteworthy black-oriented presses – Broadside, Third World, Heritage, and Lotus – to create an ever-expanding readership for African American poetry that continues to grow in the period covered by Chapter 5.

The book's final chapter addresses the contemporary period from the last decades of the twentieth century to the first two decades of the twenty-first. To demonstrate their inextricable links and parallels, this chapter examines the aftermath of the dialogue between the two most iconic periods of the African American poetry tradition, which are too often artificially separated. With Nielsen, in his brilliant and pathbreaking book, *Black Chant: Languages of African-American Postmodernism,* I situate a shift following World War II that marks a movement into a different – a postmodern – era, which does not necessitate drawing a rigid temporal or even stylistic boundary. It is an avant-garde motive and result that I am ascribing to the marginalized poets in this volume. As Chapter 5 discusses in detail, experimental poetry and African American poetry are often viewed as unrelated phenomena. Anthony Reed, Nielsen, Timothy Yu, Brent Hayes Edwards, and Shockley are among those critics who represent a new wave of interest in correlating innovative or experimental poetry with race, when it is true that lineages of experimental poetry have historically overlooked poets of color. When Nielsen published *Black Chant* in 1997, it was a novel perspective that a black author might use related forms of resistant, disruptive, oppositional, or "anti-absorptive" practices, to use the terminology of Charles Bernstein, as white authors.[31] Such an idea is no longer a novelty, in part because of Nielsen's body of critical writing, but there has still been slow progress in recognizing that an unimpeded range of creative freedoms is available to all poets regardless of their race.

---

[31] See, for example, Charles Bernstein, *Artifice of Absorption* (Philadelphia: Singing Horse Press, 1987).

The challenges of rationalizing possibilities of canon formation and periodization for African American poetry parallel that of modern and postmodern studies in mainstream Anglo-American literature, which has tended to center on the creative ferment inaugurating the twentieth century and the critical explosion in its final decades. Efforts at periodization have been stymied by how to categorize the century's middle decades, and even whether it has produced much work of value relative to the extended era in which it was produced. The gap in scholarly attention is perplexing since this tumultuous era encompasses a second world war and political events with lasting consequences. One recent solution within the academy has been to discuss the long twentieth century by shifting to an economic model to recalibrate measurements of aesthetic and cultural value. The same dilemma applies to mid-century African American poetry, which makes it important to counteract impressions that little of value was produced in mid-century.

In the last decades of the twentieth century, we see a continued increase in presses specializing in black literature, and new receptivity to publishing black poets in non-race-based forums. There is further growth of African American poetry in an international, diasporic, and postmodern framework. Reflecting curricular changes in American universities that now stress the value of ethnic, minority, and multicultural studies, there has been a wave of reconsideration and re-envisioning of American literature with increased recognition for the experiences, viewpoints, and expressions of various groups of minority and underrepresented poets. Poetry often is acknowledged to be on the margins of literature, and minority poetry – including African American – has been particularly, and deliberately in some corners, neglected. As the voice of correction and critique, African American poetry historically has been an especially marginalized genre.

Since the 1970s, African American postmodernism has reflected trends of neo-realism, verbal jazz improvisation, L=A=N=G=U=A=G=E poetry-inspired textual innovation, visual and conceptual poetries, hip-hop-inflected lyrics, sound environments and experiments, conceptual and multi-media projects, documentary poetics, music and poetry explorations, and an extraordinary expansion and extension of four centuries of prior creativity. There have been many artistic advances in this body of writing since the 1980s that pay tribute to and move forward the features discussed in the first four chapters of this book. By the contemporary period, we clearly see the very wholeness and continuity that Henderson asked to be noticed and honored. Progress does not indicate loss of memory. Instead, as we see African American poetry become increasingly influential nationally and internationally, a resounding case is made that this genre has fully articulated its own identity as a body of writing with distinctive features that remain engrained in consciousness of their origins, which they have the capacity to evolve meaningfully. Critical race theory grows in relevance in the context of a contemporary environment of racial mixing and claims of post-racialism, and in conjunction with pressing issues of American nationalism, ownership, migration, and identity. This book offers brief summaries of the existing canon but proposes a new alternative by placing special emphasis on the threads that have continued from the start of the tradition. Chief among these are a history of African American poetry as social and political action, the integral connection of innovation to tradition, stylistic and thematic diversity which have expanded and flourished with unprecedented variety since the closing years of the twentieth century, the massive recent growth of a racially diverse readership, changes to higher education that require sensitivity and exposure to ethnic studies, and all indications that these trends will continue. This body of writing is special and unique, while at the same time, it has played an integral role in the American and Anglophone literary and cultural tradition, though its contribution often is not fully recognized. It is a cohesive body of literature with its own tradition, worthy of study for its own value, and indispensable to any vision of American identity, literature, and culture.

This is an important moment to recognize the essential contribution of African American poetry to the Anglo-American literary canon. At this moment in time, HBCUs face unprecedented threats to their survival, African Americans face ongoing challenges to obtain equal treatment by law enforcement agencies, the prison-industrial complex has created what many consider to be a new system of enslavement, and issues of racial discrimination remain unresolved. As expected, African American poetry remains a potent venue to express outcry over these conditions with an increasing variety of platforms from the Internet to café settings. African American poetry has maintained its traditional role by articulating both individual and communal concerns, using music, language, and performance to convey resistance, and creating unity and self-determined expression. It also has expanded in a wide array of styles and forms. A constant in African American poetry has been a belief that art can produce social change and challenge the status quo. African American poetry holds an inextricable role in reflecting and defining the truth and totality of American experience, expression, and identity.

CHAPTER 2

The Origins of African American Poetry

Oh Freedom, oh Freedom,
Oh Freedom, over me!
Before I'll be a slave
I'll be buried in my grave,
And go home to my Lord and be free!

African American slave song

According to Henry Louis Gates, Jr., "The birth of the Afro-American literary tradition occurred in 1773, when Phillis Wheatley published a book of poetry."[1] It is widely accepted that the African American poetry tradition starts with Wheatley (c. 1753–84). Kidnapped from her birthplace in Gambia, West Africa, and sold into slavery as a child of only six or seven, Wheatley is an unusual case of a "slave" whose education, companionship, and prestige as a literary prodigy were of paramount importance to the Wheatley family who "purchased" her. Wheatley's volume *Poems on Various Subjects, Religious and Moral*, published in London, is regarded as the first poetry collection to be published by an African American. Many anthologies and books on the history of African American poetry start with the poems of Wheatley, who was manumitted by her owner, John Wheatley, in the same year that her only poetry collection was published.[2] During her sadly brief lifetime, Wheatley was famous both nationally and internationally for her extraordinary

---

[1] Henry Louis Gates, Jr., "Foreword: In Her Own Write," in Maria W. Stewart, Jarena Lee, Julia A. J. Foote, and Virginia W. Broughton, *Spiritual Narratives* (New York and Oxford: Oxford University Press, 1988), p. vii.

[2] Some examples of anthologies and historically important books that start with Wheatley as the first figure in the African American poetry tradition are Benjamin Brawley, *The Negro in Literature and Art in the United States*; Brown, Davis, and Lee, eds., *The Negro Caravan*; Richard Barksdale and Keneth Kinnamon, eds., *Black Writers of America*; Arthur P. Davis, J. Saunders Redding, and Joyce Ann Joyce, eds., *The New Cavalcade*, Vol. 1; Rochelle Smith and Sharon L. Jones, eds., *The Prentice Hall Anthology of African American Literature*; and Joan R. Sherman, ed., *African-American Poetry, 1773–1927*.

linguistic precociousness and literary talent. She has maintained her stature until the present day as one of the first Americans to publish a body of verse, an especially remarkable achievement considering her status as a young enslaved black woman. Wheatley's significance has been controversial: was she merely a novelty, or a poet of value? What does it mean to say that the African American poetry tradition starts with Wheatley? Are there other options? These are the first in a series of questions about the African American poetry tradition and canon – not necessarily the same things – that we will address throughout this chapter and book.

It is a common critical perspective that Wheatley would not have been able to gain acclaim as a serious poet had she not proven herself by emulating recognizable conventions associated with the esteemed white male poets of the day, such as Alexander Pope and John Milton. Of course, this is speculative, but is the claim true? Is it necessary for black poets to show mastery of mainstream literary modes to build an audience, have impact, and achieve respect? This question has been raised since the beginnings of this genre and demonstrates the complex relationship between style and esteem for black poets. Many critics note that Wheatley, who was widely acclaimed as a prodigy and genius during her lifetime, was extremely adept in mimicry, both linguistically and literarily. As discussed by Gates and others, she had to undergo a formal examination by a group of eminent white Bostonians to determine whether she was truly the author of her poetry. Without an "Attestation" of authenticity, she was assured that it would be nearly impossible to secure a publisher for her poetry collection.[3] This curious need for Wheatley's "proof" of authorship suggests the fraught dynamic between two concepts that are interwoven throughout the history of this genre: authenticity and originality. The idea of authenticity often correlates poems with racialized ideas about the poet's identity. When African American poems have been considered "authentic," they also have been called primitive and childish, which is part of the history of critical reception of the foundational slave songs, which will be addressed later in this chapter. Too often throughout American and European history, "originality" has been associated with white authors. African American poems that are deemed to be "inauthentic" are frequently called imitative and unoriginal.

---

[3] This experience is discussed by Henry Louis Gates, Jr. in several places, including "Foreword: In Her Own Write," pp. vii–x, and "Preface to Blackness: Text and Pretext," in Winston Napier, ed., *African American Literary Theory: A Reader* (New York and London: New York University Press, 2000), pp. 147–50.

Many of Wheatley's poems are Augustan apostrophes to ideals, such as "On Virtue," and paeans to esteemed pillars of colonial America, such as "To His Excellency General Washington." Critics have extolled Wheatley for interleaving her formalist verse with a subtle vein of subversion. For example, the first stanza of "To the University of Cambridge, in New-England" reads:

> 'Twas not long since I left my native shore
> The land of errors, and Egyptian gloom:
> Father of mercy, 'twas thy gracious hand
> Brought me in safety from those dark abodes.

The word "left," which implies a decision and volition, is a curious choice for someone who was the victim of the unthinkable crime of child-snatching. This poem is a hymn of praise to God for bringing her from her native land, described as a dark place of errors and gloom. The final stanza concludes with advice addressed to "Ye pupils" on avoiding sin:

> Ye blooming plants of human race devine,
> An *Ethiop* tells you 'tis your greatest foe;
> Its transient sweetness turns to endless pain,
> And in immense perdition sinks the soul.

The speaker, whose self-described origins are in a dark land of wrongs, transforms herself, through her deliverance, into the source of sage moral wisdom ("an *Ethiop* tells you ...") to Harvard College students about the correct path to save their souls by making religion their priority. We could view this maneuver as extreme audacity, a projection of a prophetic voice, or a manifestation of the Magical Negro topos. The contrast between her negative comments on her place of birth and her implicit claim of moral authority as a teacher demonstrates some of the fascinating tensions in teasing out the rhetorical posture and self-positioning of Wheatley.

Many critics have defended Wheatley's style and content by recognizing that it inevitably reflected the accepted verse of the period. While the use of standard literary forms and conventions would have been judged appropriate for the admired poets of her era, who were mainly white males, this style was questioned when used by someone of a different race and sex. It is no coincidence that one of the earliest books on the connection between literary racism and sexism, *The Sexual Mountain and Black Women Writers* by Calvin C. Hernton, opens with an epigraph from Wheatley.[4] Wheatley's critical reception was bifurcated: she was patronizingly admired for being able to imitate the poets who were held in the highest esteem, and simultaneously criticized for writing in a way that was deemed artificial and imitative for a black woman. Her status as a young black enslaved woman in colonial America made it necessary to reveal her talents strategically and with caution to keep up appearances of humility and propriety.

While she has been lauded as an originator, feminist, and cunning spokesperson for racial equality, Wheatley also has been criticized for modeling neoclassical formalist poets and writing without sufficient consciousness of her race. Some of the early major black critics who first formulated the concept and contents of an African American poetry canon shared misgivings about her seriousness and quality as a mature poet. Her use of wit, heroic couplets, learned allusions, decorous imagery, and moralizing platitudes in the School of Pope were called competent but second-rate copies. Like most critics, Brawley lauded Wheatley's accomplishments as being remarkable in the context of her disadvantages. Brawley wrote, "Alexander Pope was still an important force in English literature, and the young student [at about age fourteen] became his ready pupil ... one of the most interesting of her efforts is the pathetic little juvenile poem, 'On Being Brought from Africa to America,'" which has become one of her most famous and often anthologized poems.[5] Sterling A. Brown drew the same comparison and found Wheatley to be inferior and wanting: "Where Pope was intellectual and satiric, Phillis Wheatley was sentimental and pious; and where he was bold, she

---

[4] As an epigraph to *The Sexual Mountain and Black Women Writers: Adventures in Sex, Literature, and Real Life*, Calvin C. Hernton quotes the whole third stanza of Wheatley's poem, "To the Right Honorable William, Earl of Dartmouth:"

> Should you, my lord, while you peruse my song,
> Wonder from whence my love of Freedom sprung,
> Whence flow these wishes for the common good,
> By feeling hearts alone best understood,
> I, young in life, by seeming cruel fate
> Was snatched from Afric's fancy'd happy seat:
> What pangs excruciating must molest,
> What sorrows labour in my parent's breast?
> Steel'd was that soul and by no misery mov'd
> That from a father seiz'd his babe belov'd:
> Such, such my case. And can I then but pray
> Others may never feel tyrranic sway?

[5] Benjamin Brawley, *The Negro in Literature and Art in the United States* (San Bernardino, CA, 2016), p. 7.

was ... shyly imitative."[6] Similar dismissals of Wheatley's impact and influence as a black poet have appeared in all eras. Misspelling her name, Thomas Jefferson issued his famed critique which measured Wheatley unfavorably against Pope, one of her literary heroes: "Religion indeed has produced a Phyllis Whately [sic]; but it could not produce a poet. The compositions published under her name are below the dignity of criticism. The heroes of the *Dunciad* are to her, as Hercules to the author of that poem."[7] James Weldon Johnson also focused on the significance of Wheatley's being a "first" or an "early." Johnson claimed that Wheatley's frequent omission from textbooks of the era was "some sort of conspiracy," which is a tantalizing comment since the nature of this perceived conspiracy remains suggested but not explained. Johnson did not connect Wheatley's importance – or, presumably, her exclusion – to her race or to her literary quality, but rather to her sex, and stressed her place in the national order over the racial order:

> Of course, she is not a *great* American poet – and in her day there were no great American poets – but she is an important American poet. Her importance, if for no other reason, rests on the fact that, save one, she is the first in order of time of all the women poets of America. And she is among the first of all American poets to issue a volume."[8]

For Alice Walker, Wheatley's importance was *that* she wrote, not what she wrote: "It is not so much what you sang, as that you kept alive, in so many of our ancestors, *the notion of song*."[9]

Another popular perspective, especially in recent decades, is to name Lucy Terry (1724/6–1821), as the founding figure of African American poetry. Although a relatively late addition to the canon, and absent from many early anthologies and critical studies, Terry (who is also referred to by her married names of Luce Abijah and Lucy Prince) is viewed by many as the founding mother of African American poetry for her symbolic role rather than her literary contribution.[10] The only known poem to be attributed to Terry, "Bars Fight, August 28th, 1746," is considered

---

[6] Sterling A. Brown, *Negro Poetry and Drama and The Negro in American Fiction* (New York: Atheneum, 1972), p. 5.

[7] Houston A. Baker, Jr., *Afro-American Poetics: Revisions of Harlem and the Black Aesthetic* (Madison, WI: University of Wisconsin Press, 1988), p. 115.

[8] James Weldon Johnson, ed., *The Book of American Negro Poetry* (CreateSpace Independent Publishing Platform edition, 2018), p. 12.

[9] Angelyn Mitchell, ed., *Within the Circle: An Anthology of African American Literary Criticism from the Harlem Renaissance to the Present* (Durham and London: Duke University Press, 1994), p. 405.

[10] Langston Hughes and Arna Bontemps are often credited with introducing Terry and her poem into the canon by including her in their co-edited volume, *The Poetry of the Negro, 1746–1949*.

the first written by an African American. Although she lived well into her nineties, and was renowned for her rhetorical skills, the only surviving piece of her writing is this poem created when she was a young woman. Her date of birth usually appears as 1730, which makes this poem the product of a sixteen-year old. But in her brilliantly authoritative biography, *Mr. and Mrs. Prince: How an Extraordinary Eighteenth-Century Family Moved Out of Slavery and Into Legend* (2008), Gretchen Holbrook Gerzina proves that Terry was a young girl of five or six in 1730 when she arrived in Deerfield, Massachusetts from Africa, and not an infant, as is often claimed. "Bars Fight" was reduced by Redmond to "twenty-eight-line doggerel," and even Gerzina acknowledges it as "a singsongy ballad."[11] Gerzina's painstakingly researched and revelatory biography of Terry and her family describes in detail the circumstances that produced this occasional poem. The subject is an unexpected and bloody raid on a community of settlers. This twenty-eight-line ballad, loosely metered in the iambic tetrameter that formed a popular pattern for song lyrics of the era, commemorated an attack on an area of Deerfield, Massachusetts called the Bars, which consisted of "two deserted houses and a field of corn and vegetables."[12] Thought to have been written in about 1746, it was not published until thirty years after her death, in 1855.[13] The poem was well enough known during Terry's lifetime that it was perpetuated, most likely as song lyrics, until its first publication in the *Springfield Daily Republican* more than a century after it was written.[14]

This poem has been criticized, like the writing of Wheatley, for identifying with the perspective of the society that enslaved her and was called "doggerel" and worse. The frequent use of the descriptive and evaluative term "doggerel" by the earliest serious African American literary critics in describing the perceived founders of the tradition cannot be overlooked.

[11] Redmond, *Drumvoices*, p. 50; Gretchen Holbrook Gerzina, *Mr. and Mrs. Prince: How an Extraordinary Eighteenth-Century Family Moved Out of Slavery and Into Legend* (New York: Amistad/HarperCollins, 2009), p. 3.

[12] Gerzina, *Mr. and Mrs. Prince*, p. 77.

[13] Some anthologies (in addition to Hughes and Bontemps's) that open with Terry (Prince) as the first African American poet are Jerry W. Ward, Jr., ed., *Trouble the Water*; Valerie Lee, ed., *The Prentice Hall Anthology of African American Women's Literature*; and Dudley Randall, ed., *The Black Poets*.

[14] Before its first publication on the front page of the November 20, 1854 edition of the *Springfield Daily Republican*, the only known copy of this poem was handwritten and located in Pliny Arms's papers at the Pocumtuck Valley Memorial Association in Deerfield (Arms Family Papers, box 13, folder 17), according to Gerzina (*Mr. and Mrs. Prince*, note 80, p. 221). It is not possible to have an accurate understanding of the facts versus the romanticized fictions about Lucy Terry Prince and her life without reading Gerzina's book, which is a major contribution to our knowledge of this previously mysterious figure.

An onomatopoetic word that derives from "dog," it contains tones of burlesquing, and making the poems and their creators the butt of a joke. "Doggerel" elevates the position and judgment of the critic to the proverbial catbird seat. This gesture simultaneously transforms perceptions of the poet into a domesticated pet, which evokes the animal imagery often used to describe African Americans by slave-holders in plantation culture. The frequent use of this word by multiple African American critics reinforces the argument that I am building about the attitude of scholarship towards the "originators" of the tradition, and the complications of anointing these figures as the sole originators of the canon.

Regardless of dismissals of its quality, "Bars Fight" may be viewed generously as a precursor of several dominant features that continue to appear in the African American poetry genre. Music and poetry are connected since this poem is believed to have originally been intended as song lyrics. It is written in ballad form rather than a poetic form that was more culturally esteemed in this era, such as blank verse. The subject is political and topical. Its purpose is to protest and witness for the innocent and overmatched sufferers of racial discrimination and violence, in this case the white victims of a Native American raid. The diction is conversational and colloquial rather than elaborated figures, and ornate or Latinate diction. It shows empathy and value for the lives of ordinary individuals and calls out their names and personal details. Nonetheless, it would be difficult to make a case that the poem has had significant literary influence, just as it would be difficult to make the case that the actual tone, content, and style of Wheatley have had a major impact on generations of poets to follow.

African American poetry is a discipline full of opportunities for much-needed research and better understanding, but there has been progress in interest and knowledge. As one example, what we now know about Terry has increased immensely from the late twentieth century. In 1963, Bontemps wrote that she remained a slave for her entire life, which is now known to be untrue. Like Wheatley, Terry was abducted from Africa as a child, and enslaved until she married a freeman, Abijah Prince, who purchased her freedom. Her remarkable life after becoming Lucy Terry Prince has been critically and creatively researched and imagined. Although no additional poems by Terry (Prince) have been found, her long and courageous life has been well-documented. Two valuable biographies are the volume by Gerzina, and a biography for young readers, *Black Woman: A Fictionalized Biography of Lucy Terry Prince* by Bernard and Jonathan Katz.[15] Terry's situation as the author of one known poem differs from that of Wheatley, who published an entire poetry collection, but her single effort also has been met with ambivalent critical reception and regard.

Yet another perspective launches the African American poetry tradition with Jupiter Hammon (1711– c. 1806), who did live his entire life in chattel enslavement. Hammon wrote a poem in 1760 titled "An Evening Thought, Salvation by Christ, with Penitential Cries," which was published in 1761. Although written fifteen years after Terry's poem, Hammon's poem is widely regarded as the first to be published by a person of African descent in the country that became the United States of America. Hammon was considered by J. Saunders Redding – whom Gates called "the veritable Dean of Afro-American literary critics" – to be "the first Negro writer in America" and "the first American Negro to see his name in print as a maker of verse."[16] Yet Hammon's poetry too was reviled by critics. Jean Wagner writes, "If the quality of his verse were the only criterion [versus the fact that he wrote "the oldest extant poem by an American Negro"] we might well consign him to oblivion forthwith."[17] Sterling A. Brown found it "noteworthy" that broadsides were being published by "a Negro slave" when most American colonists were too busy homesteading to write poetry. But "these were by no means good poems," which Brown summarized as "crude doggerel." Brown identified Wheatley and Hammon as suffering from the same shortcoming: they gave back only what they "had got from others." If they had been more themselves, their literary place "might have been greater than that of a curiosity."[18]

What is the significance of designating these figures and documents as the foundations of the African American poetry tradition? All three poets were enslaved at the time of their landmark writing. All three learned to read and write and produced their poetry in written form. They have been widely judged as unique or exemplary individuals, not as typical of

---

[15] The Lucy Terry Prince collection, which contains research materials relating to *Black Woman: A Fictionalized Biography of Lucy Terry Prince* (1973) by Bernard Katz and Jonathan Katz, is housed in the Schomburg Center for Research in Black Culture, Manuscripts, Archives and Rare Books Division, New York Public Library.

[16] J. Saunders Redding, *To Make a Poet Black* (Ithaca: Cornell University Press, 1988), pp. 3–4 and vii.

[17] Jean Wagner, *Black Poets of the United States: From Paul Laurence Dunbar to Langston Hughes*, tr. Kenneth Douglas (Urbana and Chicago: University of Illinois Press, 1973), p. 17.

[18] Brown, *Negro Poetry and Drama*, pp. 4–5 and 5–6.

African Americans, although – paradoxically and ironically – they also were evaluated based on their race and as group representatives. Their achievements were considered notable in the contexts of their tragic life circumstances in a state of enslavement, which inevitably positioned them as pitiable. We must ask what is the significance and value of the position of "first" in relation to a literary canon, and what does this designation particularly imply in an African American context? In his introduction to Redding's classic text *To Make A Poet Black*, originally published in 1939, Gates calls Brawley the first to introduce the notion of a canon – a tradition of African American writing, by calling it out – "to *assert* the existence of this 'great' black aesthetic tradition..."[19] Gates considers Redding to be "the tradition's first eminent scholar-critic," who built on Brawley's foundation to produce "the first sophisticated book of literary criticism published about Afro-American literature." Gates credits Redding with producing a "system" of defining and connecting the constituent units (p. xvi).

With Redding in this preeminent position, his views on the founding figures, who he calls "The Forerunners," are of paramount importance. Redding opens his study with this important claim: "The literature of the Negro in America, motivated as it is by his very practical desire to adjust himself to the American environment, is 'literature of necessity.'" By needing to maintain "two faces," Redding points out that black writers needed to satisfy two different audiences, black and white, which were "opposed when not entirely opposite" (p. 3). Like "threads through the whole cloth," these positions – he claims – run straight through the African American literary tradition from its origins. Redding describes the poetry of Hammon as "rhymed prose, doggerel," which encapsulated his "homely thoughts" in "limping phrases" (p. 4) Wheatley was castigated as one of "The Mocking-Bird School of Poets" for her lack of originality, authenticity, and racial consciousness; being little more than a curiosity for having a good memory and an aptitude that enabled her to master culturally admired skills; and succeeding only in ineptly imitating the prevailing tastes in European culture, including the poetry of Pope, Milton, and Homer.[20] "This early group of poets suffered from too great decorousness," we read in *The Negro Caravan*. Though *The Negro Caravan*

---

[19] Redding, *To Make a Poet Black*, p. xv. Subsequent page references are given in parentheses in the text.

[20] See the section called "Part I, The Negro in American Poetry, Early American Negro Poetry" in *Negro Poetry and Drama and The Negro in American Fiction*, pp. 4–31.

modulates these criticisms with empathy for the poets' circumstances, Brown stands by the accusations in his assessment of Hammon's poetry as "crude doggerel" and Wheatley's poetry as the product of "a cultured Bostonian whose chief interests were in the library."[21]

Here we arrive at a critical dilemma that haunts this genre to the present. One would expect the "originators" of a literary tradition to be judged as exemplary in quality and as making a truly original contribution, yet the literary achievements and legacies of these three figures have been treated with ambivalence at best. They have been assessed largely for their questionable ability and ambitions to reflect the prevailing tastes and dominant features of the contemporaneous Anglo-American poetry canon. Even when these poets exhibited self-awareness as members of a marginalized population with an alternative history, they were measured by their skill at enrobing their poems in conventional literary garb. Although Walt Whitman has been revered for his efforts to create an authentic "American" style, form, and diction as distinct from British exemplars, African American poets were not comparably rewarded for striving to forge their own self-determined modes of poetic originality. In fact, the situation is the opposite: efforts to generate an African American poetic mode that builds on and acknowledges its own history and traditions have been mocked and dismissed. African American poetry that used the conventions of the white canon has been judged as substandard. It should be made clear that I am summarizing the complicated history of critical reception, and not endorsing its perspectives or judgments. At moments throughout the history of African American literary criticism, Wheatley, Terry, and Hammon all have been denigrated as amateurish, reviled as inauthentic, and ridiculed as imitative. The earliest critics of African American poetry, such as Brawley and Redding, would have been the most influential in establishing the existence and definition of an African American poetry canon. Their views on these three foundational figures were, at best, grudgingly respectful and, at worst, outright dismissive. How did these figures come to be seen and taught as the cornerstones of the African American poetry canon? Is there only one African American poetry canon, or have there always been canons in the plural from the outset which we continue to see played out today?

Throughout this book, we will ask the questions "why this text and not that text?" or "why not this text *and* that text?" Is there a way that

---

[21] Brown, Davis, and Lee, eds., *The Negro Caravan*, pp. 275, 5 and 13.

visions and traditions can be valuably seen together? While I do not propose definitive answers, I hope to raise provocations and reconsiderations. Canons by their nature tend to be conservative, but I believe the stakes in canon formation are raised for a population that is already silenced and marginalized. In addition to qualifications about their literary value and originality, there are further problems in viewing Terry, Hammon, and Wheatley as the sole founding figures of the tradition. Referred to not only as "slave poets," but also as exemplars of the so-called "literary tradition," all three represent the print culture, and publication as the standard of literary value, which overlooks the essential role of oral and unpublished literature. All three represent the voices and perspectives of enslaved African Americans, which erases the African origins of black people in America, and the literature – both written and oral – of free African Americans. In relation to the presence of a black population in the nation that became the United States of America, they are chronologically too late to represent the origins of the tradition. John Rolfe documented the arrival in 1619 of an English warship to the colony at Jamestown, Virginia with a cargo of "20 and odd Negroes" to live in servitude, before slavery existed as a full-fledged institution.[22] It is an often-cited statistic that this date and event mark the origins of black people in the land of the future United States. The influential compilation *The Negro Caravan* reflects this standard belief. Its chronology of major historical and literary events lists 1619 as the year that the "First Negroes landed in Virginia" (p. 1062).

However, there is ample evidence that black people, both free and in various forms of indenture, were in the future United States at least a century earlier. Several figures have been cited as "the first" black person to arrive well before 1619. For example, Gates identifies a free man and conquistador named Juan Garrido as "the first documented black person to arrive in this country" when he accompanied Ponce de Leon on his 1513 expedition to Florida seeking the Fountain of Youth, and later traveled to California in the 1530s.[23] *The Norton Anthology of African American Literature* starts its chronology in 1492, with Pedro Alonzo Nino, "traditionally considered the first person of many New World

---

[22] For example, see the website of historic Jamestown for a reference to "The first documented arrival of Africans to the colony of Virginia": www.nps.gov/jame/learn/historyculture/african-americans-at-jamestown.htm (last accessed August 23, 2018).

[23] The source of this information is The Root: www.theroot.com/articles/history/2012/10/who_was_the_first_african_american_100_amazing_facts_about_the_negro/ (last accessed August 23, 2018).

explorers of African descent," who sailed with Christopher Columbus. The next date listed in Norton's chronology is 1526, when the Spanish brought the first African slaves to the country that became the United States. The year 1619 is the third date listed in this chronology.[24] As early as 1790, the census of this new nation reported that there was a population of 697,897 "slaves," and 59,466 "free colored." By the time of the 1860 census, just before the start of the Civil War, we find 487,970 "free colored" and 3,953,760 "slaves" in the United States, with both populations having increased dramatically since the 1850 census.[25]

While it is inarguable that the majority of black people in America are descendants of kidnapped Africans sold into slavery, it is equally true that there has always been a significant population of free black people in America, either manumitted slaves, or born and always free. If the African American poetry tradition is widely perceived to be based solely on the writing of enslaved people of African ancestry in English-speaking America, and whose primary stylistic influences come from the Western canon, what are the implications? It is a common belief that most, or even all, black people in colonial and antebellum America were the victims, or their descendants, of kidnapping in Africa who were sold into slavery. It is another common perspective that virtually all black Americans were illiterate before the Civil War because of laws prohibiting enslaved African Americans from reading and writing, but as an indication of the rapid increase in knowledge since the late twentieth century about African American literature, history, and culture, we now know that far more enslaved African Americans could read and write than had been believed previously. Most estimates are that between 10 and 30 percent of enslaved blacks had basic levels of literacy and numeracy, while African Americans in the North could read and write at far higher levels. For the enslaved, this figure may well be underestimated, owing to the necessary circumstances of secrecy.

The notion prevails that there was a miniscule body of "early" African American poetry – meaning before the twentieth century – which necessitated that virtually all poems and poets be included in the canonical record almost as artifacts. But we gain a clearer perspective of the prevalence and value placed on writing, including poems, from scholars who have done foundational work that still has not been fully built upon. Starting in 1974 with her revelatory anthology, *Invisible Poets: Afro-Americans*

---

[24] Henry Louis Gates, Jr., and Valerie Smith, gen. eds., *The Norton Anthology of African American Literature*, 3rd edn. (New York: Norton, 2014), Vol. 1, p. 1373.

[25] www2.census.gov/prod2/decennial/documents/1860a-02.pdf (last accessed August 23, 2018).

of the Nineteenth Century, followed by *African-American Poetry of the Nineteenth-Century: An Anthology* (1992), Joan R. Sherman has brought attention to numerous fascinating and diverse poets who too often remain invisible even in the present. *Beyond Bondage: An Anthology of Verse by African Americans of the Nineteenth Century*, edited by Erika DeSimone and Fidel Louis represents a marvelous contribution to scholarship which presents a selection of poems by African Americans published between 1827 and 1899 by black presses. Presumably "beyond bondage" means freedom by means of inscribed and published poetic expression, since many of these poems were written well before Emancipation, and the contributors were "slaves, former slaves, the children of slaves, or free people of African descent."[26] Even the choice of publisher extends the lineage of this documentary project of revisionism. NewSouth Books, whose origins are in a cooperative founded in 1984 called the Black Belt Communications Group, is committed to printing "regional books of national interest," which is an apt description of the voices represented in this anthology. One hundred and fifty poems have been selected and are presented with invaluable editorial commentary and a superb introductory essay, offering fresh insight into the relationship between black poets and black presses, which becomes a topic of continuing importance as this tradition develops. Though the topic of black-owned presses was addressed most prominently during the 1960s and 1970s, that limited perspective overlooks the legacy established by many earlier African American poets who published newspapers and journals, including Alfred Gibbs Campbell and Fenton Johnson. Highlighting early publishers such as Samuel E. Cornish, John B. Russworm, David Ruggles, Frederick Douglass, T. Thomas Fortune, and Peter Williams, Jr., DeSimone and Louis show that poetry was an essential component at the birth of black publishing from the colonial period onwards, ranging from "news" handsewn into quilts, to early black pamphlets, to the establishment of the nation's first black-owned and operated newspaper, *Freedom's Journal*, in 1827, all of which routinely featured poems. The extent of African Americans writing poetry becomes evident by the presentation of better-known poets such as Horton side by side with many iterations of "Anonymous" who were still, like Horton, in the bonds of enslavement but felt compelled to give voice to their emotions, ideas, and experiences.

---

[26] Erika DeSimone and Fidel Louis, eds., *Voices Beyond Bondage: An Anthology of Verse by African Americans of the 19th Century* (Montgomery: NewSouth Books, 2014), p. vii.

The earliest and largest canon of African American poetry is the oral poetry of slave songs, or spirituals, which will be discussed in detail later in this chapter. As I have written elsewhere, my preference is to use the word "slave songs" for this term's more inclusive suggestion, and to redirect critical attention to their value and function as poetic texts rather than as Christian folk hymns. "Slave songs" is a more historically and aesthetically appropriate term. It echoes the title of the first major compilation of these poems, *Slave Songs of the United States* (1867) edited by William Francis Allen, Charles Ware, and Lucy McKim Garrison. It is a misperception that these sung poems were all "spiritual" in nature, an image perpetuated by abolitionists who wanted to convey the impression that enslaved African Americans were all placid and pious Christians who cared for nothing but religion and reaching Heaven. "Slave songs" articulates the conditions and circumstances of their production as an essential part of their meaning and significance.[27] Representing African survivals melded with the experience of the Middle Passage and plantation culture, the origins of slave songs date to the moment of kidnap in Africa.

They function as a composite of African and American experiences – in this sense, they may be the most authentic record of how "African Americans" came to be. They present an alternative way to perceive the origins of the genre. The result is to illuminate how the canon developed over time and recover important literature that was lost or omitted through the currently limited view of the tradition's birth. By relocating the roots of the African American poetry tradition, we see more clearly the integral role of music. That view applies not only to Lucy Terry's poem as popular song lyrics, but also to the extraordinary endeavor of such marginalized figures as Joshua McCarter Simpson to produce counter-songs to erase and revise the body of American music and lyrics that reviled African Americans. This perspective also allows us to see the close connections among music, poetry, and social protest that date to the origins of this tradition and have never abated. The influence of slave songs on African American poetry as it has evolved is far more pronounced than that of the so-called originators. The voluminous quantity of African American poetry that has been influenced by slave songs may even exceed those poems without allusions to these truly foundational texts.

In the eighteenth and nineteenth centuries, numerous literate African Americans were writing verse. These poets, both free and enslaved,

[27] Ramey, *Slave Songs and the Birth of African American Poetry*, p. 10.

knew about and alluded to a black American literary tradition, as well
as the Anglo-American canon. In anthologies as early as *Old Plantation
Hymns: a collection of hitherto unpublished melodies of the slave and the
freeman, with historical and descriptive notes*, edited by William E. Barton
(1899), we already see the development of a self-referencing tradition.
Formal diversity is notable: some poems are in conventional canonical
forms; some reflect the structures, diction, perspectives, and imagery of
slave songs, hymns, and African survivals; and some presage the more
open forms that will follow in the periods ahead. Many contain signifiers of race and key themes: African American Christianity and biblical
imagery, slave songs, plantation culture, black dialect, Abraham Lincoln,
Frederick Douglass, freedom, black Civil War regiments and soldiers,
slavery, Emancipation, the Negro race, and struggles and progress. As
with the work collected by Sherman, and DeSimone and Louis, these
writings remain little known. Some nineteenth-century poets, such as the
sophisticated and often bitterly ironic voices of James Monroe Whitfield
(1822–71) and Alfred Gibbs Campbell (1827–84), were famed and
extolled during their lifetimes, yet are unjustly overlooked or entirely forgotten today. This pattern of erasure, and failure to recognize continuities
connected to progressions, appears in the twentieth century, which will
be discussed in later chapters.

Despite other significant sources and voices – including slave songs –
the canon is based on the premise that its foundational texts were written by one of three enslaved African Americans. These are remarkable
and essential voices to be represented. The direct experience of slavery,
and the ability to speak from and about that state, is an integral part of
American and African American history and culture. In the case of Terry
and Wheatley, we even encounter the voices of individuals who were
born in Africa, experienced the horror of being kidnapped in childhood,
and survived the Middle Passage. Wheatley, Terry, and Hammon have
earned their stature as figures of historical importance, and perhaps of literary value, though we have seen the differences of opinion on this matter. But by presenting them as the sole originators of this tradition, other
traditions have been marginalized that have equal claim to be foundational to the canon. Their exclusions also reveal important insight about
what has been suppressed and why. Some features that are described as
later developments in the African American poetry tradition – such as
formal innovation and voices of protest – are shown to have far earlier
roots. Throughout each subsequent generation, the African American
poets themselves certainly have been aware of many of these other and
more diverse influences and literary ancestors.

The problem with the existing scenario rests in the ideological implications of the exclusions, as well as the significance of those marginalized writings. The two most important bodies of literature to be excluded at the start of the tradition are the voices of free African Americans and oral literature, which is as literary as the written discourse in this tradition. The canon as it now stands is discriminatory and ideological. It starts too late and is insufficiently inclusive and representative. In the Introduction to *American Negro Poetry* (1963), Bontemps writes, "Lucy Terry and Phillis Wheatley, along with such other American Negroes as Jupiter Hammon and George Moses Horton, belong to a tradition of writers in bondage which goes back to Aesop and Terence."[28] By starting with Wheatley, Hammon, and Terry, the medium of print – both as the method of production and the mode of dissemination through publication – is valorized, as is the setting of the (future) United States of America, which ignores the diasporic history of this transnational, intercultural, inter-linguistic, and transatlantic population. By using the existing touchstones, the entirety of the African American poetry tradition is perceived to have been founded by enslaved people of African descent in the eighteenth century. The tradition also is reductively misrecognized as being more uniform in style, content, and purpose than is accurate when its full breadth and diversity are recognized.

From the earliest recorded material, there have been observations about the importance of song, poetry, dance, and storytelling in the cultures of Africa. It is well documented as early as the seventeenth century that this propensity was used against the kidnapped Africans by their white captors as a method of degradation. At the same time, it was used by the kidnapped Africans, and later during enslavement, for their own wellbeing and survival. Captors used these deeply embedded practices to reinforce perceptions that the kidnapped Africans were different and inferior, to inflict control and humiliation, and to debase them into the positions of comic entertainers. The enslaved Africans used the same practices to facilitate communication, retain self-esteem, reinforce their identity as sentient subjects, subversively reject the belief systems of their captors, preserve ancestral traditions, augment community, and convey refusal and resistance towards their imposed objectification and state of unwilling captivity.

Sea captain Richard Jobson wrote in his 1623 report on the West African slave trade, "There is without doubt, no people on the earth more

---

[28] Arna Bontemps, ed., *American Negro Poetry* (New York: Hill and Wang, 1963), p. xvii.

naturally affected to the sound of musicke than these people." Describing his experience in the Gambia River region, Jobson explained that "they use the singing of Songs" to exalt their history, important people and acts, and, in his particular case, "praise of us white men" – for a gratuity.[29] Olaudah Equiano, kidnapped from his birthplace in Benin, wrote this famous line in one of the earliest "slave narratives" (1789): "We are almost a nation of dancers, musicians, and poets."[30] Scottish surgeon Mungo Park, who explored the region of the Niger River between 1795 and 1797, described the centrality of music and poetry to the African daily social fabric: "With the love of music is naturally connected a taste for poetry, and fortunately for the poets of Africa, they are in a great measure exempted from that neglect and indigence, which in more polished countries commonly attend the votaries of the Muses." Park explained that there were two classes of singers. The first was those who "sing extempore songs in honor of their chief men, or any other persons who are willing to give 'solid pudding for empty praise.'" This class of singers also preserved historical events and great deeds of ancestors. The other class sang religious hymns and performed religious services, mainly Muslim. Park also described the function, style, and content of songs spontaneously created by the women as they spun cotton. This singing while working together was an integral part of West African cultures, which also registered emphatic consciousness of the white outsiders who functioned as the recorders:

> They lightened their labour by songs, one of which was composed ex tempore, for I myself was the subject of it. It was sung by one of the young women, the rest joining in a sort of chorus: The air was sweet and plaintive, and the words literally translated, were these: "The winds roared, and the rains fell:–The poor white man, faint and weary, came and sat under our tree: He has no mother to bring him milk; no wife to grind his corn. Chorus: Let us pity the white man; no mother has he, &c. &c."[31]

Several qualities discussed here are precursors of the oral tradition and slave songs that are entitled to be seen as the foundation of African American – and American – poetry. Here we find the tradition of group

---

[29] Quoted in Eileen Southern, ed., *Readings in Black American Music*, 2nd edn. (New York: Norton, 1983) p. 1.

[30] Olaudah Equiano, *The Interesting Narrative of the Life of Olaudah Equiano, or Gustavus Vassa, the African. Written by Himself* (1789), Vol. 1, p. 14. Electronic edition http://abolition.nypl.org/content/docs/text/life_of_equiano.pdf (last accessed August 19, 2018).

[31] Mungo Park's *Travels in the Interior Districts of Africa*, first published in 1799. Quoted in Southern, ed., *Readings in Black American Music*, pp. 5–6.

singing to lighten the load of labor, the antiphonal structure of call-and-response with a solo voice followed by a chorus, an attitude of pity for anyone who is separated from family, a perspective of strength in community action ("let us"), and the correlation of nature with human emotions and circumstances. Proposing that the African American poetry tradition starts with printed texts in the eighteenth century that is patently imitative of contemporaneous British exemplars such as Pope and Milton denies the African values, practices, traditions, and memories that are the birthright of African Americans.

An example of a slave song that echoes the tropes and ethos of the song recalled by Park is "Sometimes I Feel Like a Motherless Child," also performed as call-and-response between a leader and the group:

> Sometimes I feel like a motherless child,
> Sometimes I feel like a motherless child,
> Sometimes I feel like a motherless child,
> A long way from home.
>
> Sometimes I feel like a feather in the air,
> Sometimes I feel like a feather in the air,
> Sometimes I feel like a feather in the air,
> A long way from home.
>
> Sometimes I feel like I'm almost gone,
> Sometimes I feel like I'm almost gone,
> Sometimes I feel like I'm almost gone,
> A long way from home.
>
> True believer, true believer,
> A long way from home.

Early white observers noted the centrality of music, dance, and song to Africans. Dena J. Epstein cites Prince Henry the Navigator of Portugal who, in 1445, described the sad and incomprehensible (to him), singing of captured Africans, who "made their lamentations in songs, according to the customs of their country, which, although we could not understand their language, we saw corresponded well to the height of their sorrow."[32] Plentiful historical documents about life in Africa record the rich oral culture and expressive modes of verbal communication for creative, emotional, and documentary purposes. Linguistic expression was integrally connected to music and dance. It was a social

---

[32] Epstein, *Sinful Tunes and Spirituals*, p. 3, n. 3.

phenomenon, mainly addressed to other members of the same group for worship, building and sustaining community, and preserving history. Documentary evidence shows that members of the African diaspora carried their traditions and practices with them, as they communicated while in transit, and, after their arrival, blended their past with new experiences in a distant land. The multiplicities of languages necessitated finding common linguistic ground after groups of kidnapped Africans were joined together during the long process of transporting them to the slave ships and their frightful destinations. Many scholars have observed that the diverse groups shared greater commonalities of practices, beliefs, and attitudes than differences, despite their differing languages and dialects.

There is extensive evidence that African survivals from oral culture are present in the earliest poetry of the enslaved African Americans in plantation culture. Part One of *The Music of Black Americans: A History* by Eileen Southern is a superb resource on the role of poetry and music in West Africa from 1619 to 1775, and their omnipresent function in the lives of individuals and the community for purposes of work, recreation, historical records, holidays, news, advice, emotional sustenance, topical commentary, and worship. Southern's opening section is followed by an outstanding history and analysis of the continued influence and evolutions of African traditions and practices in America through the twentieth century. Interdisciplinary scholars find overwhelming proof that slave songs preserved African survivals as well as musical, liturgical, theological, historical, sociological, linguistic, and experiential influences of plantation culture in a state of enslavement. In his indispensable book *The African Imagination: Literature in Africa and the Black Diaspora*, F. Abiola Irele constructs the argument that both oral and written texts must be considered literary in the discourse system of African and African diasporic literature. If we look at the origins of African American literature as coming from African survivals and other products of oral culture including slave songs, as well as poetry by free African Americans in colonial and antebellum culture, the diverse totality of this genre emerges in a much more exciting and dynamic way than if it is limited to Hammon, Wheatley, and Terry. It also is more accurate to look at the influence of slave songs as far stronger for twenty-first century and future generations than the poetry of Wheatley, Hammon, and Terry, as will be shown in later chapters. This point of view will form an important thread throughout this book in defining and defending an African American poetry tradition with roots that are innovative and original, self-invented and self-reflexive, resistant and assertive, and transnational and international.

It is naïve to imagine that the process of becoming an African American started on plantations on American soil. For the kidnapped Africans, the journey from their former lives to enslavement was unimaginably cruel, treacherous, and debilitating physically, emotionally, and psychologically. The process of becoming African Americans, and producers of African American cultural products, began at the nightmare moment of irrevocable capture. Extensive resources document the history of North American slavery as the crucible of a new form of community, which centrally entailed creative uses of language and culture inspired by West African traditions. In-depth scholarship on this topic can be found in many outstanding texts, including *Scenes of Subjection: Terror, Slavery, and Self-Making in Nineteenth Century America* by Saidiya V. Hartman, *Culture on the Margins: The Black Spiritual and The Rise of American Cultural Interpretation* by Jon Cruz, and two classic texts, *Roll, Jordan, Roll* by Eugene D. Genovese, and *Black Culture, Black Consciousness* by Lawrence Levine. *The Slave Ship: A Human History* by Marcus Rediker, *Ring Shout, Wheel About: The Racial Politics of Music and Dance in North American Slavery* by Katrina Dyonne Thompson, and *Reversing Sail: A History of the African Diaspora* by Michael A. Gomez provide well-detailed accounts of the experiences and operations of the journey to and through the Middle Passage. The concept of Afro-Pessimism, addressed in an essay collection called *Afro-Pessimism: An Introduction*, builds on the work of esteemed scholar of slavery, Orlando Patterson. This theoretical lens asserts that "The social death of the slave goes to the very level of their being, defining their ontology," leaving a legacy of "anti-blackness" which lingers today.[33]

Kidnapped Africans were bound together, often stripped naked, and forced to walk in processions called coffles to their point of embarkation, where they could remain for another few months while recovering from the journey or awaiting the next slave ship. The physically restrained people in the coffles were made to carry materials and provisions, and forced either to be silent or to entertain their captors by singing and dancing. An expressive community of language and gesture would have begun to evolve as soon as the coffles were organized, to create a bridge between multiple African languages and dialects. The cruelty, indignities, suffering, and perils to health were unimaginable, and the death rate along the journey was extraordinary. Rediker shares a chilling sailor rhyme on the

---

[33] The Editors, *Afro-Pessimism: An Introduction* (Minneapolis: racked & dispatched. January 2017). Rackedanddispatched.noblogs.org (last accessed August 19, 2018).

odds of survival: "Beware and take care / Of the Bight of Benin; / For the one that comes out, / There are forty go in."[34] Gomez writes that it could take four months or longer simply to reach the coast, where captives could spend several additional months convalescing or awaiting a slaver.[35] Usually the captives were incarcerated in what were essentially holding pens called barracoons, often exposed to the elements, and sometimes moved from one barracoon to another before entering the hell of the slave ship itself.

Rediker discusses the necessary development on board the slave ships of a rich interchange in languages consisting largely of English and African pidgins. Will Coleman claims that the rhetorical foundation of West Africans and the first African Americans can be understood only by recognizing the role and importance of the Dahomean god Legba (Eshu Elegbara), who "crossed the Atlantic Ocean along with the slaves." Legba is "the master of language" and "the quintessential trickster," who "knows how to use and manipulate semiotic codes to his own advantage in every conceivable (con)text." As the "vodun of communication," Legba serves, through language, as an ever-present bridge between worlds and modes of existence.[36] These traits were differentially exploited by the captors and captives and perpetuated on the ships. Women were often kept above decks, where they were forced to sing and dance, ostensibly for "exercise," for the amusement of the sailors who routinely sexually abused them. Often the enslaved Africans were deprived of clothing during the ocean voyage, branded, and made the objects of torture and amusement. It could take as long as one year from the moment of capture until kidnapped Africans reached the shores of America. The physical and psychological damage for survivors was such that many never fully recovered. Suicides, resulting from maltreatment, depression, shock, and terror, were common.

The population that arrived in America, and their descendents, surely incorporated the effects of post-traumatic stress into the people that they became. After the traumatized survivors arrived on plantations, they rapidly became a source of status and entertainment for slave owners. Advertisements for slaves listed prized and desirable skills in music, singing, recitation, and dancing. According to Thompson,

---

[34] Marcus Rediker, *The Slave Ship: A Human History* (New York: Penguin Books, 2007), p. 7.

[35] Michael A. Gomez, *Reversing Sail: A History of the African Diaspora* (Cambridge: Cambridge University Press, 2005), p. 73.

[36] Will Coleman, *Tribal Talk: Black Theology, Hermeneutics and African/American Ways of "Telling the Story"* (University Park, PA: The Pennsylvania State University Press, 2000), pp. 8 and 9.

For more than two centuries, the performance of music, song, and dance was an integral part of every aspect of the Southern slave experience. Ethnomusicologists, historians, and folk scholars have explored the dance movements and song lyrics of the enslaved community, recognizing that these traditions were adaptations of West African cultures that contributed to the creation of distinct African American communities.[37]

Thompson builds a persuasive argument that "African captives gained power within the Atlantic voyage through their songs, which acted as a form of rebellion that often has been ignored in historical texts" (p. 60). The creative expressions that represented coercion and domination by white society equally represented resistance, rebellion, and retention of identity for the African Americans. The defining moments in African American history can be retro-constructed by observing their presence as recurring poetic themes. Poems about coffles appear in all eras of this tradition, and serve a powerful mnemohistorical function to recall, reexamine, and preserve the traumatic cycle of this terrifying and humiliating experience. Coffles were employed once again when the enslaved people reached America and were moved to the auction block. The pattern of forcing captives to sing under conditions of the greatest duress is a constant in this tradition.

Singing and dancing, even when it was ordered and under the most painful conditions, were used as a public display of the ostensible happiness of the enslaved people, as Frederick Douglass vividly recounts in a famous passage from his autobiography: "I have often been utterly astonished, since I came to the north, to find persons who could speak of the singing, among slaves, as evidence of their contentment and happiness. It is almost impossible to think of a greater mistake. Slaves sing most when they are most unhappy."[38] As a number of critics have observed, the centrality of oral communication, music, song, dance, and the role of the griot are features of African culture that led to exploitative stereotypes. The strong correlation between descriptions of West African cultural practices and later commentaries on slave songs from American plantations urges us to look for African origins and oral traditions as the original source from which the African American poetry tradition sprung.

---

[37] Katrina Dyonne Thompson, *Ring Shout, Wheel About: The Racial Politics of Music and Dance in North American Slavery* (Urbana: University of Illinois Press, 2014), p. 6.
[38] Frederick Douglass, *Narrative of the Life of Frederick Douglass, An American Slave, Written by Himself* [1845]. Norton Critical Edition, ed. William L. Andrews and William S. Feely (New York: W. W. Norton, 1997), p. 131.

It is especially important to incorporate the oral tradition in the canon because it represents the strength of African and African diasporic survivals such as the inextricability of community, performance, language, song, dance, and memory. While liturgical forms, particularly sermons and hymns, often serve as allusions or echoes in the so-called "slave poets," other forms of performativity – such as poetic dialogues, dramatic poems, call-and-response structure, and song lyrics – are far more characteristic of slave songs as well as the poems of antebellum free blacks. A common – and accurate – view of African American poetry is that two of its essential traits are its connections to orality and to musicality. Yet the figures credited with founding this tradition show relatively little relationship to either of these features. As we know, the sole poem attributed to Terry, "Bars Fight, August 28, 1746," appears to have been created as song lyrics. Though the music does not survive, the poem's rhyme scheme and ballad pattern are indicative of the Western tradition, not of African structures and features. Similarly, the poetry of Hammon and Wheatley shows no pronounced influence of these features and is obviously the product of the Western canon. It is more common for critics to ascribe references to orality and vernacular culture to the laws against literacy – a deprivation – rather than to African survivals – a strength. Here is an example of viewing African American poetry, from the origins of the tradition, as aspirational to white models, and/or the products of deprivation and diminishment. In the history of reception of African American poetry, we see perceptions foregrounded of inadequacy, incompetency, and incompletion manifested in multiple ways. A foundational example is the accusation against slave songs that they were the result of poor emulation of white Protestant hymns, and therefore, absent of originality and mastery. The distinctive theology, lyrics, performance style, and musical features of slave songs were attributed to partial absorption and incompetent application of Western influences rather than the authentic power of African survivals, astounding resiliency of spirit, and supernal creativity.

Based on the root of the word, meaning to create or imaginatively start something new, it is reasonable to think of the "originators" of a canon as truly original. It is reasonable to expect their literary quality to achieve a level of greatness – even indispensability – as perceived by most critics. Foundational figures in the canon are expected to be major sources of influence and allusions. Yet there have been reservations by critics throughout the tradition on both issues as they relate to the so-called "originators." There are radical implications for how the bedrock of the canon is perceived, and how we can productively and excitingly reimagine a canon that has developed organically from newly reconceived roots. Formally innovative poetry is a constant in the African American poetry canon, though the experimental motives may not be mainly or wholly intended as a rejection or affront to the mainstream. Yet critical perspectives have tended to create dichotomies or binary oppositions about the themes and techniques of African American poetry, which reflect being either inside or outside the values of the Western lyric tradition. The criteria often point to some failure, lack, absence, or insufficiency: is black poetry formal or dialect, folk or literary, oral or print, difficult or populist, accommodationist or protest? The mainstream is the center, hence the perceived origins of the African American poetry canon, and the lineage that follows. But if we look beyond the figures who are identified as the originators, we become better equipped to recognize and appreciate the truly original poets who have defined their own goals and methods to sidestep this reductionist and reactive pigeonholing.

There has been little critical appetite and admiration for experimental African American poetry, especially as a thread through the tradition, yet it is present and traceable throughout the history of this genre. It is precisely the writing that cannot be easily naturalized and explained by the conventional modes of Western literary interpretation and assessment that has been marginalized, starting with slave songs. The pattern moves forward to L=A=N=G=U=A=G=E Poetry and figures such as Harryette Mullen and Erica Hunt, whose formally oppositional and experimental writing did not receive the critical attention enjoyed by white poets working in related trajectories. The same pattern of neglect occurs throughout the tradition, which explains why a long lineage of experimentalists has been disparaged, neglected, and ultimately underappreciated or lost. How often do we find classes or general anthologies today that routinely feature writing by Oliver Pitcher, De Leon Harrison, Lloyd Addison, or Allen Polite, to name only a few? To complicate matters even more, there are poets like Julia Fields and Jay Wright that chose to actively limit or prevent their own inclusion in anthologies.

According to Paul Gilroy in *The Black Atlantic: Modernity and Double Consciousness*, we should expect the fractal patterns associated with innovation, experimentation, and fragmentation to be normal compositional and conceptual modes for members of the black diaspora, based on their history of dislocation, disruption, and alienation from the heritage of the cultural center. But the African American, black and ethnic minority British, and African diasporic canons tend to be fundamentally conservative and reflective of centrist standards. That circumstance helps to explain the historical disassociation of black poetry from avant-garde practices, which deliberately addresses mainstream practices and expectations to subvert them. The African American poetry tradition has always been innovative, with a history of progressive transformation of its core materials, values, and concepts. If poets are locked out of the mainstream of power by factors such as race, their situation is different from that of poets who are granted access by means of privileges such as race, class, and sex, but who choose to reject mainstream modes and values.

I stand with scholars who find any critical maneuvers that do not grow from the history of the African American experience to be wholly inadequate. Addison Gayle, Jr. articulates the dilemma in his 1972 essay, "Cultural Strangulation: Black Literature and the White Aesthetic." Gayle opens by recounting negative reviews of *Black Fire: An Anthology of Afro-American Writing*, edited by Amiri Baraka and Larry Neal (1968), in the *New York Review of Books* and the *Saturday Review*. The criticism is that America is "one predominant culture," so the reviewers argue that to speak of a black aesthetic is to practice racial chauvinism. With this colonial mindset, where black is bad and white is good, "the extent of the cultural strangulation of Black literature by white critics has been the extent to which they have been allowed to define the terms in which the Black artist will deal with his own experience." For Gayle, the most striking example of this circumstance is Paul Laurence Dunbar from the late nineteenth and early twentieth century:

> Like so many Black writers, past and present, Dunbar was trapped by the definitions of other men, never capable of realizing until near the end of his life, that those definitions were not god-given, but man-given; and so circumscribed by tradition and culture that they were irrelevant to an evaluation of either his life or his art.[39]

Antebellum "protest literature," which attacks institutionalized racism, discrimination, injustice, and prejudice, is usually associated with slave narratives, essays, and novels.[40] It is a common critical perspective that protest poetry is mainly a twentieth century phenomenon, which started to flower during the Harlem Renaissance with poems such as "A Litany of Atlanta" by W. E. B. Du Bois and "If We Must Die" by Claude McKay,

---

[39] Mitchell, *Within the Circle*, p. 212.
[40] Some of the texts that are often identified as the earliest protest literature are Benjamin Banneker's "Open Letter to Thomas Jefferson" (1791), David Walker's "Walker's Appeal" (1829), and Henry Highland Garnet's "An Address to the Slaves of the United States of America" (1843).

and exploded during and after the Civil Rights Movement. In fact, the first truly incendiary period of African American protest poetry is well before the Civil War with slave songs, followed by numerous examples in the mid-nineteenth century, with such powerful voices of outrage and resistance as Elymas Payson Rogers (1814?–61), Charles Lewis Reason (1818–98), Joshua McCarter Simpson (1820?–76), James Robert Watkins (*c.* 1821–?), James Monroe Whitfield (1822–71), and Alfred Gibbs Campbell (1828–84).

African American poetry as a field of public and academic interest is dramatically escalating, propelled in part by remarkable new discoveries and access to information. Some of the brilliant recent research has resulted from digital access to materials, which has been transformative. Canons are built on access to information, and that which is made visible and available stands the greatest chance of entering awareness and recirculating. Conversely, and of immense relevance and concern to this tradition, the invisible eventually becomes lost and devalued. As examples of some of the tremendous forward strides in access and respect, The Freedmen's Bureau Project has digitized and provided full free online access to 1.5 million handwritten records from newly freed slaves, mentioning the names of 4 million individuals, that were collected in 1865 by the Freedmen's Bureau.[41]

As another example of the power of digital humanities, for over one hundred and fifty years, it was accepted among scholars that the first poetry pamphlet by Frances Ellen Watkins Harper (1825–1911), *Forest Leaves*, was a lost text. We read in *Drumvoices*, "Her first work, *Forest Leaves* has not been located."[42] The biographical comments in the third edition of the *Norton Anthology of African American Literature* state, "around 1845 Harper reportedly published a small collection of poems called *Forest Leaves* (no copy is known to have survived)."[43] Johanna Ortner, a doctoral student conducting research for her dissertation on Harper, made the historic discovery of finding a copy of this manuscript through the traditional method of archival research.[44] Melding conventional scholarship with digital humanities, the complete manuscript has been made freely available online in the context of the transformational

---

[41] Accessible at www.discoverfreedmen.org/ (last accessed August 23, 2018).

[42] Redmond, *Drumvoices*, p. 76.

[43] Gates and Smith, *The Norton Anthology of African American Literature*, Vol. 1, p. 445.

[44] Johanna Ortner, "Lost no More: Recovering Frances Ellen Watkins Harper's *Forest Leaves*," *Common-place.org.* 15, no. 4 (Summer 2015). http://common-place.org/book/lost-no-more-recovering-frances-ellen-watkins-harpers-forest-leaves/ (last accessed August 20, 2018).

work being accomplished by Commonplace.org and its sister project, Just Teach One: Early African American Print.[45] The aim of this project is to rediscover pre-twentieth century African American literature for the purposes of "changing an academic landscape reified by decades of neglect, dismissal, and other forms of racism" and "to create points of access to these rediscoveries that appropriately frame and present these critical pieces of African American (and so American) literature and culture and that allow individuals to work in responsible, well-informed, dialogic ways to benefit teaching, learning, and further scholarship." Here is an example of the ways in which digital humanities has the potential to profoundly reshape concepts of African American poetry and American culture. In another major discovery, scholar Jonathan Senchyne found a previously unknown handwritten 500-word essay called "Individual Influence" by Horton at the New York Public Library.[46] Resources such as hathitrust.org have digitized many rare African American poetry volumes, and a vast trove of little magazines has been digitized by sources including the University of Wisconsin.[47]

Such developments enabled by technology have fueled interest in this field as the enormity of exciting and potential discoveries is revealed by the democratization of information and ease of access. Because this field has not been studied with full depth and seriousness, it is a certainty that many more poets and manuscripts have been overlooked and lost, hopefully to be recovered if we know they exist. Digital humanities and increasingly open access to information will probably continue to unravel some of the mysteries that especially apply to the earliest period of the tradition and have prevented a clear overview of the enormous quantity of poetic production by African Americans in the nineteenth century and earlier. Precise birth and death dates, as well as bibliographical and biographical details, are often questionable and incomplete for the earliest figures in this genre, especially but not exclusively for those who were enslaved. This situation indicates the tremendous opportunities to conduct landmark research in this field, and proves its relative neglect, compared with the British and American poetry canons. For example, the birth and death dates for Alfred Gibbs Campbell have always appeared

[45] http://jtoaa.common-place.org/welcome-to-just-teach-one-african-american/frances-ellen-watkins-harpers-forest-leaves-introduction/ (last accessed August 20, 2018).
[46] https://mobile.nytimes.com/images/100000005427432/2017/09/25/arts/george-moses-horton-essay.html (last accessed August 20, 2018).
[47] https://uwdc.library.wisc.edu/collections/LittleMagInt/ (last accessed August 20, 2018).

in anthologies as uncertain or unknown, including the laborious efforts by Sherman. We now know from his *New York Times* obituary (January 11, 1884), as well as digital images of his gravesite, that Campbell died in 1884 at age 57.[48]

Other gaps and mysteries may result from an element of literary self-fashioning, strategic representation by abolitionists, subterfuge for safety, or simply mistaken attribution, which may all apply to the case of James Watkins, also known by the "slave names" of Ensor Sam and Sam Berry. The literary confusion may result from well-intended desires by abolitionists to portray enslaved and fugitive African Americans in an admirable light, as they did by referring to the sung poems of the slaves as "spirituals." As shown by its cover, *Narrative of the Life of James Watkins* by Watkins is presented as an autobiography. In a similar statement to the Attestation of the authenticity of Wheatley's poetry, the book contains numerous prefatory testimonials, mostly about the character of Watkins, and recommending that he be assisted in England, where he fled in 1850 after the Fugitive Slave Law was passed. J. W. C. Pennington, D.D. wrote, "I have seen his letters, and from the long intercourse I have had with all the gentlemen, I am satisfied of their genuineness."[49] The Preface is written by "H.R., (Bolton, February 5,[th] 1852)," who is perhaps Robert Heywood, Esq., named as one of the gentlemen who presided over the meetings held by Mr. Watkins in Bolton, England. The volume's "authorship" is suggested more than stated. "H.R." provides another example of the complexities of African American authorship, which includes the suggestion of a Christian motive in abolitionism, and a telling implied definition of authorship itself. Here we encounter one of the continuing strands of this genre

---

[48] I wish to pay my thanks to Col. Rob Burrows, Ivanhoe Wheelhouse Museum and Art Gallery History Curator, who is a seventh generation Patersonian, and ardent preserver of the legacy and importance of Campbell as an esteemed resident of Paterson. Col. Burrows has read Campbell's writing at public poetry readings, and generously shared with me his unique collection of Campbell photographs and ephemera.

[49] James Watkins, *Narrative of the Life of James Watkins, Formerly a "Chattel" in Maryland, U.S.; Containing an Account of His Escape from Slavery, Together with an Appeal on Behalf of Three Millions of Such "Pieces of Property," Still Held Under the Standard of the Eagle* (Bolton: Kenyon and Abbatt, Printers, Market Street, 1852). A facsimile edition of the original is made available by University of North Carolina at: http://docsouth.unc.edu/neh/watkin52/watkin52.html (last accessed August 20, 2018). In addition to the third edition's subtitle, listed in the Bibliography, the Kessinger Publishing reprint lists the subtitle "Narrative of the Life of James Watkins, Formerly a 'Chattel' in Maryland, U.S.; Containing an Account of His Escape from Slavery, Together with an Appeal on Behalf of Three Million of Such 'Pieces of Property,' Still Held Under the Standard of the Eagle."

which identifies the social realist themes of racial hardship as the definition of authenticity, and the role of the publisher as the validated pre-
senter of the truth. The Preface states that the many testimonials in this
book, and the many more that were excluded for lack of space,

> will be sufficient to inspire confidence in the simple, ungarnished, truth-
> ful Narrative presented in these pages, which speaks at once to the heart,
> and draws out our holiest sympathies. Properly speaking, it is an Auto-
> biography, written down as the words dropped from the lips of Mr.
> WATKINS, by a *friend*, a "Friend indeed," and afterwards arranged for
> the press by the writer, with a few remarks bearing on this monstrous
> iniquity – Slavery.[50]

Accessed through the ProQuest database, the electronic files provided
by Chadwyck-Healey Inc. are identified as "Poems, Original & Selected,
By James Watkins, A Fugitive Slave, Manchester, England," from the
press Abel Heywood in Bolton, published in "*[1859?]*," and labeled
"Only verse by Watkins included." In conjunction with the dramatic
"Auto-biography," *Narrative of the Life of James Watkins* by Watkins
(1852), his *Poems, Original & Selected* suggests that Watkins may be an
original and unjustly overlooked author. However, stylistic variations,
anachronisms of diction, and familiar echoes become apparent. In fact,
"The Blind Slave Boy," attributed to Watkins by Chadwyck-Healey,
appeared eleven years earlier in the collection *The Anti-Slavery Harp:
A Collection of Songs for Anti-Slavery Meetings* (1848), "Compiled by
William Wells Brown, A Fugitive Slave," and attributed to "Mrs. Bailey."
The poem from Watkins's collection titled "Slave's Escape to Canada" is
recognized as "Away to Canada" by Joshua McCarter Simpson, which
was published seven years earlier in Simpson's first poetry book, *Original
Anti-Slavery Songs* (1852).[51] "The Poor Slave's Joy" appears to be a variant
on "Come Join the Abolitionists" attributed to "Anonymous" in Brown's
The Anti-Slavery Harp.

My purpose is not to criticize Chadwyck-Healey's highly respected and
invaluably useful database as an academic resource. Rather this mistaken
attribution indicates a crucial pattern where voices of African American
poets are too often taken as speaking for the aggregate, and not differen-
tiated from each other as individuals. Several of Simpson's poems have
been attributed either to "Anonymous" or to authors other than himself,

---

[50] Watkins, *Narrative of the Life of James Watkins*, p. 2.
[51] It was reprinted in 1874 in Simpson's magnum opus, *The Emancipation Car*, which expanded on
the contents of the earlier slim self-published volume.

and similarly to the situation of Wheatley and so many others, "proof" was offered by the poet himself of his ownership of the poems' creation. Simpson's first book was called *Original Anti-Slavery Songs*, with the stress on "original." His second extraordinary book, *The Emancipation Car* (1874), includes the statement, "This work is all original, though several of the songs have been republished several times, under other names, and by other persons, *they are my own Composition*." The poems are stylistically and tonally cohesive, and there are no appearances prior to the publications of his two books, so there is no reason to doubt Simpson's claim that he has authored these poems. The point is that such a claim would remain needed at all, even for a free black man in the late nineteenth century. Slave songs created a condition where anonymity and denial of ownership represented discretion over ego, and safety over renown. Simpson, an underground railroad conductor and ardent abolitionist, was able to assert his ownership and literary aspirations. It is interesting that the Poetry Foundation lists Simpson on its website, and calls him "a well-known abolitionist songwriter, herbal physician, and Underground Railroad conductor," but does not refer to him as a "poet." The biographical entry states that he was "Subversive in his use of familiar tunes" and "created a 'double voicing' in songs of emancipation that included an antislavery rendition of 'America.'" These sound like similarly sophisticated literary processes to those of slave songs, but slave songs are almost never categorized as lyric poetry. This metonymic process of part representing the whole started, of necessity, with slave songs. But it has continued through the centuries, including its manifestation of the issue of literary tokenism – which we see with Dunbar, Hughes, and later Jones/Baraka – where one black poet's inclusion in an anthology was taken as sufficient representation of all black poets. As a result, poems by Simpson are co-opted by a variety of anthologies as communal "black songs" of protest. An issue that is endemic in the tradition is exemplified in this situation: how does one speak for a group and maintain individual identity?

Sherman pointed out that at least 130 black Americans, whom she calls "invisible poets" in American society, published their writing during the nineteenth century. Judging from recent scholarship that takes account of the omnipresence of poetry in black newspapers and journals throughout the nation, this is probably a conservative estimate. Yet these unjustly overlooked published writers did not just form a tradition: they also entered one. An extraordinary body of diverse and stirring poetry has been marginalized from the canon of early African American poetry, which makes it invisible in dictating several different significant trajectories for the tradition. Rather than dividing African American literature into "vernacular" and "literary" traditions, they are clearly all one body of writing. Breaking down these barriers freshly illuminates the breadth as well as the cohesion of African American poetry. It also highlights the definitional features of this genre and supports the importance of seeing it as a varied body of indispensable verse to American and world literature. One defining trait is an adamant cry for freedom for all Americans, the insistence that this value is what America was based on, and a commitment to the ideal that this nation is morally and religiously obligated to fulfill. Related to that idea is a stress on physical safety, equal opportunities, and treatment with respect. Other common qualities are physicality, orality, performance, and oratory. Another is an integral connection between the individual and the community, which is often conveyed in various forms of dialogue, including call-and-response, and examples like the verse plays of Simpson, where individuals engage in dialogue with choruses. Double consciousness and double voicing also are dominant features.

Only by considering the songs and oral poetry of antebellum enslaved blacks, and the written poetry of free blacks, can it be judged fairly whether, how, and to what extent Wheatley deserves credit for her role as the mother of the tradition. Literary history is quite familiar with poems such as Wheatley's "On Being Brought from Africa to America" and its opening line, "'Twas mercy brought me from my *Pagan* land." More commonly found is the inverse of Wheatley's stated sentiment, which starts in the earliest period of this tradition: accusations to America for its failure to live up to its ideals.[52] Many poets in this earliest period – among them Harper, Whitfield, Simpson, Alfred Gibbs Campbell, and Josephine Delphine Henderson Heard – called the nation to task for its hypocrisy in fighting for human liberty, with many black soldiers participating in this cause, and then creating a culture of oppression. The voices are strong that say that blacks would never have fought for America's freedom if they realized that they were helping to establish a nation that would enslave their own descendants. This theme is a commonplace, and it is impossible to read "protest poetry" of the Civil Rights Movement outside the context of these early precursors, who are far less well known than white abolitionist poets such as John Greenleaf Whittier. Why are

---

[52] I am not overlooking but leaving aside the issue of whether she was "obligated" to make such statements and expressed them only with irony, as some critics believe.

the antebellum free black abolitionist poets not better known but we know the voices of the enslaved who have been accused of being imitative, accommodating, and substandard in literary quality? "Protest literature," which rails against institutionalized prejudice, injustice, and discrimination, often is thought of as a twentieth century phenomenon. Sometimes the slave narratives and early African American essays and fiction are identified as the earliest protest literature, but colonial and antebellum African American poetry is wrongly ignored as an example of early revolutionary writing.

Whitfield produced one poetry collection titled *America* (1853) that deserves to be far better known for its own value and as proof of the under-recognized variety, originality, pre-modernity, and power of antebellum African American poetry. A landmark volume, *The Works of James M. Whitfield: America and Other Writings by a Nineteenth-Century African American Poet* (2011), co-edited by Robert S. Levine and Ivy G. Wilson, collects all of Whitfield's poems, essays, and letters for the first time since the middle of the nineteenth century, and offers marvelous editorial commentary and insight. This much-needed and definitive book should dramatically increase the stature and awareness of Whitfield's accomplishments and importance. Whitfield, known by many as "the" great African American poet during his lifetime, is among the numerous examples of poets discussed in this book who were famed during their lifetimes, and now have undeservedly faded into complete obscurity or relative disregard.

Whitfield – with Campbell, Simpson, Harper, and others – leads readers to once again confront this question: what is the relationship between African Americans and America? This question was raised about slave songs. We also find this tradition of questioning America in the earliest period of African American poetry – poets who embrace America as their home and call for it to fulfill its promise as the land of the free. Levine and Wilson argue that *America* should be viewed as a single integrated entity comparable to Walt Whitman's monumental *Leaves of Grass*. It is one of several cohesively developed poetry collections from the period, including the remarkable *The Emancipation Car* (1874) by Simpson and *Poems* by Campbell. In several of Whitfield's poems, America's boast of itself, its self-image, is portrayed as a standard that has never been and must be lived up to. The opening of Whitfield's poem "America" majestically and forcefully articulates these themes and surely belongs in the canon:

> AMERICA, it is to thee,
> Thou boasted land of liberty,–

It is to thee I raise my song,
Thou land of blood, and crime, and wrong.
It is to thee, my native land,
From whence has issued many a band
To tear the black man from his soil,
And force him here to delve and toil;
Chained on your blood-bemoistened sod,
Cringing beneath a tyrant's rod,
Stripped of those rights which Nature's God
Bequeathed to all the human race,
Bound to a petty tyrant's nod,
Because he wears a paler face.
Was it for this, that freedom's fires
Were kindled by your patriot sires?
Was it for this, they shed their blood,
On hill and plain, on field and flood?
Was it for this, that wealth and life

Were staked upon that desperate strife,
Which drenched this land for seven long years
With blood of men, and women's tears?
When black and white fought side by side,–

The contrast is striking between the tone of the book's Introduction – presented anonymously in first person plural and presumed to have been written by Whitfield – and the opening salvo of the first poem, "America." In the topos of mock humility and self-effacement that may well be taken as theatricalized and at least partly ironic, the Introduction describes the poet as "one of the proscribed race, whose lot has been ignorance and servitude," and "a poor colored man of this city, engaged in the humble, yet honorable and useful occupation of a barber" who "feels the 'Divine Spark' within him." The poet calls himself "uneducated," and writes that his "genius is native and uncultivated." His hope is that this book's sales will "put money in the purse" to allow him to develop his God-given talent. Considering what we know about Whitfield, it is hard to take this tone as anything other than an expression of double consciousness or playing the dozens in over- or rewriting a national anthem as counter-discourse. In the context of African American poetry, his writing falls into the too-often overlooked tradition of counter-song, which includes examples by Dunbar, Simpson, and slave songs.

Whitfield, James David Corrothers, Simpson, Campbell, Albery A. Whitman, and Harper are some of the free black poets whose important voices are essential examples of extraordinary individuals who spoke loudly and bravely for the cause of human rights when the dehuman-izing condition of slavery could be legal for any African Americans. The unfolding of the African American poetry canon, from its origins in Africa to its full flowering in the twenty-first century, is seen from an entirely different perspective if the roots of this genre are rethought. The progressions and the continuities come to light in ways that only strengthen the sense of this canon's originality, impact, and indispensabil-ity to the world's great bodies of literature.

There has been an uptick in scholarship that proposes a surge in experimental African American poetry starting in the middle of the twen-tieth century. This criticism suggests the existence of a "hidden canon" of modern and postmodern writing that foregrounds "difficult" or avant-garde methods and motivations. Experimentation has radically increased since the advent of modernism and an attendant array of sociohistorical factors, but we now can see that this phenomenon is the natural exten-sion of a process that is inherent in the poetry of African Americans from its earliest manifestations. Little critical attention has been paid to the bold originality and experimentalism that have been present in the African American poetry tradition since its origins. African American poetry, of brilliant necessity, has always been innovative. By examining the earliest examples, and using the lens of experimentalism, the features associated with this practice are in clear evidence.

Just as we find with the exclusion of many avant-garde or oppositional texts from the mainstream canon, so we find – perhaps even more so – that some of the most subversive texts created by African Americans also have been overlooked and marginalized from the canon as it has evolved, even if they were well known in earlier times. Barbara Herrnstein Smith addresses the role of "value" as a changing and mutable property in liter-ary evaluation and canon formation and invokes Hughes's 1926 state-ment in "The Negro Artist and the Racial Mountain:" "If white people are pleased, we are glad. If they are not, it doesn't matter."[53] Considering the role of anthologies in establishing taste and value, Smith believes that the repeated inclusion of certain texts both promotes and creates their value. More and more readers encounter the work, and therefore its

---

[53] Barbara Herrnstein Smith, "Contingencies of Value," in *Canons*, ed. Robert von Hallberg (Chicago and London: University of Chicago Press, 1984), p. 13. Within the article, the quotation of Hughes comes within a quotation from poet-critic Onwuchekwa Jemie, where Hughes's statement is preceded by this comment from Jemie: "In this day and age, British preferences do not count in the Black World." Subsequent page references to this article are given in parentheses in the text.

value is reinforced through its continuous supply, making "it more likely both that the work will be experienced at all and also that it will be experienced as valuable" (p. 29). Then what determines what she calls the "survival" or "endurance" of a text so that it does become "a classic" or part of the canon? It is "a series of continuous interactions among a variably constituted object, emergent conditions, and mechanisms of cultural selection and transmission" (p. 30). A circular process ensues by which the objects that are perpetuated as culturally valuable are precisely those that articulate the standards of cultural value, and "since those with cultural power tend to be members of socially, economically, and politically established classes (or to serve them and identify their interests with theirs), the texts that survive will tend to be those that appear to reflect and reinforce establishment ideologies" (p. 30). What about the canonical texts that seem to offer cultural critique or corrective? Smith believes that they are essentially little more than prompts to "question," "remind," and "confront" precisely the shared values that the establishment is already committed to upholding. Such texts of questioning must remain within narrow parameters: they cannot too radically "subvert the ideologies that support them *effectively*" (p. 34). Smith's theory goes far towards explaining why the most subversive and ideologically independent African American poetry would be almost guaranteed from its beginnings to enter neither the mainstream canon nor the African American poetry canon if those in power were disposed towards modeling the values of the American mainstream.

Jacob Korg called experiment "an essential element" of modernism.[54] It is a common view that myriad factors led to a social revolution at the start of the twentieth century, which resulted in techniques that are strongly associated with experimentation, among them citationality, fragmentation, parody, irony, collage, and problematical views of the self and the lyric "I." In African American poetry, set against a different set of historical circumstances entirely, which is to say a profound state of temporal, spatial, and relational dislocation, experiment has been essential and unavoidable since the start of the tradition. This is not the Poundian "Make it new" of the Anglo-American tradition: this is seizing workable components from utter destruction and applying the most remarkable ingenuity to adapt these remnants of psychic and material shrapnel of the past, in Darwinian fashion, into usable substances in the present. How could it

---

[54] Jacob Korg, *Language in Modern Literature: Innovation and Experiment* (Pepperell, MA: Branch Line, 1979), p. 1.

have been otherwise? When we look closely at the foundations of this tradition, and the texts that evolved from its true roots, it becomes evident that we have inherited a partial, skewed, and highly selective version, which has privileged certain types of African American poetry and erased others. The existing canon is largely oriented towards a conservative and what we might think of as "controllable" literary body. Ranging from the seventeenth to the nineteenth century, three examples offer a counter-discourse to Wheatley, Hammon, and Terry: slave songs, Alfred Gibbs Campbell, and Joshua McCarter Simpson. This writing represents bodies of truly original and self-determined poetry and poetics that unsurprisingly have become invisible. This perspective gives us the opportunity to reconsider the entire African American poetry canon as a unique historical record of sparkling artistic and conceptual innovation and originality.

These examples of marginalized experimental works from colonial and antebellum America serve as expansions as well as counter-examples to the texts usually identified as foundational, such as "Bars Fight" by Terry, "An Evening Thought" by Hammon, and "His Excellency General Washington" by Wheatley. While it is essential to incorporate written texts by enslaved black people in any conception of the origins of this genre, we can see how printed poems by free black people and oral poems by enslaved black people are routinely omitted, but especially the examples that display the greatest stylistic and thematic independence, which is often conveyed in formal experimentation. It also should be noted that the oral poems of slave songs and poetry by free blacks were often more innovative than the early African American written poetry by the so-called "slave poets," which makes their exclusion an especially potent piece of information. They tended to actively exploit the conventional literary feature of ambiguity, as masterfully developed in the classic text on this trope, *Seven Types of Ambiguity* by William Empson. Ambiguity is inherent both in poetry and in biblical rhetoric. We find this operation foregrounded in many sections of the Bible, such as the parables, where it is stated that Jesus deliberately employed modes of obfuscation to be selectively unclear to some audiences. In that sense, we can view the poets of the slave songs as among the earliest American biblical hermeneuticians: they cleverly employed a central property that existed within the biblical text as a formal model for their own communicative benefit. In contrast, it was ironic that slave holders who used the Bible as transparent and uncoded "proof" of divine support for slavery were less sophisticated than the African Americans in understanding the nuances of what can be revealed to whom and in what manner.

To further underscore the contrast between the canonical and marginalized early poems, there is a common perspective that to read and write were universally banned for enslaved African Americans who all were supposedly illiterate. Therefore, Terry, Hammon, and Wheatley could be viewed as anomalies rather than representatives of a larger group – a threat to slave-holding society. By the early nineteenth century, perhaps 30 percent of the enslaved people could read and/or write, and most of the half million free black people were educated. It also is a common, and accurate, understanding that African literary traditions are oral, which makes our current early canonical foundations appear even more misleading. To underscore the point, why are the origins of this genre based on written conventional poetry by enslaved writers who were viewed as exceptional individuals mainly writing for audiences of educated white readers? As we have seen, it is inarguable that the perceived canon is based on a so-called "literary tradition" of African American poetry produced by enslaved writers who aimed to validate the worth of their poems by formally emulating white Classical and Neoclassical texts. Therefore, perceptions of their "difference" reside in two manifestations related not to form, but to content, and assumptions about authorial identity. When the poets did not utilize themes based on the suffering or oppression of their race, they too often were judged negatively as copies of originals. When they did utilize themes based on the suffering or oppression of their race, they were frequently seen as the expressions of an underclass evoking pity in audiences of others who perceived themselves, in contrast, as privileged and elevated. Difference was guaranteed either way, accompanied by judgments of inauthenticity, incompetency, or unoriginality.

The first and earliest example of African American poetic innovation, predating any of the currently identified founders of the canon, are slave songs, which, as mentioned, are also known as spirituals, as well as plantation hymns, cabin songs, sorrow songs, or Negro religious folk-songs. These oral texts created by enslaved African Americans probably extend from the lyrics produced in the African slave coffles. Here we apply the view of Irele that a distinguishing feature of African diasporic literature is its foundation in orality, and oral texts are as literary as written texts in this tradition. Slave songs are a remarkably fresh and composite product, unlike anything pre-existing in either Africa or white America. They contain elements of African survivals, of the lyrics created in the coffles during the initial state of captivity and treacherous journey to the eventual destination of America, and the influence of American plantation culture. The result was something radically innovative and different; the way that early auditors most often described the slave songs was as "weird" and "strange." Although they often are described as quintessentially American cultural products and an authentic and indispensable part of its cultural heritage, they rarely are considered as lyric poetry, and certainly are not "canonical" in the conventional sense. The Oxford University Press *Anthology of Modern American Poetry* opens with poems from the 1860s when slave songs were first being actively transcribed and disseminated, yet they do not appear here. Surprisingly, they also do not appear in most African American poetry anthologies, including *The New Cavalcade, African American Poetry: An Anthology, 1773–1927, American Negro Poetry, The Vintage Book of African American Poetry, The Prentice Hall Anthology of African American Literature*, and others. In the few where they do appear – such as *The Black Poets, Black Writers of America, The Norton Anthology of African American Literature*, and *The Negro Caravan* – they are relegated to separate sections from "lyric" or "literary" poetry, generally called "spirituals" or "vernacular" or "folk" products.

In the origins of this tradition, with slave songs, no premium was placed on authorial credit or ownership. Though it is likely that each song was originally created by a gifted enslaved poet, they were intended to be performed and shared by the community, deliberately modified and creatively adapted, and passed along in different versions. Another practical issue that explained the slave songs' anonymity was the prohibition against literacy, which meant that lyrics could not be written down safely – quite a significant contrast to the standard canon, which extols authorship and credit. The enslaved people used the African survival of the oral tradition for their benefit when deprived of literacy. Further, the subversive content would have put anyone identified as the author in peril. As we have clearly seen, one of the distinguishing features of the African American poetry tradition is the complex issue of ownership and production.

In deciding whether this exclusion is justified, we may consider this example that was a favorite of both Du Bois and Thomas Wentworth Higginson:

> I know moon-rise, I know star-rise,
>   Lay dis body down.
> I walk in de moonlight, I walk in de starlight,
>   To lay dis body down.
> I'll walk in de graveyard, I walk through de graveyard,
>   To lay dis body down.

I lay in de graveyard and stretch out my arms,
    Lay dis body down.
I go to de judgment in de evenin' of de' day,
    When I lay dis body down.
And my soul and your soul will meet in de day,
    When I lay dis body down.

The compositional principle of this slave song, like many others, is unlike conventional practices in the text-based Western lyric tradition. The lyrics could be different each time it was performed with no set authoritative finished product. The segments were interchangeable, and often realigned to create new correspondences, though their presentation as printed texts and when set to music in the concert tradition misleadingly suggests otherwise. This form allowed them to be endlessly regenerative and creative to serve new purposes through a process that has been called "mosaics" and "wandering choruses." As oral products, they obviously would not have been lineated or presented with punctuation so even their appearance in anthologies is only a transcription based on editorial incursions which hides one of the most original aspects of these poems, their adaptability. Like many other slave songs, this example is rich with cognitive blends, where there is a disanalogy – instead of a correspondence as in conventional metaphor – between source and target domains. Creative blends typically appear in situations where the desire is to convey something new, as would be the case for the enslaved people who had to create their own tradition. The poem is built on a series of tensions between body and spirit, earth and heaven, which generate clashing temporal grounds and spatial planes. A body walking through a graveyard would be assumed to be alive, yet this body is walking through the graveyard to lay itself down in a grave, which is in a state of death. Death and life form a blended space where the body is both dead and alive. The disembodied soul, which is outside the state of life, will meet another disembodied soul during the day, and meet Christian judgment in the evening of the day, another creative blend. In the blended space, we encounter a life on earth for the enslaved people that feels like a state of living death.

The next example is Alfred Gibbs Campbell, who was a remarkable free black man from Paterson, New Jersey. Campbell was so well known and revered in his lifetime that the *New York Times* published an extended obituary when he died at age fifty-seven in 1884 and he was buried in a well-marked grave with headstone, which were unusual for a black person in that era. According to his obituary in the *New York Times* on January 11, 1884:

> He was an Abolitionist from his youth, and so earnestly in the cause that he would not vote in a country that tolerated slavery. Many years ago he became interested in the preparation of patent medicines, perfumes, &c., and some of his productions in this line brought him a large fortune ... Having left the Methodist church for the Congregational, he became dissatisfied, and asked to be dismissed. It was decided by the authorities to whom the matter was referred that he could get out only in one of two ways – by dying or by expulsion. He said he had done nothing meriting expulsion, and he was not ready to die; so the matter hung in abeyance a long time, to the great annoyance of the church people. He had a faculty for versifying, and some of his poems were extremely graceful. A collection of these was published last year [*Poems*, Newark, NJ, Advertiser Printing House, 1883]. He is to be buried at Paterson tomorrow.

Now a virtually forgotten author, Campbell is absent from all anthologies of American poetry that I have found, and of African American literature anthologies, he only appears in Sherman. He is not mentioned in *Drumvoices*, which is famed for its encyclopedic listings of even the most minor figures. A prosperous entrepreneur in real estate, the paper industry, and marketing products, as well as an anti-slavery and temperance activist, Campbell also edited and published a newspaper called *The Alarm Bell* from 1851 to 1852. In Volume 1, issue 5 of *The Alarm Bell*, in 1852, Campbell published his own poem called "Song of the Decanter," which is historically significant because it is probably the first concrete poem created by any poet in America.

In addition to its appearance in *The Alarm Bell*, Campbell distributed this poem on a postcard from his home address promoting the cause of temperance. A fine example of this postcard, mailed in 1874, is found in the Ivanhoe Wheelhouse Museum and Art Gallery provided to me by courtesy of Colonel Rob Burrows, the Curator. A broadside of the poem (dated "18—") is shown in Figure 1.

The lyrics, spoken from the perspective of a bottle of alcohol, show the poet's aim to utilize formal poetic innovation as a radical device of defamiliarization and a means to achieve social and political efficacy, which becomes a hallmark of the subsequent African American poetry tradition. So, why have Campbell and his poetry (though "The Decanter" or some variation on that title frequently appears in varied forms with anonymous authorship on the Internet) become all but forgotten? Why have slave songs, the anonymous brilliant oral poems of the enslaved

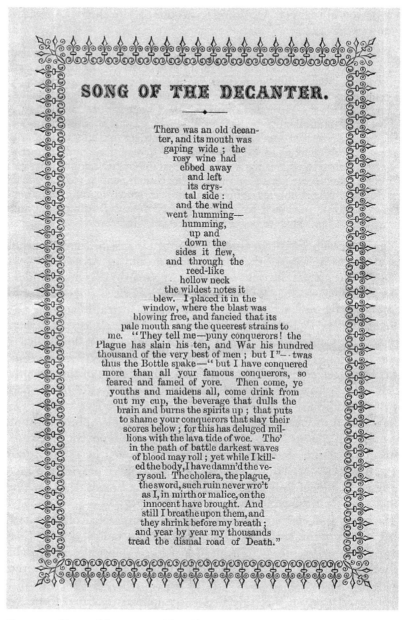

Figure 1   "Song of the Decanter" by Alfred Gibbs Campbell, from the Hay Harris
Broadside Collection, Brown University Library

African Americans, systematically been excluded from the early canon of so-called "literary" African American poetry in favor of Wheatley, Hammon, and Terry? The approximately 6,000 combinatory slave songs were produced a century before those figures lived, had far greater impact on the culture and tradition, and entail a much larger corpus of magnificent poems. The most truly self-determined and innovative African American poetry, following its own path and evading any possible accusation of imitation or copying, has been excluded from the canon as it has developed.

Finally, we turn to Simpson (1820?– 76), also a free black man in nineteenth century Ohio. Briefly mentioned in *Drumvoices*, his work is virtually invisible apart from small representation in the two Sherman anthologies. He produced the two books previously discussed, one essentially a very early prototype of the full-length volume to follow. Simpson received no formal education until he attended Oberlin College for two years as an adult. He did not complete his program and prided himself on being self-taught apart from that institutional aberration, which he basically dismissed as a waste of time. He subsequently called himself "Dr." and treated the local population with folk medicine. Like Whitman with *Leaves of Grass*, Simpson spent a lifetime writing and rewriting a single book, which is his magnum opus. If it were in print and available, which it is not, this would be an incredible volume to use in the classroom, which is the position that it deserves to be in based on its originality, quality, and historical value. The first version of this book, *Original Anti-Slavery Songs* expanded into *The Emancipation Car*, an indescribable compilation of polemic, essays, meditations, poetic scripts that combine features of Greek drama with call-and-response (for example, "Queen Victoria Conversing with Her Slave Children"), and poems that Simpson describes as "airs" – parodies of popular songs that he wrote with the intent to "kill the degrading influence of those comic Negro Songs … and change the flow of those sweet melodies into more appropriate and useful channels." An ardent anti-slavery activist like Campbell, Simpson was serious in his ambition of hoping that what he called his "little book" would "find its way and lodging place in every house and family in the land of the free and home of the brave."[55]

---

[55] Joshua McCarter Simpson, *The Emancipation Car, being an Original Composition of Anti-Slavery Ballads, composed exclusively for the Under Ground Rail Road* (Zanesville, OH: Sullivan and Brown, 1874), preface, n.p.

The Greek root of the word parody translates into "counter-song," which is a fitting literal and metaphorical description of the process that we see in the works of Simpson. With Simpson's work, we encounter parody and irony, which may be akin to but are profoundly different from either allusion or emulation. Unlike Wheatley, Simpson comes full bore at admired traditions, and demands that they be seen in the light of their inhumanity, evil, and hypocrisy. The first two stanzas of "Song of 'The Aliened American,'" which is a counter-song to "America the Beautiful," offer a glimpse of Simpson's unabashedly harsh criticism and use of form for purposes of expressing protest and rage:

> My country, 'tis of thee,
> Dark land of Slavery,
> In thee we groan.
> Long have our chains been worn—
> Long has our grief been borne—
> Our flesh has long been torn,
> E'en from our bones.
>
> The white man rules the day—
> He bears despotic sway,
> O'er all the land.
> He wields the Tyrant's rod,
> Fearless of man or God,
> And at his impious nod,
> We "fall or stand."
>
> O! shall we longer bleed?

In a startlingly contemporary voice, especially in Simpson's prose in this volume, we view early examples of the traditions of satire, protest, and musicality, features that were always present in African American poetry and have become even more visibly prominent in the twentieth and twenty-first centuries. The trickster mode and double-voicing that are characteristic of Simpson's style also are found in many of the slave songs and poems by Campbell, which drip with sarcasm and burlesque, and demand that America stand by its own stated principles.

So here we have examples of three – among many – truly experimental African American bodies of poetry and poetics in the earliest period of the tradition. Such texts, and their exclusion from the canon, should raise questions about how and why a fundamentally conservative view of the African American poetry tradition became normative. The roots and trajectory of this tradition emerge in a wholly different light if we recognize the contributions of brilliant and self-determining innovators from the start of this genre. "Anthologies of Afro-American literature typically imply that black poetry began with Phillis Wheatley (1753–84), disappeared for over one hundred years, and only reemerged with Paul Laurence Dunbar (1872–1906)," wrote Sherman in the 1989 Preface to *Invisible Poets: Afro-Americans of the Nineteenth Century* (p. vii). In 1974, Sherman wrote, "Afro-Americans of the nineteenth century are the invisible poets of our national literature." In 2010, I wrote, "the relationship of slave songs to either 'American' or 'African American' poetry has been one of curious disregard."[56] There has been progress in recovering some of these "invisible" voices, but the origins of the canon remain accepted as historical fact, when far too many poets are overlooked whose words are essential to a true understanding of what African American poetry is and how it began. Throughout this book, the "outsiders" and the unjustly forgotten are recuperated, with a call to reconsider what this body of writing would look like in its totality with their inclusion. The opportunities for further study, discovery, and theorizing remain open and enticing.

---

[56] Ramey, *Slave Songs and the Birth of African American Poetry*, p. 1.

CHAPTER 3

Emancipation to African American Modernism

Though slavery's dead, yet there remains
A work for those from whom the chains
Today are falling one by one;
Nor should they deem their labor done,
Nor shrink the task, however hard,
While it insures a great reward,
And bids them on its might depend
For perfect freedom in the end.

James Madison Bell, from "An Anniversary Poem
Entitled the Progress of Liberty"

'Tis your brothers sigh,
O! ye wicked men take warning,
The judgment day will come by and by.

Joshua McCarter Simpson, from
"To the White People of America"

The momentous period following the end of the Civil War, and extending to the abrupt termination of Radical Reconstruction, was the time often known as "the Nadir" of social conditions in America, the onset of the Great Depression, and the advent of World War I. In a society that had not fully prepared for this period of transition, Emancipation brought with it both elation and confusion for the newly freed African Americans, many of whom were understandably ill-prepared to sustain their basic needs. The formerly enslaved people gathered at sites such as what is now called the Emancipation Oak on the grounds of what was to become Hampton University to read aloud and celebrate President Abraham Lincoln's Emancipation Proclamation. But local government and documentary records such as the Works Progress Administration (WPA) interviews demonstrate the confusion felt by many formerly enslaved people over the practical and emotional meanings and implications of "freedom." Released from what was often the only home they had ever known, and without the paternalistic function of slave culture, some of the newly emancipated African Americans were terrified and mystified about where to go and what to do. Many important successes were achieved by the Freedmen's Bureau, local churches, the American Missionary Association, the African Methodist Episcopal Church, educators, former Northern military officers, abolitionists, and the consortium of HBCUs founded to educate the newly freed African Americans. But these efforts could not wholly combat and eradicate the exploitation and poisonous hatred that erupted into lynching; the rise of white supremacist movements such as the Ku Klux Klan (KKK) spurred on by the "myth of the lost cause" perpetuated in both the North and the South in political action and literary works; and working conditions that essentially operated as slavery by any other name. It quickly became clear that the hoped-for promise of freedom and full civil rights would not be provided willingly in America, and attitudes of racial prejudice had not materially changed for many white Americans. The lowest point arrived with the 1876 election of the openly racist President Rutherford B. Hayes, which ended Reconstruction by the removal of the protective Federal troops from formerly slave-holding southern states.

In his study, *The Betrayal of the Negro: From Rutherford B. Hayes to Woodrow Wilson*, historian Rayford W. Logan calls the period from 1877 to 1901 "the Nadir" of race relations in America.[1] In this tumultuous historical period in a still-torn American society, the literary world also reflected this betrayal. The role of newly freed African Americans was unclear, and the emergence of major poets on highly individualized literary paths reflected the era's divisiveness and uncertainty. Although some of these figures and their contemporaries were productive during the period to follow, they appear in this chapter because they also served as stylistic and thematic precursors to what comes next, and several poets throughout this book will be mentioned in more than one chapter. Some of the key figures of this period that Redding referred to as "Adjustment" are Frances Ellen Watkins Harper (1825–1911), James Madison Bell (1826–1902), Henrietta Cordelia Ray (1850–1916), Albery Allson Whitman (1851–1902), Joseph Seamon Cotter, Sr. (1861–1949), Daniel Webster Davis (1862–1913), James Edwin Campbell (1867–96), James David Corrothers (1869–1917), J. Mord (Junius Mordecai) Allen

---

[1] Rayford W. Logan, *The Betrayal of the Negro: From Rutherford B. Hayes to Woodrow Wilson* (New York: Da Capo Press, 1997), p. 52.

(1875–?), W. S. Braithwaite (1878–1962), Anne Spencer [Annie Bethel Scales Bannister] (1882–1975), Walter Everette Hawkins (1883/6–?), Georgia Douglas Johnson (1885–1966), Fenton Johnson (1888–1958), and the first "African American Man of Letters," Paul Laurence Dunbar (1872–1906).

In this era called "Accommodation and Protest" by *The New Cavalcade*[2] – an intriguing riposte to "Adjustment" – there was now steady, if challenging, progress of African American literary and intellectual culture, much of it tied to the growth of various types of religious, social, and educational institutions, including HBCUs, as well as the American mainstream, including the military; industries of housing, travel, and leisure; and career and employment opportunities. The struggles of self-determination in African American culture inevitably are reflected in the poetry of this era and become an increasing concern in the times that are ahead. The role of women poets remains visible in this and the next period as well, and a key figure is certainly Alice Ruth Moore Dunbar Nelson (1875–1935) through her poetry as well as her letters, while other unique and talented poets include Helene Johnson (1907–1995) and Jessie Redmon Fauset (1882–1961), who have only increased in their critical attention and esteem in recent decades.

Henry Louis Gates, Jr.'s perspective that the African American poetry tradition starts with Phillis Wheatley makes her "the progenitor" of the entire canon, which becomes a matrilinear inheritance through her founding role.[3] In the past, Wheatley was also one of a small number of women whose verse routinely appeared in compilations of the earliest American poetry, along with a meagre handful of others such as Anne Bradstreet and Elizabeth Barrett Browning. General anthologies, such as the most current edition of the *Norton Anthology of Poetry*, edited by Margaret Ferguson et al., have started to include a far greater representation of women poets prior to the modern and contemporary eras. As we examine these neglected and forgotten figures from the past of this tradition and conceptualize a more diverse and inclusive canon, it is certainly time to start reevaluating the place of women in the history of African American poetry, including those foremothers who have been overlooked. There is

---

[2] Arthur P. Davis, J. Saunders Redding, and Joyce Ann Joyce, eds., *The New Cavalcade: African American Writing from 1760 to the Present* (Washington, DC: Howard University Press, 1991), Vol. 1, pp. 183–7.
[3] Gates, "Foreword: In Her Own Write," p. x.

ample room for further scholarship, but some useful critical resources are *Lyrics of Sunshine and Shadow: The Tragic Courtship and Marriage of Paul Laurence Dunbar and Alice Ruth Moore: A History of Love and Violence among the African American Elite* by Eleanor Alexander (2001), and *Color, Sex, and Poetry: Three Women Writers of the Harlem Renaissance* (Blacks in the Diaspora) by Gloria T. Hull (1987), which focuses on both Dunbar Nelson and Georgia Douglas Johnson (1880–1966).

This period saw the publication of early modern works of literary scholarship that significantly addressed African American poetry. *The Souls of Black Folk* by W. E. B. Du Bois, with its classic chapter on the spirituals called "The Sorrow Songs," appeared in 1903. Benjamin Brawley is often credited with launching the field of African American literary criticism with *The Negro in Literature and Art in the United States* (1918). Some other significant books of this era dealing with African American poetry are *The Singing Campaign for Ten Thousand Pounds; or, The Jubilee Singers* by the Rev. Gustavus D. Pike (1873), *Afro-American Folk Song: A Study in Racial and National Music* by Henry Edward Krehbiel (1914), and *A Bibliographical Checklist of American Negro Poetry* by Arthur A. Schomburg (1916). A brief sampling of magazine and journal articles on the subject includes: "Negro Spirituals" by Higginson, *The Atlantic Monthly* (Vol. 19, June 1867, p. 685); "Old Plantation Hymns" by William E. Barton, *New England Magazine* (Vol. 19, December 1898, p. 443); "Hymns of the Slave and the Freedman," *New England Magazine* (Vol. 19, January 1899, p. 609); "Recent Negro Melodies" by William E. Barton, *New England Magazine* (Vol. 19, February 1899, p. 707); "Paul Laurence Dunbar" by Mary Church Terrell, *Voice of the Negro* (Vol. 3, April 1906, p. 271); and "George Moses Horton: Slave Poet" by Stephen B. Weeks, *The Southern Workman* (Vol. 43, October 1914, p. 571).

Important new scholarship on under-recognized poets of the earliest periods should promote reconsideration of these individual voices and invite spirited re-imaginings of what the canon would look like with their inclusion. The current canon is filled with stylistic and chronological gaps which inevitably impact ideas about this genre, including misperceptions that all black poetry falls into a social realist tradition, and Wheatley and Dunbar were the only black poets before the Negro Renaissance. The work by Ivy G. Wilson on Albery Allson Whitman (1851–1901) is a noteworthy example. Whitman's name has appeared as Alberry Alston Whitman, Albery A. Whitman, and Albery Allson Whitman (Redmond 85), and with vacillating dates of death (1902 in

Redmond)[4]. *At the Dawn of Dusk: Selected Poetry and Prose of Albery Allson Whitman* – superbly compiled, edited, and introduced by Wilson – clarifies his correct name, and offers brilliant scholarship on the author of *Not a Man and Yet a Man* and *Twasinta's Seminoles: Or Rape of Florida*. This book is an essential resource for an authentically unique figure with every right to be included in the early canon for his inventive exploration of form and structure in producing an epic or documentary lyric encompassing history across cultures and eras. A mulatto who was born into slavery, Whitman famously stated, "I was born in bondage – I was never a slave." Robert Thomas Kerlin wrote that Whitman (along with James Madison Bell), is "too important to be omitted even from a swift survey."[5] Redmond notes Whitman's "brilliant gift of descriptive prosaic prose" in conveying in poetic form such issues as tragic romance, social oppression, self-alienation, and racial mixing, and perceptively compares him to such modern and contemporary writers as Gil Scott-Heron, the Last Poets, and James Baldwin.[6] Redmond wrote in 1976 that an edition of Whitman's complete work was "long overdue," raising the question of why Whitman would appear in older studies and anthologies such as those by Sherman, Redmond, and Kerlin, but be excluded from more recent collections such as *The Norton Anthology of African American Literature* and *The New Cavalcade*. Hopefully, this situation will be rectified by the growing interest in the "invisible" poets.

Recent scholarship has already dramatically increased attention and respect for the inventiveness and seriousness of Dunbar and Whitman. Joanne M. Braxton's edition of *The Collected Poetry of Paul Laurence Dunbar* (1993), with its superb introduction, has provided an invaluable resource on the magnitude and scope of Dunbar's poetic breadth and boldness – contrary to past judgments – that remains definitive. In 2006, Stanford University hosted a Paul Laurence Dunbar Centennial Conference, which resulted in a special issue of *African American Review* (Vol. 41, No. 2, Summer 2007), edited by Shelley Fisher Fishkin, Gavin Jones, Meta DuEwa Jones, Arnold Rampersad, and Richard Yarborough which has wonderfully progressed respect for Dunbar after decades of scholarly ambivalence coupled with disregard.

[4] In, respectively, Joan Sherman, ed., *African-American Poetry: An Anthology, 1773–1927* (Mineola, NY: Dover, 1997), p. 30; Mark A. Sanders, "Toward a Modernist Poetics," in Graham and Ward, eds., *Cambridge History of African American Literature*, pp. 220–37; p. 227; Redmond, *Drumvoices: The Mission of Afro-American Poetry*, p. 85.
[5] Robert Thomas Kerlin, *Negro Poets and their Poems*, 3rd edn. (Washington, DC: The Associated Publishers, Inc., 1935), p. 32.
[6] Redmond, *Drumvoices: The Mission of Afro-American Poetry*, pp. 100–3.

But the negative or mixed critical reception of the earliest generations of African American poets has continued for this next generation
of poets when they receive any attention at all. *Cavalcade* damned with
faint praise the poets James Edwin Campbell and Daniel Webster Davis,
whom the editors called "fairly good as imitators."[7] *The New Cavalcade*
offers this modest affirmation: "Harper's verse was conventional and,
measured by the standards of her era, competent."[8] Of Davis, Redding
wrote, "there is in his buffoonery a peculiar sincerity."[9] Conflicting with
the positive appraisals of Whitman by Kerlin, Redmond, and Sherman,
the editors of *Cavalcade* called him "by turns a 'black Longfellow,' a
'black Byron,' a 'black Spenser.' Lacking originality, Whitman's work was
not truly significant, and he is remembered only for his versatility and for
having composed the longest poem ever written by a Negro, 'Not a Man
and Yet a Man.'"[10]

No one met with as much controversy as Dunbar. The critical record
shows that Dunbar has been a problematical poet for more than a century, a situation often attributed to his use of vernacular diction, which
was seen by many as a degrading and pandering accommodation to negative white racial stereotypes, and accusations of sentimentalized nostalgia
for the plantation culture that he, as an Ohioan born after Emancipation,
never experienced first-hand. Many of the poets discussed in the next
chapter reacted strongly against Dunbar in inventing themselves for a new
era. In *The New Cavalcade*, co-editors Davis, Redding, and Joyce wrote
about Dunbar and his use of vernacular diction in his best-known poems:

> His poetry, of course, did no violence to the acceptable notions of black
> life and character or mind and spirit. The widely held opinion of Dunbar
> the poet was best expressed by William Dean Howells, who was prob-
> ably the most highly regarded of contemporary critics: "In nothing is
> [Dunbar's] essentially refined and delicate art so well shown as in those
> pieces, which ... describe the range between appetite and emotion ...
> which is the range of the race. He reveals in these a finely ironic percep-
> tion of the Negro's limitations."[11]

Dunbar's ex-wife, Alice Moore Dunbar Nelson, wrote that he never
recovered from the humiliation of Howells's review.

---

[7] Arthur P. Davis and J. Saunders Redding, eds., *Cavalcade: Negro American Writing from 1760 to the Present* (Boston: Houghton Mifflin, 1971), p. 185.
[8] Davis, Redding, and Joyce, eds., *The New Cavalcade*, Vol. 1, pp. 184–5.
[9] Redding, *To Make a Poet Black*, p. 53.
[10] Davis and Redding, eds., *Cavalcade*, p. 185.
[11] Davis, Redding, and Joyce, eds., *The New Cavalcade*, Vol. 1, pp. 184–5.

Some of the same challenges facing this era's poets continued from antebellum conditions: to determine the best means to gain respect, whether by following a path of self-determination or by demonstrating a refined mastery of the signposts of Anglo-American culture; to interrogate and represent the nature of the black experience both as individuals and as poets; to navigate post-slavery discrimination and oppression; to cope with the ironic worsening of racial conditions after Emancipation; to engage in the establishment and operations of African American educational and cultural institutions; to choose individual modes and methods of poetic communication in light of African American society; to forge a relationship between American and African American identity; and to examine the symbol versus the reality of America on matters of race and freedom.

While some of these issues remain relevant threads from the earliest era of this genre, new themes emerge with increasing relevance after Emancipation: the desirability and practicality of separatism versus integration; the recording and disseminating of the truth of African American history; the enforcement of legal rights and freedoms for African Americans; and the role of African Americans in the American national imaginary and operation. Some of the stylistic, aesthetic, and formal questions that have been inherent in the tradition since its origins in the colonial and antebellum periods remain compelling: who are the audience(s) for black poetry? What is the purpose of poetry for an African American writer and reader? Should it be different from the purpose for white poets? What is the nature of "authenticity" in this racialized framework? Should an African American aim to emulate the most admired and erudite mainstream (white) poets or strike out on a path of originality that might be mistaken for ignorance or ineptitude? What are the implications of using vernacular or spoken models of language versus standard diction associated with print culture? What are the literary models that are deemed appropriate (and by whom?) for an African American poet? Is there a special set of critical standards or theoretical approaches for an African American poet? What is the role of African American poets in relation to themselves, to America, and to the black American community? These issues were addressed in a variety of ways by poets representing poles as diverse as Whitman, Helene Johnson, and Dunbar, all of whom were extraordinarily original and innovative in their own rights, and none of whom received the regard for which they hoped.

Many poems of this second major period are dedicated to figures, experiences, and events of special significance to African Americans.

This feature supports the idea that African American poetry is on some levels an autonomous and self-defining body of writing apart from, or in addition to, its relationship with American literature and culture. How likely are we to read poems by white authors with the same dedications, sets of concerns, and foregrounded experiences with the same level of frequency? Or received in the same interpretive context? In contrast with the allusions typically found in the conventional Anglo-American poetry tradition, this period contains poems dedicated to Dunbar by James Weldon Johnson ("Dunbar"), Anne Spencer ("Dunbar"), Walter Everette Hawkins ("Dunbar"), and James David Corrothers ("The Black Man's Soul" and "Paul Laurence Dunbar"); to Joshua McCarter Simpson by Whitman ("The Lute of Afric's Tribe"); to slave songs by James Weldon Johnson ("O Black and Unknown Bards"); to white Union officer Col. Robert Gould Shaw, who led the black 54th Massachusetts Regiment in the Civil War by Henrietta Cordelia Ray ("Robert G. Shaw"); to Frederick Douglass ("Frederick Douglass") by Joseph Seamon Cotter, Sr.; to Du Bois by Hawkins ("To W.E. Burghardt Du Bois"); and to Booker T. Washington by Hawkins ("To Booker T. Washington") and Joseph Seamon Cotter, Sr. ("Dr. Booker T. Washington to the National Negro Business League"). Themes of enslavement, violence, discrimination, and freedom appear in countless poems, such as "Remember Brownsville" by Hawkins. The development of a canon of African American poetry and its attendant scholarship displays a trajectory from its origins – continuing in this period – of building its own reference points of significant figures, events, and topics. Based on the pattern of dedications, allusions, and citations, African American poets were forming and drawing on their own self-determined canon of writings since the genre originated.

Through this system of citationality, slave songs became a foundational and self-referential body of texts that functioned from the outset as its own canon for the earliest African Americans. The earliest and best-known compilations of slave songs, such as *Slave Songs of the United States*, edited by Allen, Ware, and Garrison (1867), and *Army Life in a Black Regiment and Other Writings* by Higginson (1870) presented the lyrics as if they were concretized and finished literary products.[12] F. Abiola Irele ascribes such misperceptions to the limitations of applied

---

[12] Higginson's article, "Negro Spiritual," originally appeared in the June 1867 issue of the *Atlantic Monthly*. It was the first substantial record of slave songs' lyrics to be published. Higginson transcribed the words himself by listening, in secret, to the black soldiers under his command. The article was subsequently published as a chapter in his book.

systems of Western classification.[13] As noted in Chapter 5, the same situation arises once again with the issues of transcription of hip-hop lyrics. Sharing the reservations of Plato and Augustine about the value placed on writing, Irele defends the authenticity, immediacy, and naturalness of oral speech versus the "fixed spatiality of writing" which depends on "technology for the transmission of thought."[14] The privileging of orality was transformed by auditors, editors, transcribers, and readers into the paradigm of print instead of recognizing – as some critics have, such as musicologist Eileen Southern in chapter 5 of *The Music of Black Americans: A History* (1997) – that the spontaneous, interactive, physical, social, and immediate nature of slave songs' orality was integral to their form and meaning. As oral literature, slave songs were based on a combination of structural familiarity and the delight of improvisation. Anchored by a foundation of several forms and styles to suit varying situations, the slave songs' wandering choruses or mosaics of words, phrases, ideas, images, references, allusions, and metaphors were used as building blocks to be moved freely among the songs. Looking at many different collections of the slave songs reveals that various units of language and ideas appear in multiple contexts, which results in a rich and revelatory set of intertexts.

Dunbar used slave songs as a major source of allusions, including some of his most famous poems, such as "When Malindy Sings," "Ode to Ethiopia," "An Ante-Bellum Sermon," "We Wear the Mask," and "Sympathy." These fusions of music and language would have resonated particularly for Dunbar because of his equivocal status as a serious black poet in early modern America, and his biographical roots in slave culture through his parents and their generation. Since the genre's beginnings, African American poetry has been integrally connected to music. According to Rowan Ricardo Phillips, it is "impossible to ignore the strong and seemingly unshakeable correlation between music and African American poetry."[15] As Phillips rightly claims, music may be foregrounded in African American poetry, but this feature does not

[13] This argument suffuses *The African Imagination*, and Irele's brilliant work in general, where he meticulously identifies and explains the operations of an African counter-discourse, for example on pp. 10, 86 ff., 112 ff., and 118 ff.

[14] F. Abiola Irele, "Sounds of a Tradition: The Souls of Black Folk," in Graham and Ward, eds., *Cambridge History of African American Literature*, p. 21.

[15] Rowan Ricardo Phillips, "The Blue Century: Brief Notes on Twentieth-Century African-American Poetry," in Stephen Fredman, ed., *A Concise Companion to Twentieth-Century American Poetry* (Oxford: Blackwell Publishing, 2005), pp. 135–50; p. 137.

differentiate it from other poetry. In fact, music is one of the most prominent and abiding qualities that connects African American poetry to the
classical Western lyric tradition. The musicality of slave songs' language
and structure is a key reason to categorize them as lyric poetry, rather
than "folk ditties" or versified Bible lessons, as they generally have been
perceived. Once we see them in that light, their pervasive influence on
poets from Dunbar through to contemporary innovators such as giovanni
singleton, Harryette Mullen, Nathaniel Mackey, and Douglas Kearney
becomes blazingly clear. The music in slave songs is part of what enabled
them to function on multiple levels of meaning in conjunction with
magnificently sophisticated use of poetic metaphors. Their conceptual
and auditory layers of meaning allowed practical, emotional, and psychological messages to be passed among the enslaved people undetected
by the overseers; and served to bond disparate groups of kidnapped
Africans in a literary tradition of their own making.[16] Dunbar's ability to
constructively re-animate slave songs in his poetry is significant because
it displays the inextricable connection between music and language in
African American poetry, and establishes a formal trajectory for this genre
from its start to the present.

The critical histories of Dunbar and slave songs are strikingly similar
and integrally connected in their receptions, evaluations, methods, and
themes. Both have been deprived of the full literary appreciation that
they rightfully deserve, and for similar reasons: Dunbar's poetry and slave
songs are very difficult to categorize, and criticism often aspires to clas-
sify. Slave songs have been denigrated, paradoxically, throughout their
recorded history – from the mid-nineteenth century to the present – for
being both imitative and weird, primitive and transcendent, repetitive
and chaotic, religious and sacrilegious. Owing to his tremendously skillful ability to handle varied dictions, styles, and structures, Dunbar's critical reception – as a black poet "denied" such versatility – similarly has
left him open to criticism and confusion. Rather than being extolled as
a unique originator in multiple modes, Dunbar often has been critiqued
for his tragic duality as a black imitator of two white traditions that were
not rightfully his to claim: Plantation Tradition poetry using dialect, and
the formal lyric poetry tradition using "standard" diction. We have a con-
tinuation here of the critical reception of Wheatley.

---

[16] My definition of African diasporic literature is founded on assertions by Irele, among others, that
it comprises both oral and written traditions. See especially chapters 2 and 3 in Irele's *The African
Imagination*.

Dunbar, literally a son of slavery via his parents, experienced tribulations in his life and career that are well-known and documented.[17] Dunbar himself may have expressed disappointment over the popularity of his dialect poems compared to his "literary" works. But this bifurcation of his lyric styles and themes – perhaps an inevitable mindset at the turn of the twentieth century – ultimately has proven to be not critically useful, and perhaps even misleading. Dunbar was called the author of "unworthy perpetuations of plantation sentimentalities" by Brown.[18] In the highly ambivalent estimation of Redding, Dunbar's own concerns – that his lasting reputation would be as the praised poet of "A jingle in a broken tongue" – were duly realized.[19] Redding saw Dunbar as the writer of a "bastard form" of dialect mainly for white audiences (p. 52). He concurred with James Weldon Johnson that Dunbar himself was responsible for the shortcomings that prevented his writing from entering the highest literary echelons for African American verse: "He was more concerned with singing than with blackness" (p. 65). Consistent with the criticism launched against Wheatley, Dunbar was castigated for perceptions that he privileged lyricism over racial concerns and identification. Redding's establishment of an elevated African American poetry canon that excluded Dunbar's "dialect" poetry also applied to the critic's scant consideration of slave songs, and his qualified or even limited admiration for Wheatley. In the book that Gates calls "the first sophisticated book of literary criticism published about African American literature," Redding briefly mentions spirituals, work songs, prayers, and sermons as "folk literature," but does not include them in his detailed analysis of the foundations of African American poetry (p. xvi). Similarly, reflecting the views of the age, James Weldon Johnson may have collected slave songs in two volumes, but still considered them primarily to be naïve folk expressions with minimal literary worth:

> What can be said about the poetry of the texts of the Spirituals? Naturally, not so much as about the music. In the use of the English language both

---

[17] An excellent discussion of this period is provided in the introduction to Barbara McCaskill and Caroline Gebhard, eds., *Post-Bellum, Pre-Harlem: African American Literature and Culture, 1877–1919* (New York and London: New York University Press, 2006), pp. 1–14. McCaskill and Gebhard persuasively argue that this era – though a hotbed of segregation and discrimination – also deserves reappraisal as "a crucial stage in African American culture and literary history and a period of high aesthetic experimentation and political dynamism" (p. 2). Certainly Dunbar, as much as any literary or cultural figure, was central to the era's positive developments, while still a victim of its abiding racism.

[18] Brown, *Negro Poetry and Drama*, p. 33.

[19] Redding, *To Make a Poet Black*, p. 67. Subsequent page references are given in parentheses in the text.

the bards and the group worked under limitations that might appear to be hopeless. Many of the lines are less than trite, and irrelevant repetition often becomes tiresome. They are often saved alone by their naivete.[20]

The history of slave songs' critical reception includes accolades as "not simply as the sole American music, but as the most beautiful expression of human experience born this side [of] the seas."[21] Slave songs also have been referred to as every kind of abomination under the sun for a range of reasons: their religious unseemliness for being delivered with wild physical abandon; their inauthentic derivativeness and poor copying of more successful white hymns; and the silly, childlike, and repetitive nature of their nonsensical lyrics. While the lyric tradition historically connects music and lyrics, contrastingly, this dual mode of production and reception in slave songs instead has been used as a means to diminish the value of their lyrics because they are embodied in song. However, the potency and efficacy of slave songs for their target audiences rested precisely in the sophisticated metaphorical imagery and operations of the words. To emphasize the primary value of the music over the lyrics, rather than a seamless integration – or to dismiss these poems because they are connected to music – is to profoundly misunderstand the totality of this art form and its poetic quality.

Slave songs and Dunbar's poetry fall into the same specious category of being loved and honored for what they tragically represent and failed to articulate – or could only articulate – because of their authors' harsh circumstances. This double bind peculiarly has excluded them from the canon of the most honored and revered literature. The sentimentalized history of Dunbar starts with Benjamin Brawley's *Paul Laurence Dunbar: Poet of his People* (1936), an adulatory portrait that nonetheless focuses on the poet's tragic example as part of the inspiring message of his legacy. Brawley opens his biography with this archetypal rags-to-renown (not the same as rags-to-riches) description: "This is the story of a young Negro who struggled against the most grinding poverty, who never completed his education as he desired, and who yet became famous when only twenty-four years of age."[22]

---

[20] James Weldon Johnson and J. Rosamond Johnson, eds., *The Books of American Negro Spirituals* (New York: Da Capo Press Edition, 1969), Vol. 1, p. 38.

[21] W. E. B. Du Bois, *The Souls of Black Folk* [1903] (Boston: Bedford, 1997), p. 231.

[22] Benjamin Brawley, *Paul Laurence Dunbar: Poet of his People* (Chapel Hill: University of North Carolina Press, 1936), p. 1.

Brawley's image of the poet is the one that has lasted, in contrast to the radically different portrait of Dunbar's resilience and exuberance depicted by Will Marion Cook, Dunbar's collaborator on "Clorindy; or, the Origin of the Cakewalk" – another critically overlooked project of Dunbar's linking music with language. Its lyrics – as with much of Dunbar's poetry – draw directly on slave songs as well as the African folk traditions from which they evolved. According to Cook – a gifted protégé of composer Antonin Dvorak, who himself championed slave songs in his "New World Symphony" – Dunbar brooked no disrespect, carried himself like royalty, and refused to accept any whiff of the pitiable image perpetuated by both black and white culture: "The colored folks of Chicago made open fun of the rusty clothed elevator boy from Dayton, Ohio. Did he care a damn – not hardly. Holding himself like the Prince out of Dahomey – he passed out his *Oak and Ivy* – the small book of most exquisite Negro and white verse – and made them like it – at a dollar a throw."

First introduced to Dunbar by Frederick Douglass at the 1893 Chicago World's Fair, Cook effused: "Oh what a man! What a character, what a genius, what a warm lovable fellow ... Dunbar had everything that it takes."[23] Cook paints a picture of Dunbar as the rarest of men and the life of the party, with an immense ability to give and experience pleasure ("He could spread some joy"), and a supremely proficient and self-confident artist: "he could write quicker, more beautifully and with less erasures than any body [sic] I've seen ... I've seen a lot – for I've been around." As described by Cook, and as exemplified by Dunbar's poetic *oeuvre* – especially when viewed as inspired by slave songs' multiplicities of registers, themes, and intended audiences for diverse messages – Dunbar was a self-determined and self-aware artist who succeeded far more often than he failed in achieving his goals. In the view of Paula Bernat Bennett, it is "precisely his contradictions" that made Dunbar "such a generative figure for other poets."[24] If so, that description equally well suits slave songs and their impact. His writing must be viewed as a totality, just as slave songs – from the rousing "My Lord, What a

---

[23] Cook's unpublished autobiography, which he died before completing, was to be called "A Hell of a Life." A section believed to be part of this manuscript is found in the Will Mercer Cook Papers, Will Marion Cook Collection, Correspondence A-D File, at the Moorland-Spingarn Research Center at Howard University. The quotations in this chapter come from pp. 1–3 of the document labeled "Paul Laurence Dunbar Up to and beyond Clorindy."

[24] Paula Bernat Bennett, "Rewriting Dunbar," in McCaskill and Gebhard, eds., *Post-Bellum, Pre-Harlem*, p. 148.

Morning!" to the incendiary "No More Auction Block for Me" to the mournful "Sometimes I Feel Like a Motherless Child" – also must be regarded in full to see their magnificent representation of the depths and breadth of human experience.

In addition to their parallel histories of mixed and mis-recognizing critical reception, Dunbar's poems and slave songs also found favor together through the intervention of HBCUs during the period of this chapter. Institutions such as Hampton Institute and Fisk University are credited with respectfully re-conceptualizing, preserving, and disseminating the past of African American culture at a time when many Americans – black and white – were eager to leave behind anything connected to slavery. The Jubilee Singers of Fisk University promoted slave songs and Dunbar's poems, nationally and internationally, by making early recordings of them together. As Tim Brooks's meticulous documentation so clearly demonstrates, the popularization of both slave songs and Dunbar's poetry to wider inter-racial audiences went hand-in-hand.[25] His research also undermines Redding's prediction that Dunbar's most lasting poetry – his so-called "vernacular" verse – would ultimately appeal mainly to white audiences. As Brooks also suggests, Dunbar's poetry and slave songs have been plagued in parallel with questions of "authenticity" as part of their critical assessment, and in tandem, have periodically waxed and waned in popularity.

The first recording made of the Fisk Jubilee Singers' repertoire featured a male quartet led by John Wesley Work. Containing material from the period 1908–11, it was intended to preserve the style and spirit of slave songs as sung by the troupe at the time of its origins in 1871 – one year before Dunbar's birth.[26] Four of the twenty tracks, comprising 20 percent of this first released record, consisted of poetry recitations, all of them works by Dunbar. Each of these poems, recited by the legendary Rev. J. A. Myers, refers directly to African American musical traditions and the slave songs themselves: "Banjo Song," "When Malindy Sings," and

---

[25] Tim Brooks, *Lost Sounds: Blacks and the Birth of the Recording Industry, 1890–1919* (Urbana and Chicago: University of Illinois Press, 2004), p. 549.

[26] For additional background, see the liner notes written by Duck Baker for the CD issued by Austria's Document Records, and Andrew Ward's thorough study, *Dark Midnight When I Rise: The Story of the Fisk Jubilee Singers: How Black Music Changed America and the World*, pp. 404–5. Though these commentators differ slightly in speculating on how closely the songbook and material represented the company's original performances – and by implication, the origins of slave songs – they agree that the intention of the recording was to present the material in a preservationist spirit, in the light of cultural recuperation and respect, and with fidelity to African American literary and musical traditions and styles.

"The Ol' Tunes" from Dunbar's *Lyrics of Lowly Life* (1896), and "In the Morning" from Dunbar's *Lyrics of Love and Laughter* (1903). According to Duck Baker's liner notes for Volume 3, with material from the period of 1924–40, "His [Rev. Myers] declamations of Paul Laurence Dunbar poems ... were high points of the concerts of the Fisk singers under James Work II's direction from 1901–1916."[27]

In the Volume 1 recording, made shortly after Dunbar's death, we have a moment of coalescence of the past, present, and future of African American poetry and music. When Dunbar himself recited his poetry publicly, the reviews described him as "performing," "singing," and "declaiming" his poetry in ways associated with music and theatre, rather than merely reading it as text. In recitations of "When Malindy Sings" – by Dunbar as well as those who followed his example, such as Margaret Walker – allusions in the poem taken from slave songs were sung ("Come to Jesus," "Swing Low, Sweet Chariot"). In addition to the common dramatic and performative properties shared by Dunbar's poems and slave songs, there also are thematic connections: the message of racial entrapment, duality, and invisibility in Dunbar's "Sympathy" ("I know why the caged bird sings!") echoes the theme and rhythm of the classic slave song "Nobody knows the trouble I've seen."

As Harry J. Elam, Jr. points out, the relationship between survival and racial masking was established in slave songs and perpetuated by Dunbar in reaction to his own era's oppressions:

> In slavery times, Negro spirituals such as "Swing Low, Sweet Chariot" contained coded, rather than explicit messages, messages about real plans for escape to the North within the figurative tale of a chariot coming to carry them in the afterlife to Heaven. Such "masking" enabled black performances to function on a variety of levels.[28]

The same process is enacted in Dunbar's poem "We Wear the Mask," as it "powerfully expresses the historic employment of the mask of racial performance as a strategy of black survival."[29] In Dunbar, we have a mask over the mask already worn in slave songs. Just as their full messages of uplift, pride, faith, and insurrection could not be safely on display for all

[27] "Every Time I Feel the Spirit." *Fisk University Jubilee Singers* (1924–40), Vol. 3. Compiled and Produced by Johnny Parth. Booklet Notes by Duck Baker. Document Records, 1977, DOCD-5535.
[28] Harry J. Elam, Jr. "We Wear the Mask: Performance, Social Dramas, and Race," in Hazel Rose Markus and Paula M. L. Moya, eds., *Doing Race: 21 Essays for the 21st Century* (New York and London: Norton, 2010), pp. 545–61; p. 549.
[29] Elam, "We Wear the Mask," p. 549.

audiences during slavery, Dunbar's allusions to the subtle multiplicities of slave songs had to be underground in his own era of lynching and racism.

Since the history of slave songs has been one of general disregard as lyric poetry, it stands to reason that their allusive presence, including their use as Dunbar's model and source of inspiration, has not been fully explored as a primary artistic reservoir in the African American canon. One of the defining features of canonical lyric poetry, in addition to its musicality, is its potential to serve as a source of allusions. By viewing the operation of slave songs allusively in Dunbar's poetry, we not only see the growth of the African American poetic tradition, but also see Dunbar's poetry freshly brought to light in that context. Many of Dunbar's poems refer directly to "spirituals" – or "hymns" or "the old tunes" euphe- mistically. These more overt nods to plantation culture – such as "The Deserted Plantation" and "Temptation" – are crowd-pleasers, acting out nostalgic tableaux where slave songs are props to set the stage of planta- tion life. Some of Dunbar's most popular poems superficially appear to evoke slave songs – for example, "A Corn-Song," "The Voice of the Banjo," and "The Ol' Tunes" – in their use of vernacular diction, nostal- gia for plantation culture, and causal relationship between humble music and emotional sustenance. Other poems that owe even more to slave songs are less obvious since they are designed – like slave songs – to con- vey coded and differential messages to black and white audiences.

A sly poem such as "An Antebellum Sermon" contains vernacular dic- tion sufficiently broad to represent a true parody of white stereotypes of plantation culture. As Keith Gilyard astutely notes, the speaker-preacher's protestations that he is only discussing freedom "in a Bibleistic way" is Dunbar's imitation of "the double voiced quality often attributed to the spirituals."[30] In the poem "A Spiritual," we read the repeated line, echoing the repetition of significant lines in slave songs, that instructs the listener to "Lif' up yo' haid w'en de King go by" – expressing a politically accept- able statement of God's eternal primacy. That exhortation is juxtaposed with "safe" instructions to "Bow down, bow 'way down, bow down" – in temporary and transient deference to the slave master, whose dominion was solely terrestrial.

Countless slave songs contain these non-threatening depictions of "freedom" and "a heavenly home with Jesus," where deliverance is delib- erately and cleverly posited as a future event in the afterlife rather than

---

[30] Keith Gilyard, "The Bible and African American Poetry," in Vincent L. Wimbush, ed., *African Americans and the Bible* (New York and London: Continuum, 2001), p. 208.

a realistic hope or possibility for enslaved people on earth. Consistent with the finest lyric poetry, slave songs operate on literal and metaphorical planes replete with symbols and layers of meaning conveyed through pivotal terms such as "freedom," "home," "travel," "the city," and "justice." These concepts and locations are carefully presented in poetic metaphors to avoid any suggestions of insurgency – though it would ever be audible to the slaves themselves. The double voicing of this imagery – representing escape routes to the North, as well as Christian belief in God's future deliverance of the slaves on earth, and retribution to the masters – would have been selectively communicated by metaphor. For example, a listening overseer in the fields might hear with suspicion the first three repeated lines of this slave song, taken as encouragement and exhortation by slaves working nearby, but then would be wholly reassured of the message's innocence and propriety by the self-protective turn in its last line:

> I am hunting for a city, to stay awhile,
> I am hunting for a city, to stay awhile,
> I am hunting for a city, to stay awhile,
> O believer got a home at las.[31]

We have another example of this process with the turn in line four of "Children, We All Shall Be Free:"

> Children, we all shall be free,
> Children, we all shall be free,
> Children, we all shall be free,
> When the Lord shall appear.[32]

As poet Clarence Major writes, Dunbar has created many engaging and "deceptively simple" pastoral poems in the dialect tradition by making full use of the entire range of African American folk traditions.[33] Like slave songs, some of Dunbar's seemingly anodyne poems that have been taken to extol plantation culture, and which sound like slave songs, are simulacra hiding challenging messages. "Hymn" is an almost parodic echo of slave songs, with this opening stanza:

> O Li'l' lamb out in de col',
> De Mastah call you to de fol',
> O l'il' lamb!

---

[31] Allen, Ware, and Garrison, eds., *Slave Songs of the United States*, p. 18.
[32] Allen, Ware, and Garrison, eds., *Slave Songs of the United States*, p. 107.
[33] Clarence Major, *Necessary Distance: Essays and Criticism* (St. Paul: Coffee House Press, 2001), p. 81.

> He hyeah you bleatin' on de hill;
> Come hyeah an' keep yo' mou'nin' still,
> O l'il' lamb![34]

This poem uses some familiar apparatus in its diction and themes: lost and suffering "lambs" are seeking to follow "De Mastah," who pastorally wants them by his side as described in vernacular diction. In this poem, the lambs conventionally experience spiritual and natural trials (wind, brambles, hiding through fear, wandering adrift from weakness), as does the prophet-like Shepherd figure – representing the back-firing Christian evangelism of the slave owners – appearing in the poem's second, third, and final stanzas – who has been sent by the master to retrieve the lambs. Using some common metaphorical touchstones of slave songs, this "hymn" is cohesive in using Christian reference points to trigger a coded dual meaning: "De Mastah" would refer to God in the ears of slave-holders but would simultaneously refer to the plantation masters for the slaves themselves. Keep quiet for your own safety, and don't let your sorrows be seen by the Mastah, this poet warns. "Hymn" – apparently bland, obedient, pious, and inoffensive – ends with the little lamb answering the Shepherd's call: "I's a-comin' quick." Slave audiences would take this final message to mean that the slaves should follow and would be protected by the Christ/Moses figure of the Shepherd, not by the Mastah who has sent the Shepherd in the form of "pattyrollers" to round up the "lost" sheep, the escaped slaves. The sheep comparison itself – safely ensconced in Christian imagery – would reinforce the plantation-era view of slaves as chattel or livestock. This poem's example mirrors some of the less overtly political slave songs which can be as incendiary as the more overt anthems such as "No More Auction Block for Me." As noted by Major, Dunbar's poetry skillfully hides and reveals the themes and guarded methods of slave songs, storytelling, sermons, and other products of African folk culture: "Diplomatic and optimistic at the same time, his was a careful militancy."[35]

A further example of this hidden influence in operation may be found in another seemingly simple Dunbar poem, "Keep A-Pluggin' Away." In the opening stanza – with striking similarity to slave songs – we see a suggested call-and-response structure with the speaker or leader continuously reinforcing the message of fortitude with the repeated advice,

---

[34] Paul Laurence Dunbar, *The Collected Poetry of Paul Laurence Dunbar*, ed. with an introduction by Joanne M. Braxton (Charlottesville, VA: University of Virginia Press, 1993), p. 133.
[35] Major, *Necessary Distance*, p. 79.

"Keep a-pluggin' away," directed to himself and the whole community. "Away" – suggesting escape – is the most frequently repeated word in the poem. Rhyme is of secondary importance to rhythm in the poem's musicality; the rhythm is cleverly uneven and bumpy to emulate life's roads of tribulation. This poem's primary means of musicality is through repetition of the title line. The final stanza incorporates a conventional religious exhortation that might have been taken directly from a slave song:

> If you've got your eye on heaven,
> Some bright day you'll wake up there, –
> I've a humble little motto
> That is homely, though it's true –
>   Keep a-pluggin' away.
> It's a thing when I've an object
> That I always try to do, –
>   Keep a-pluggin' away.[36]

This poem – with its challenges depicted by natural disasters ("rising storms," "opposing waters swell," "rain come down in torrents") and human scorn ("There'll be lots of sneers to swallow") – harmonizes with the themes of uplift, perseverance, and encouragement in a slave song with the same central themes and images, "Inching Along:"

> Keep a-inching along,
> Keep a-inching along,
> Jesus will come by and by.
> Keep a-inching along like a poor inchworm,
> Jesus will come by and by.[37]

Trials, troubles, and tribulations are predicted for the weary traveler in this slave song's verses, with the chorus continuing to echo the same advice to not give up but "keep a-inching along." Though Dunbar's poem – like the slave song – might be read as cheerfully upbeat and benignly aphoristic, the advice to survive and not give up becomes veritably revolutionary if viewed as an allusion to a slave song in the context of the Nadir. By mapping plantation culture over his own society, Dunbar's poem invites readers to make sense of two worlds and shows how the earlier poem's themes have continued to have meaning and value in his present era. As the ancestors survived, so too can Dunbar's African American contemporaries.

[36] Dunbar, *Collected Poetry*, p. 46.
[37] Work, *American Negro Songs*, p. 125.

Allusion can occur through a variety of formal means and achieve several purposes. Global allusions invoke an entire world view, for instance when Augustan poets refer to Graeco-Roman standards and values by alluding to Homer, Horace, and Virgil. Biblical allusions offer an interpretive framework for readers to understand characters as moral archetypes, such as when Thomas Hardy alludes to the Job-like circumstances and character of Jude the Obscure. Writers can intend their allusions to be caught by virtually everyone within their linguistic community, or – as is more common with slave songs and Dunbar's poems – for certain allusions to be understood selectively only by certain segments of the public – African American audiences in this case. It can be easy or challenging for readers to catch certain allusions, and to decide how allusions reflect the aims of the texts in which they appear. However, even the most heavily veiled allusion is intended to be caught and used to shed light on the new literary work that serves as its context. The audience's participation in the game is what makes the allusion work. It is a way of bringing together the worlds of the original and the alluding sources, while also joining together the writer and audience in the act of making meaning from this correspondence.

There is a clear lineage building on a foundational reservoir which provides us with the critical ability to see that Dunbar is recognizing and reinforcing the existence of an African American literary canon by basing his poems on slave songs. Further proof of this action's aesthetic efficacy is the omnipresence of allusions to both Dunbar and slave songs in subsequent generations of poets, including Melvin B. Tolson in the period to come. Dunbar's global allusions bring together comparatively large-scale worldviews and cultural circumstances using thematic reference points and technical resources found in the earlier body of work: these notably include music, rhythm, double voicing, address of two audiences, irony, hyperbole, and other conventional figures. Dunbar has heavily relied for his allusions on slave songs as models in important ways, including his depictions and adaptations of music and language as signifiers of racial identity.

As further evidence of the way slave songs become a body of echo and allusion in African American poetry through the mediation of Dunbar and others, their omnipresent imagery of home with a complicated set of inputs and implications resonates throughout Dunbar's poems. Dunbar appropriates, reconstructs, and adapts slave songs' imaginaries of home, which – for both Dunbar and the slaves in their respective moments of American history – remained a concept charged with ambiguity, uncertainty, and desire, particularly for an African American society that was embarking on major new geographical, professional, societal, and educational transitions on the verge of massive northward migration. The Kiquotan Kamera Klub of what was then Hampton Institute produced photographic illustrations of Dunbar's poems that reflected images of plantation culture together with iconographic representations of slave songs. These photographs work in fascinating conjunction with the literary imagery of home reflecting both Dunbar's poems and the slave culture to which they allude. The Kamera Klub photos often narrow the viewer's angle of perspective to a circumscribed space that looms large in the imagery of home in slave songs and in Dunbar's poetry: the vestibule or doorway. Many photos show figures – often males – in the vestibule of a cabin, in full scrutiny of the perceiver, not ensconced within safe private space. This liminal state remained a disturbing vestige of the past carried into the twentieth century that Dunbar barely lived to see.

In the illustration that accompanies Dunbar's poem "Long Ago," which appeared in *Joggin' Erlong* (1906), we see three separate images of male figures in the doorway of a cabin. These images accompany the first three stanzas of the poem. Stanzas one and two focus on the loss of the "old times" and slave songs – the hymns of the past – which are explicitly connected to community through nostalgia for the "meetin':"

> De ol' time's gone, de new time's hyeah
> Wid all hits fuss an' feddahs;
> I done fu'got de joy an' cheah
>   We knowed all kin's o' weddah,
> I done fu'got each ol-time hymn
>   We ust to sing in meetin';
> I'd leahned de prah's, so neat an' trim,
>   De preachah keeps us 'peatin'.
>
> Hang a vine by de chimney side,
>   An' one by de cabin do';
> An' sing a song fu' de day dat died,
>   De day of long ergo.[38]

The old tunes are not what some people want to hear anymore because they serve as a reminder of the failures of Emancipation and the unrealized hopefulness of slave songs. Plantation life as depicted contemporaneously in slave songs was even then characterized by inescapable

---

[38] Dunbar, *Collected Poetry*, pp. 192–3.

ambiguities associated with the state of being deprived of a stable and unitary sense of home, homeland, and being at home in the world. "Long Ago" explicitly addresses romantic nostalgia exemplified by the old age of the central figure, and we recall that even at the time that the slave songs were first being collected by Allen, Ware, and Garrison, they were already considered sentimental relics of a rapidly passing earlier era. The dramatic situation is generated by the evocation of the persona's youth on the plantation, as visually represented by a dual image of a man perched half in and half out. In other illustrated poems, we see a photo of a male figure standing on the steps of a home in "At Candle-Lightin' Time," a woman leaning against the door of a house in "The Deserted Plantation," and a man sitting immediately outside a home in the same poem, all of which are infused with plantation culture music. To accompany "A Banjo Song," the illustrative photo shows a group of individuals sitting and leaning against the perimeter of a house, including two men against the front door and one against the front window. This is the poem that is recited on recordings by the Jubilee Singers, reinforcing the mood of temporal and spatial dislocation that connects Dunbar's poetic world to that of slave songs, even at the dawn of the twentieth century.

The anonymous and torturous circumstances of the slave songs' authorship do not impinge on a full appreciation of their inventive imagery, rhetorical sophistication, and emotional pathos – and no wonder they had compelling appeal for Dunbar. In his goal of being a great poet, and a voice for his people, he could look to the lyrics of slave songs as a foundational body of inspiration connected to his own family history, which reflected the identities of the individual and collective African Americans who created them. Voice, identity, language, and music are inextricably connected in slave songs. During the Nadir and after Reconstruction, the identity of the formerly enslaved people and their descendants was on the perimeter, not categorized, not claimed, hanging in the cultural balance, and not fully dealt with. Dunbar's poetry – as the bridge from the earliest eras into modern African American poetry – was the vehicle to move African American poetry forward while honoring the past in an era that still suffered from escalating post-slavery racism. Slave songs were critically received with perplexity and contradictions: they were called American but not American, authentic black songs but poor imitations of white culture, naïve yet tricky, hauntingly sad and cheerfully uplifting. The dilemmas of categorizing their voices and identities were those inherited by Dunbar and his literary contemporaries and correspond to the critical restrictions placed on their poetic output.

On the verge of the twentieth century, it was unclear in this new world what the role would be of African Americans, but the roots of this uncertainty had already appeared in slave songs in their representations of a home that was, almost by definition, "elsewhere" and in the future: "I got a home in dat rock don't you see / between the earth and sky," "I hope dat trump might blow me home," "Fare you well by de grace of God, for I'se gwinen home."[39] There are a range of meanings of "home" in slave songs and the allusions in Dunbar's poems to slave songs often engage with concepts of home. These tensions suggest the way Dunbar was mediating between worlds in his poetry, often through imagery of home and by allusions to the world represented in image and substance by slave songs. Like the representations of home in slave songs, being at home in Dunbar's poetry often refers to an evanescent constellation of fragments in the speaker's imagination in a new era at the dawn of the twentieth century. Even if these are images of past slavery, they are still the only available images of home as the foundation of the African American present. For instance, "The Old Cabin" ends: "An' hit hu'ts me w'en I membahs / Dat I'll nevah see no mo' / Dem ah faces gathered smilin' / Roun' dat po' ol' cabin do'."[40] This frame of mind is reflected in Dunbar's stylized and strategized mourning for slave songs themselves, which rapidly were seen during and after Reconstruction by the newly freed people as part of the history of slavery. In his allusions to slave songs, Dunbar's representations of home belong to the old times and old ways. They mark a lost path to familiar comforts and signal the uncertainties of an unknown and unreached place of future peace and stasis. Like slave songs, Dunbar's poems are indelible depictions of late nineteenth-century America and its legacy which also look ahead to a better time – hoped for, if not realized – to construct a new and modern sense of African American place, history, community, and identity. The lasting power of slave songs and Dunbar's poems does not reside in the tragic pathos of their conditions of production: it derives from their resounding songs of glorious triumphalism in two of the most challenging periods of African American experience.

From the roots that were previously established at the origins of the genre, this era also sees the further growth of the canon of African American poetics and criticism. This does not mean that the earlier critical split vanished as the tradition developed. The perceived dichotomies

---

[39] In "I Got a Home in Dat Rock," "Blow You Trumpet, Gabriel," and "De Ol' Ark's A-Moverin'."
[40] Dunbar, *Collected Poetry*, p. 262.

that were applied in evaluating the poetry of this and earlier periods have repercussions even today – for example, the idea that African American poetry was authentic, oral, populist, and a folk expression, or that it proved its worth by literary, traditional, high art verse tradition. This perspective of dualism can be readily understood in the context of the Anglo-American literary tradition whose history, especially in the last three hundred years, is to differentiate written from oral texts by privileging print over oratory in esteem. However, there are greater benefits in applying an integrated approach with African American poetry. Many African American poets – from the earliest figures such as Frances Ellen Watkins Harper and George Moses Horton to this "postbellum/ pre-Harlem" generation of James David Corrothers, James Edwin Campbell, and Dunbar – were working in the interstices between oral and print culture, formal and folk art, vernacular and formal language, and black and white audiences. Illuminating this bifurcation casts fresh light on the problems faced by Dunbar, as well as those who would follow in the future such as Langston Hughes, who did not neatly fit into one "tradition" or the other. Canon formation has tended to reward the most "acceptable" verse depending on who created it, and that has been especially true for African American poets. Bifurcated identity became increasingly a feature of African American life and identity in the late nineteenth and early twentieth century. The idea is powerfully articulated in Du Bois's concept of double consciousness; Hughes's later construct of "the racial mountain" faced by black artists; the ideology of the Pan-Africanist Garveyism and the Universal Negro Improvement Association and African Communities League (UNIA-ACL);[41] and the succeeding Black Nationalism that intensified as part of the Black Power and Black Arts Movements. Direct address of the state of black identity, as an artist and as a human being, in a nation where slavery was legal, appeared in the earliest African American poetry, in such poets as Horton, Whitfield, Harper, Simpson, Alfred Gibbs Campbell, and sub-textually in Wheatley. This theme is equally prominent in the postbellum period of unresolved

---

[41] Marcus Garvey (1887–1940) was an influential organizer, activist, thinker, and proponent of Pan-African diasporic consciousness and black national identity. According to The National Humanities Center, "Marcus Garvey and his organization, the Universal Negro Improvement Association (UNIA), represent the largest mass movement in African-American history. Proclaiming a black nationalist 'Back to Africa' message, Garvey and the UNIA established 700 branches in thirty-eight states by the early 1920s." http://nationalhumanitiescenter.org/tserve/twenty/tkeyinfo/garvey.htm (last accessed August 27, 2018).

issues of oppression and discrimination. We find an example in the third stanza of "At the Closed Gate of Justice" by Corrothers:

> To be a Negro in a day like this
> > Demands strange loyalty. We serve a flag
> Which is to us white freedom's emphasis.
> > Ah! one must love when Truth and Justice lag,
> To be a Negro in a day like this.[42]

This poem combines the figures of metonymy and apostrophe with an inventive rhyme scheme and clever choice of rhyming words (this/emphasis, flag/lag), the presentness of time and orality through caesura ("Ah!"), and a framing structure ("To be a Negro in a day like this" as the first and last line of each stanza until the powerful closing line: "'Merely a Negro' – in a day like this!"), and stress on repetition, internal rhyme, and enjambment that echoes slave songs. The ironic tone, and the paradoxical circumstances and content ("strange loyalty") that criticize freedom as being "white" depict the present-day social conditions for an African American. That combination identifies the poem thematically as an anthem of anger, an early protest poem with America as the target. The flag that is its symbol fails to uphold the very values of truth and justice for all (not just "white") on which the nation was based. The poet's advice is to counter those failures with "love," though the sarcasm behind that word is patent. In its theme and the subject position of the lyric "I," this race-based poem is a link from the African American tradition that preceded to the one that will follow. It also serves as another of the many African American poems that are either apostrophes or direct or indirect addresses to the symbol and reality of America.

Corrothers is an early example of a poet who shows technical mastery over the Anglo-American literary tradition by writing a poem consisting of four iambic pentameter quintains. But he subtly transforms what would otherwise appear to be merely a copying of a conventional pattern and style – the accusation faced by the "Mockingbird Poets" – by adding an extra A line to an ABAB rhyme scheme. Not only do we wind up with an outlier – now forming an ABABA pattern – but he audaciously repeats the first line of the first three stanzas which confronts us with the dramatic repetition of "this" as the final word of the first and fifth lines of every stanza, as he forces readers to deal realistically with the situation. In addition, we see that the first and last lines of those three stanzas

---

[42] Sherman, ed., *African-American Poetry: An Anthology, 1773–1927*, pp. 53–4.

hold semantically different meanings. The first use of "To be a Negro in a day like this" initiates a proposition and an open enjambed question: we must continue to the next line to discover what it means "to be a Negro in a day like this." At the end of the stanza, the line becomes an underscore, a refrain, and a conclusion. We discover a different example of what it means to be a Negro in Corrothers's time in lines two, three, and four of the first three stanzas; the repetition of line one as line five becomes confirmation that we have been shown what it means. There is also a clear echo of the call-and-response structure of slave songs in this clever overwriting or counter-song of the Anglo-American tradition, with the first and fifth lines serving as choruses, and the second, third, and fourth lines for the leader. We have in Corrothers's poem a sophisticated display of what critics might have hoped to see in Wheatley and Hammon: a demonstration of poetic sophistication showing knowledge of esteemed sources but making the form their own with enhanced originality that showed more consciousness of their individual and racial identity.

Humor is one of the most marked features of avant-garde African American poetry, which is often conveyed through the use and perpetuation of dialect or vernacular diction as another allying force in the development of this genre. Though political poetry is not generally thought of as laugh-aloud comedic, a double-edged humor more closely associated with allusion, allegory, satire, irony, double voicing, signifying, surrealism, and the absurd becomes a vehicle of incisive political commentary in the hands of poets such as Corrothers, Dunbar, and Fenton Johnson (whose published books contained substantial sections of "spirituals" written in dialect, in contrast with his better-known prose poems). The tone of humor associated with vernacular diction and other forms of play with language, diction, and register continues in the poetry of later writers including Kearney, Tracie Morris, Julie Ezelle Patton, Mullen, Mark McMorris, Kim D. Hunter, Keene, Duriel E. Harris, and Dawn Lundy Martin. We identify the tone as one of sly antithesis, a trope of negation and interrogation combined with hyperbole. "Funny" is meant and actuated in the sense of semantic rupture or elongation, the strange, the uncanny, or the beggaring of belief.

As this book emphasizes, it is a common yet mistaken preconception that there is little correlation between the diasporic and the avant-garde. But much of the humor in African American poetry, which becomes increasingly prominent in this period and increases exponentially as we move into the twentieth and twenty-first centuries, derives from the creative tension between the avant-garde as a vehicle of forward-looking social commentary and cultural transformation, and the diasporic as a connection to an identity and set of values that are partially set in another time and place in the past. Philosophically speaking, there is a central disanalogy between avant-garde and diasporic concepts of temporality and location, but that slippage offers a place of very productive creative tension. Diaspora is in part a gaze towards a pre-dispersal past set elsewhere, in an African homeland, while the avant-garde looks towards the future in the location of displacement. The concept of creative blends enables us to do productive work in recognizing a correlation between the avant-garde and the diasporic. In a blended space, conflicting domains are mapped over each other, resulting in emergent features not found in either of the input spaces. In other words, something new happens when the diasporic and avant-garde are brought together which is not apparent in the individual terms.

According to Mark Turner, creative blends tend to appear in literature where conventional modes of expression are inadequate to describe a new idea. This description readily applies to African American poets who are aiming to remake American culture in such a way that their voices and perspectives are an integral part of the mainstream, and no longer the words of a marginalized underclass of outsiders. A blended space results in a vibrant and freshly illuminating perspective that offers new visions, ideas, and ways of meaning. As Turner puts it, "the blend can reveal latent contradictions and coherences between two previously separated elements. It can show us problems and lacunae in what we had previously taken for granted. Blends yield insight into the conceptual structures from which they arise."[43] When the diasporic and the avant-garde are cross-mapped in the blended space of a text, a body of literary goals and techniques emerge which demonstrates the resonances between the two domains: this includes employing a synthetic practice which brings together multiple sources in such forms as dialogue, collage, or pastiche; questioning dominant discourses and totalizing narratives; privileging demotic and oral as well as literary models of language and linguistic communication; articulating voices and perspectives of individuals coming from the margins rather than the centers of cultural power; fusing artistic and political motives for the purposes of enacting social change;

---

[43] Mark Turner, *The Literary Mind: The Origins of Thought and Language* (Oxford: Oxford University Press, 1998), p. 84.

and reflecting international, multiple, and cross-cultural references and influences rather than a single cohesive and unitary national tradition.

The diasporic and the avant-garde come together – often with wonderfully comic effect – in a great deal of African American poetry by ironizing the very fact of black people's present circumstances in America, with the awkwardness of the speaker's self-position appearing in the double-voicing of the liminal space of Homi K. Bhabha and others. The speakers are objects of ridicule, as seen internally and externally, for the circumstances in which they find themselves. As Hughes put it,

> Humor is laughing at what you haven't got when you ought to have it. Of course, you laugh by proxy. You're really laughing at the other guy's lacks, not your own. Humor is when the joke is on you but hits the other fellow first – because it boomerangs. Humor is what you wish in your own secret heart were not funny, but it is, and you must laugh. Humor can be like a dropped brick or the roar of Niagara Falls. Like a welcome summer rain, humor may suddenly cleanse and cool the earth, the air, and you.[44]

The way space is interpreted in cosmopolitan society has been a topic of keen literary and philosophical interest at least since the late nineteenth century, and this attention coincides with The Great Migration, starting in about 1910, at the end of the period that we are addressing. This time frame also reflects the moment in which the role of African Americans – and their cultural products – became an issue of major national concern following Emancipation and Reconstruction. "Space" is a highly resonant and polysemous word that readily applies to literal experiences and metaphors of materiality, orientation, home, relation, and identity. However, this term – when interpreted to privilege stable and unitary understandings – has serious limitations for individuals whose life experiences entail dual or multiple racial, cultural, and national identities; voluntary or involuntary dislocations or migrations across boundaries; and various patterns of disorientations and destabilizations. The term takes on differing literal and metaphorical meanings for members of post-slavery, postcolonial, and diasporic populations, where specific kinds of migration, alienation, accommodation, exclusion, and deprivation may be central to personal and family histories. Texts by these writers often include narratives that reconstitute community space and personal wholeness; reflect and incorporate concepts such as liminality and double consciousness; employ multiple and co-existing physical and cognitive

---

[44] Langston Hughes in *Encyclopedia of Black Folklore and Humor*, ed. Henry D. Spalding (Middle Village, NY: Jonathan David Publishers, Inc., 2010), p. 428.

locations; and display a propensity to accept and negotiate "slippery" concepts of locality, temporality, ontology, and experience. In this literature, we see that comprehensive or cosmic space must be adequately joined to socio-political and material space to form sufficient human orientational schemes. African diasporic literature that reflects multiple kinds of spatial orientation – notably, much less delineation between time and space, and the realms of life and death – often are marginalized. In an academic context, this situation raises questions of whether their exclusion from the literary canon relates to experiences and expressions of space that differ from Western intellectual and aesthetic conventions, and whether different or expanded critical paradigms of space are needed.

As we saw in Chapter 2 with the discussion of "I Know Moon-rise," (see p. 85) a frequent trait of African American poetry that originates in slave songs has been an unwillingness, refusal, or inability to articulate a fixed state of time and place – a ground of here and now that corresponds to a biologically viable state of being.[45] This poetry of disorientation uses operations that deliberately disrupt conventional literary and cognitive processes with a resulting aesthetic impact that is often affective or uncanny. Throughout the history of African American poetry, certainly during this transitional time and increasingly in the twentieth and twenty-first centuries, we find profuse examples of varied types of conceptual blending to convey this indeterminate state and perspective, including counterfactuals, fictive motion, double scope blending, spatial and temporal compression, force dynamics, and ghost physics. These manifestations at the end of the nineteenth century foreshadow the formal and cognitive shifts that will more fully bloom with the modernist revolution, such as semantic rupture, stylistic and generic mixing, and surrealism and absurdism, while they also are present throughout the history of African American and African diasporic poetry.

By recognizing these related operations in two bodies of writing often considered to be disparate, we confront the role played by race in the pattern of critically bifurcating "the formally innovative" and "the diasporic" or "the ethnic." We also address the way these manifestations differ in the context of African American history and culture. Examples of creative blends used to convey states of dual, multiple, dis-, and anti-location are replete throughout the history of African American poetry, in such exemplary figures of the early periods as the poets of slave songs, Simpson,

---

[45] See www.theatlantic.com/magazine/archive/1865/01/leaves-from-an-officers-journal/308757 (last accessed August 19, 2018).

Alfred Gibbs Campbell, Dunbar, Corrothers, Braithwaite, Whitman, and Fenton Johnson. For four hundred years, there has been an integral, necessary, and too often overlooked pattern of formal, stylistic, and conceptual innovation in African American poetry, a point asserted by Paul Gilroy which is discussed in more detail in Chapter 5. While there has been a steep increase in experimental assumptions, methods, and goals since World War II, this development is an extension of formal traits that have been found since the birth of African American poetry in slave songs in such lines as:

> I've got a home in that rock, don't you see?
> Were you there when they crucified my Lord?
> Oh Mary, don't you weep, don't you moan,
> Pharoah's army got drownded.
> I've started to make heaven my home.
> Sometimes I feel like I'm almost gone.
> Before I'll be a slave, I'll be buried in my grave.
> I walk through the graveyard, lay dis body down.

These examples are filled with creative or cognitive blends of various sorts. As we know from the work of Turner, George Lakoff, Gilles Fauconnier, and others, creative blends tend to formulate new ideas and appear when existing or conventional modes of communication are inadequate. We have the logical impossibility of enslaved people stating that they will die before they will be enslaved, suggesting the existence of a parallel or alternative simultaneous mode of existence that erases or co-exists with material reality. We have a living body placing itself in the future in a state of death in a final resting place. We have colonial and antebellum black enslaved speakers in America locating their voices in the spatial and temporal planes of the Old and New Testaments, often with all three times and spaces evoked at once.

A modern example of similar phenomena is found in the astonishingly beautiful poem, "Tired," by Fenton Johnson, which often appears in anthologies of African American (if not American) poetry:

> I AM tired of work; I am tired of building up somebody else's civilization.
> Let us take a rest, M'Lissy Jane.
> I will go down to the Last Chance Saloon, drink a gallon or two of gin, shoot
> a game or two of dice and sleep the rest of the night on one of Mike's
> barrels.
> You will let the old shanty go to rot, the white people's clothes turn to dust,
> and the Calvary Baptist Church sink to the bottomless pit.

You will spend your days forgetting you married me and your nights hunting
    the warm gin Mike serves the ladies in the rear of the Last Chance Saloon.
Throw the children into the river; civilization has given us too many. It is
    better to die than it is to grow up and find out that you are colored.
Pluck the stars out of the heavens. The stars mark our destiny. The stars
    marked my destiny.
I am tired of civilization.

We start with conversational diction in what we take to be the speaker's
contemporaneous frame of time and space addressing us, the readers; but
in the second line, the diction, time, dramatic circumstance, and setting
shift with a coded vernacular reference to slave culture being posed to a
newly inserted addressee, "M'lissy Jane," who now replaces us. We move
to the predictive future in lines three and four, where the ground appears
to return once again to modern or pre-modern America; then the level of
prediction returns once again to the past and an apocalyptic vision of
dissolution, decay, and destruction. The fascinating and constant shifts
of alternating dislocations end with the penultimate line, an elegant
example of what Pascal Boyer calls ghost physics, where the speaker
develops the agency to act from a state of transfiguration in the heavens
that formed so much of the operational ground in the slave songs at the
origins of this tradition. Though it remains a common preconception
that the diasporic and avant-garde are unconnected, much of the irony in
African American poetry derives from the creative tension between them.
They are linked through the goal of using literary means to deny, resist,
and remake the circumstances of the present time and place as a transcendent form of protest poetry.

These examples show that the tremendous sophistication of African
American poetry has not been reflected in mainstream perceptions of
this genre and has resulted in a narrow, limited, and conservative canon
that too often has been selected for its parallels to the (also conservative,
for reasons explained by Barbara Herrnstein Smith in "Contingencies of
Value") mainstream American poetry canon. The true nature of what is
possible for the African American canon has not been sufficiently understood and has been subjected to gross misrepresentation. Each period
of this literature shows the same problems that have been addressed in
this chapter and reinforce the need to establish a fresh look at the development of the canon and its exclusions and where we go from there.
The bifurcation and unjust methodologies and stereotypes are revealed
when we consider some literary treasures that achieved recognition while

ignoring equally excellent poetry produced by African Americans. Strong scholarship is called for to undo wrongs to superb literature and rectify centuries of critical judgments that are in fact racist. This body of poetry is diverse, and critical methods must accordingly be diverse. It is often claimed that African American literary theory to date has proven insufficient to wholly elucidate African American writing, which implies that a set of special criteria still is needed to apply to this canon of verse. As we examine the first two periods of African American poetry, we discover a canon that is found lacking by the critical community. The disconnection between critical expectations and the creative products to which they are applied is a situation to be explored in the next chapter, which focuses on the periods often referred to as dual Renaissances: the Harlem or New Negro Renaissance and the Sixties and Seventies. These periods, especially the earlier era, are widely perceived as the great flowering of classic African American poetry. Is this view accurate?

In 1882, the African American Rev. Marshall W. Taylor, D.D. wrote prophetically of slave songs, "Their influence is not done."[46] Created and performed by anonymous enslaved African Americans, they have been shown to be essential to the foundation as well as the progression of the African American poetry tradition. Many modern and contemporary African American poems are infused with phrases, forms, themes, techniques, and rhetorical strategies of slave songs. Through greater awareness of their presence, function, and influence, readers can better understand the wholeness and continuity that Stephen Henderson called for us to recognize in African American poetry, including its most innovative manifestations. This pattern of marginalizing slave songs as lyric art and a major source of textual appropriations also shows how an exclusionary and ideological canon has developed that misrepresents and limits the scope of African American poetry. We are reminded of Irele's contention in *The African Imagination* that difference or distinctiveness on several grounds is an inherent feature in the production and reception of African and African diasporic literature.[47] Here we have a case study in the texts that form the roots of the African American poetry tradition. Recent developments in conceptual poetry, and critical reexaminations of the

---

[46] Rev. Marshall W. Taylor, D.D., *Plantation Melodies* (Cincinnati: Marshall W. Taylor and W. C. Echols, Publishers, 1882), p. 4.

[47] See especially chapter 2, "Orality, Literacy, and African Literature," pp. 23–38, which addresses the sources of inevitable distinctiveness, including the predominance of orality.

conventional bifurcation of ethnicity and avant-garde practices, now open the way to reimagine the African American poetry canon. From the nineteenth century to today, slave songs have been alluded to and cited in diverse forms and styles of African American poetry, including some of the most formally challenging. In addition to Dunbar, Gilyard also correctly cites allusions and references to slave songs in poems by Hughes and James Weldon Johnson in the period to come. The Harlem Renaissance is associated with a blossoming of cosmopolitan East Coast literary sophistication. In this era of northern urbanity, critics and readers could easily overlook the seemingly atavistic influence of the oral, southern antebellum products that some writers were trying to reject and erase. But it would be a mistake to ignore the presence of the tradition's origins during this period. The influence of the so-called "primitive" poets is apparent in the work of many of the major figures of the Harlem Renaissance, including Gwendolyn Bennett, Alain Locke, Hughes, and Brown – as we will see next.

CHAPTER 4

The Twentieth Century Renaissances

There is a weird strangeness
In the songs of black men
Which sounds not strange
To me.

Edward S. Silvera, "Jungle Taste"

In this chapter, the periods of modernism and the advent of postmodernism are reconnected in the long history of African American poetry. Though these periods are often artificially separated in critical studies, there is more to be gained by recognizing the relationships between them from the perspectives of both theory and praxis. Many important figures enjoyed long life spans and had major impact at pivotal moments across decades and eras. Rigid periodization can lead to reductive stereotypes about eras as well as poets and focus negatively on the charge of "changes" rather than recognizing positive, productive, and progressive evolutions. It is equally problematical that figures who do not embody the stereotypes of literary periods are precisely those who are marginalized regardless of how squarely they may fit into the chronology and culture. Theoretically, by dismantling conventional concepts of periodization, we see patterns of progressions and continuities by viewing the later period as the result of the earlier moment, where otherwise both seem isolated or anomalous in the history of African American poetry. In fact, with the long perspective of this book, we see how every period in the genre contains fractals of each preceding period dating back to its origins, and the seeds of the periods yet to come. As themes, metaphors, structures, techniques, and images repeat to gain proud recursive strength, this tradition also shows a unique capacity to use its past as a creative mechanism to respond progressively to its own era as a hinge to the future. In some ways, periodization has had a more delimiting and pernicious impact on African American poetry than on the dominant canon.

In this sense, we can see the identity of the genre itself as forming a blended space, using this concept from cognitive poetics and critics such as Mark Turner in *The Literary Mind*. In the cognitive blend, the circular pattern of returning to a body of original features of identity is cross-mapped over a linear pattern of moving ever forward. This centrifugal motion echoes the relationship between the forward vision of avant-garde practices cross-mapped against the retrospective view of diasporic return. We will see these dual functions and sets of definitional characteristics played out time and again to explain some of the truly distinguishing features of this poetry, and its resilient core of identity coupled with future-defining regeneration. Afro-futurism and "back in the day" live in perfect non-discordant harmony. These are precisely the issues of theme and style discussed in Chapter 1 which have been interwoven as threads throughout this book. In these two eras in the early to late mid-twentieth century where political, cultural, and historical forces dramatically collide, it is more useful to highlight their commonalities and links rather than their separations and differences. Both moments are deeply contextualized in recurring patterns that move ever forward, as we shall see.

Now I will briefly summarize the conventions and alternatives. As part of a larger historical era, this chapter opens with the period in the first part of the twentieth century whose impact is incommensurable, yet its title and timing remain arguable. Though there is relative unanimity on certain causes, manifestations, and results, there is substantial scholarly difference of opinion on others; the naming and dating debate tends to indicate these varying interpretations. African American modernism, the New Negro Movement, the Harlem Renaissance, the Black Renaissance, the Afro-American Renaissance, the African American Renaissance, the Negro Awakening, and the New Negro Renaissance are some frequent designations. In the 1960s and 1970s, there was a period of equivalent drama and prominence that has been referred to as Afrocentric postmodernism, African-American postmodernism, the Black Arts Movement, the Black Power Movement, the Black Arts Era, the New Black Renaissance, the Second African American Renaissance, the Era of Reform and Revolution, the Freedom Movement, the Civil Rights and Post-Civil Rights Era, the Protest Era, the Contemporary Period, the Human Rights Era, and the Sixties and Seventies. Even if readers have little or no specific knowledge about African American poetry, they still are likely to have glamorous impressions of the vaunted Harlem Renaissance with its flapper clothes, house parties, bigger than life writers, romans à clef, and anthemic poems, when the Negro was in vogue, as Hughes put it.

The 1960s and 1970s are almost as likely to evoke similarly dramatic impressions, though of a different order of entertainment and intensity: sit-ins, Northern–Southern cultural divides recreating the racist Civil War mentality, protests, voter registration, Freedom Riders, intergenerational and interracial marches, officially sanctioned brutality, and students who stood up for human rights, respect, and freedom.

This chapter continues the focus on rethinking the canon and reimagining the resulting new possibilities of progression and evolution by addressing continuing themes and incorporating marginalized texts. That motive is especially important for periods that are both famed and misrepresented in the context of the African American poetry tradition. The major focus here remains on figures and ideas whose connections, contributions, and directions deserve more serious attention and respect for their own value and as factors in a broadened view of what constitutes African American poetry. There is no need to duplicate the voluminous quantity of diverse and outstanding resources available, but many will be mentioned as invaluable resources to further study of specific topics and figures. As I have emphasized, a wealth of superb material is readily accessible on key figures and themes of this era. Representative resources and ideas are mentioned here briefly as aids to further research while avoiding excessive summary of readily available materials.

With varying explanations and justifications, the dating of the period at the start of the twentieth century ranges from 1900 to 1960. Based on its oral, vernacular, and cultural influence on generations of poets to the present day, Mark A. Sanders even muses that the Harlem Renaissance never ended.[1] I will emphasize the value of recognizing African American modernism and the larger fight for Civil Rights as a coordinated progressive effort and era whose imagery and ethos have been crucial in establishing the current sociological, political, and aesthetical moment. At times it seems that arguments over these periods' proper names, and dates of onset and demise, overtake discussion of what was produced and why it is significant. I find it most helpful to avoid strict chronological delineations, and focus on literary tendencies and manifestations, though the major movements and moments will be presented and interpreted within a generally modern and postmodern framework. The basis will be the economic, political, cultural, historical, and conceptual views of "the

---

[1] Mark A. Sanders, "African American Folk Roots and Harlem Renaissance Poetry," in George Hutchinson, ed., *The Cambridge Companion to the Harlem Renaissance* (Cambridge: Cambridge University Press, 2007), p. 110.

long twentieth century," with the aim of understanding how the African American poetry canon evolved in this era. The struggle over periodicity reflects a structural problem, which is only now being revised with expansive and open critical thinking.

In her important essay, which is well worth reading in whole, "The Black Canon: Reconstructing Black American Literary Criticism," Joyce Ann Joyce too connects these eras:

> The 1960s marks a subtly contradictory change in Black academia reflective of the same contradictions inherent in the social, economic, and political strife that affected the lives of all Black Americans. Organizations like SNCC and CORE; the work of political figures like Stokely Carmichael, H. Rap Brown, Julian Bond, Huey Newton, Medgar Evers, Martin Luther King, Malcolm X, and Elijah Muhammad; the intense activity of voter registration drives, sit-ins, boycotts, and riots, the Black Arts Movement; and the work of Black innovative jazz musicians together constituted a Black social force that elicited affirmative action programs and the merger of a select number of Blacks into mainstream American society. This merger embodies the same shift in Black consciousness that Alain Locke described in 1925 in The New Negro where he suggested that the mass movement of Blacks from a rural to an urban environment thrust a large number of Blacks into contact with mainstream values.[2]

We will start with the opening decades of the twentieth century, a period that is often popularly perceived as "the first flowering" of African American culture and the arts, with literature as a leading force. As we have seen, the idea that African Americans had not produced great poetry before the twentieth century is a profound misunderstanding. This perspective reflects the problems of viewing African American history and culture as a series of stop-starts and renewals, when, in contrast, the Anglo-American canon is viewed as a continuous timeline of developments and progressions. General courses in American literature would not typically divide the twentieth century into small segments that are too often seen as disconnected and not the result of long preceding conditions. Yet academic courses in African American literature might start with a poem by Phillis Wheatley and a poem by Paul Laurence Dunbar, presenting both as relatively isolated figures in historical or political contexts, but not within *literary* contexts. Courses would typically skip forward to a period referred to as the Harlem Renaissance covering about

---

[2] Joyce Ann Joyce, "The Black Canon: Reconstructing Black American Literary Criticism," in Napier, ed., *African American Literary Theory*, pp. 290–7; p. 291.

two decades from roughly 1910 to 1929. Poets included would probably be Langston Hughes, Claude McKay, and Countee Cullen. It is a time so renowned that it has become virtually synonymous with African American poetry or at least the era of its highlights. Poems taught in schools at all academic levels – the chestnuts of the genre – are selected with notable frequency from this period.

In keeping with one of the central threads of this volume, which is to outline an alternative canon of formal innovation and self-referencing, this era of so many competing designations can also be thought of as the post-Dunbar period. The year 1906 marked the death of this towering figure, who may have been, and may remain, the dominant African American poet of the nineteenth and twentieth centuries. His role and image, complications of critical appraisal, and astonishing level and breadth of achievement are unparalleled, and indicated by the number of institutions and schools named in his honor. Dunbar was the looming figure for the generation to follow him, who inherited the burdens and inspiration of his legacy. The Harlem or New Negro Renaissance was a vibrant era with a lasting poetic legacy which has such a towering reputation and legend that it is often the only period in African American literature known to general readers. Rather than the first flowering of African American artistic originality, as it is often perceived, it follows in a long tradition, as we have seen. A relatively brief era of spectacular literary production, this period also displays more diversity and a closer connection to national and international modernism than typically is recognized. The international dimension of African American poetry is one of its often underexamined features, and avant-garde movements including surrealism and Negritude, and the influence of the ideas of Darwin and Marx, had a great impact on many poets of this era. International travel, expatriate experiences, and cross-germination of ideas and cultures for the poets of this era (notably W. E. B. Du Bois, Hughes, Richard Wright, and McKay, among many others) had inevitable aesthetic results. In this era, we also see the continuing evolution – and traceable lineage – of African American poetry into disparate threads that are still perceptible today. These directions include the formal experimentations of Jean Toomer and Melvin B. Tolson, the dual vernacular/formal styles of James Weldon Johnson, Cullen, and McKay, and performances of black identity in Owen Dodson and Hughes.

Other themes of the era are the literary impacts of cosmopolitanism, urbanization, and northern migration, and reactions against agrarian and Southern values and settings. In solidifying these themes as still meaningful for African American poets in modern times, these poets became important as literary ancestors and forebears for many who would follow. Specific issues that retain their importance from earlier periods include questions about speech-based versus literarily-based poetics; the complications, desirability, and perhaps inevitability of dual race-determined audiences; vernacular versus standard poetic diction; the relationship between African American poetry and music (slave songs, ragtime, gospel, blues, and jazz); poetry and art as mechanisms for social benefit; the role of heritage, Africa, and America intertwined and in a state of tension; and the relationship between the individual poet and the larger black community.

This is an especially crucial period in the progressive development of an African American critical tradition and impressively developing body of poetry. The year 1918 also marks the publication date of the bellwether study *The Negro in Literature and Art* by Benjamin Brawley, which arguably establishes the presence of a critical and aesthetic tradition. Literary landmarks published during this period are Fenton Johnson's *Tales of Darkest America* (1920), Toomer's *Cane* (1923), James Weldon Johnson's *Fifty Years and Other Poems* (1917), *American Negro Poetry* (1922) and *Books of American Negro Spirituals* (1925, 1926), Alain Locke's *The New Negro* (1925), Hughes's *The Weary Blues* and "The Negro Artist and the Racial Mountain" (1926), Cullen's classic anthology, *Caroling Dusk* (1927), and Sterling A. Brown's *Negro Poetry and Drama and The Negro in American Fiction* (1937).

The fraught symbol of Africa as related to "heritage" becomes increasingly prominent as a concern and literary symbol, as seen in canonical poems such as "Heritage" by Gwendolyn Bennett (1923), "Heritage" by Cullen (1925), and writing that deserves to be better known, such as Margaret Danner's extensive focus on Africa in her correspondence and poems such as "Far from Africa: Four Poems." Even Paul Breman chose the term and concept of "heritage" for the title of his publication house and literary series of chapbooks and pamphlets:

> Curiously, "deep attachment to past, present and future" was precisely the reason why I chose the name Heritage for the poetry series: the poet is a bridge between past and present, and also between present and future – he uses a heritage, and leaves one – his work is ancient, contemporary, and timeless.[3]

---

[3] Ramey, *The Heritage Series of Black Poetry*, p. 131.

The period also saw the publication of two important single magazine issues, *Harlem: A Forum of Negro Life* (1928) and *Fire!!* (1926), both edited by Wallace Thurman, which continued the important role of black newspapers and journals while becoming part of the growing trend of modern little magazines, including *Others* and *Poetry*, that were publishing avant-garde poems and manifestos. Hardly a brief and isolated spark of brilliance, this period of African American modernism built on its turn-of-the-century poetic inheritance and established the careers of some of the most important figures in the history of African American poetry. They would continue to publish writing of major importance in the decades to come.

The period from approximately 1910 to 1940 reveals radical diversity and critical arguments that bonded and divided key participants in what was essentially an avant-garde movement. Here we are dealing with the issues that arose both later and earlier regarding the mapping of race over practices considered to be innovative. Yet this era had the characteristics of an avant-garde movement or grouping of writers both connecting and disconnecting with each other as they engaged in the process of rejecting the past to create new modes of expression to best suit the present. We also have allusions and citations to the past and modes of redirecting its interpretation. Such modes of cultural correction are gestures of an avant-garde practice in the context of a heavily assimilationist history for this genre going back to its perceived origins, as we have seen in the formation of the canon as it now stands.

In the Preface to his only poetry collection, *Personals* (1963), published as Volume 4 of the Heritage Series of Black Poetry, Arna Bontemps looks back and offers a first-hand view that evokes descriptions of the historical avant-garde movements whose conceptual and technical ingenuity have been given far greater attention than this similarly situated "black awakening:"

> In some places the autumn of 1924 may have been an unremarkable season. In Harlem it was like a foretaste of paradise …
>
> And what a year for a colored boy to be leaving home for the first time! Twenty-one, sixteen months out of college, full of golden hopes and romantic dreams. I had come all the way from Los Angeles to find the job I wanted, to hear the music of my taste, to see serious plays and, God willing, to become a writer.
>
> It did not take long to discover that I was just one of many young Negroes arriving in Harlem for the first time and with many of the same thoughts and intentions. Within a year or two we began to recognize ourselves as a "group" and to become a little self-conscious about our

"significance" ... we were shown off and exhibited and presented in scores of places, to all kinds of people. And we heard the sighs of wonder, amazement and sometimes admiration when it was whispered or announced that here was one of the "New Negroes."

...

We were heralds of a dawning day. We were the first-born of the dark renaissance.

The tone of youthful exuberance in "we stayed up all night, my friends and I" that opens F. T. Marinetti's Futurist Manifesto sounds very similar to Bontemps's reminiscence on this thrilling social moment when something new and counter-cultural was being born for a cause, a quintessential description of the historical avant-gardes. There has been voluminous scholarship on futurism, Dada, surrealism, and even the Francophone Negritude, but less on this African American Renaissance, though the resemblance is clear.

As described by Bontemps, the external gaze on the strangeness of the Harlem scene ("we were shown off and exhibited") forms an uncanny parallel with descriptions by early white auditors and observers of the performance of slave songs. The twentieth century retro-romanticizing veil might seem slightly different until we recall the reveries of figures such as Mark Twain and Thomas Wentworth Higginson, who commented on the primitive, pure, and natural beauty of the enslaved people's singing. Adulation of performances perceived as primitive and uncivilized returns us to earlier periods of the critical tradition that privileged weirdness, difference, barbarity, and strangeness as the most authentic African American expressions. Anything that could not be seen in that light was a poor imitation of white culture. The othering is not a measure of respect for difference but a qualitative downward distancing: the truest and most valued African American poems have been those that display their creators as coming from a "low" point in relation to an elevated seat of judgment. The New Negro represented a progressive movement towards sophistication, yet here it is presented as a regression into racial stereotypes.[4] Bontemps's portrait of the Harlem heyday explicitly looks ahead to the future into which it evolved. Harlem could not remain a paradise in the confines of an America that was insensitive to the racial disharmony that existed all around the nation. It would eventually erupt in Harlem with rioting and its own self-dismantling once it had run its

---

[4] Arna Bontemps, *Personals* (London: Paul Breman, 1963). Reprinted London 1973. Volume 4 in the Heritage Series.

course as avant-garde movements do. By 1942–3, the fear in the streets of Harlem became the fear of muggers: "Hazel Scott and Cab Calloway and Jimmy Lunceford and the rest would certainly not have been moved by a poem which invited them to 'roam the night together' in Harlem. They lived in Westchester."[5]

It is not a coincidence that social geography dominates discussions of postbellum African American poetry, with increasing emphasis as more spatial freedoms proliferated following Reconstruction and into the twentieth century. Yet these freedoms were still tempered by restrictions of home, school, and safe passage, which prevailed in a time of lynching, housing covenants, and Jim Crow laws. The Southern "Black Belt" originally referred to regions of Alabama in the early nineteenth century named for the darkness of the topsoil, and then metaphorically applied to the enslaved African Americans who worked the soil. As Harlem imploded as a cultural center, renaissances began to spring up in other urban centers of the United States that spread to cities with high black populations that were referred to as "black belts." "The Black Belt" came to be used for areas in America – often economically, educationally, and culturally deprived sections of urban metropolises – with a majority African American population. The metaphor is negative, and suggests isolation, ghettoization, barriers, and separation from more heavily white or integrated regions. In the first half of the twentieth century, mainly in the 1930s to the 1950s, this combination of isolation, self-efficacy, and black empowerment "flowered" in Indianapolis, Detroit, Chicago, Los Angeles, Memphis and elsewhere to produce "renaissances" in urban black belts throughout the United States. Darlene Clark Hine sees the demise of the Harlem Renaissance as causal, but also points to the earlier eras as laying the foundation for what followed:

> The "New Negro" consciousness with its roots in the generation born in the last and opening decades of the nineteenth and twentieth centuries respectively, replenished and watered by migration, and solidified into the creative force, the Harlem Renaissance in the 1920s, was destined to reemerge significantly transformed in the 1930s as the Black Chicago Renaissance.[6]

In acknowledging the growth of other cultural flowerings throughout the United States, there is further support for extending this chronological

---

[5] Bontemps, *Personals*, p. 9.
[6] Darlene Clark Hine and John McCluskey, Jr. *The Black Chicago Renaissance* (Urbana: University of Illinois Press, 2012), p. xv.

period forward into the middle and second half of the twentieth century, and eschewing the Harlem Renaissance label, which spatially and temporally creates an artificial bubble implying brevity and isolation for black creativity.

Hine refers to those artists, dancers, poets, and creators as both "captives and purveyors of Great Migration fever." The Black Chicago Renaissance was no more a permanent oasis of beauty and harmony than its predecessor in Harlem, but in the face of urban challenges, the arts, culture, commerce, and community flourished in this variegated Black Belt that still displayed economic and educational hierarchies within the black community. We see Fenton Johnson as an example of the privileged life that was possible in this environment.

In another view of the segregated housing that still was the norm, we find the poet Benjamin Franklin Gardner's 1933 poem "The Black Belt:"

> Like an ugly scar from a half-healed itching sore
> It lies there near the outskirts of the town,
> With dirty unpaved streets and old house-shacks galore,
> And passers-by look on it with a frown.
>
> This is the "Black Belt," an unwanted, shameful sight
> Close by the garbage dumps and railway track,
> Where din and noises reign supreme by day and night:
> 'Tis where we live, we men with faces black.

It cannot be missed that cultural progress and challenges are both described with metaphors that heavily draw on natural, temporal, spatial, and musical source domains, with binary oppositions of vegetation/barrenness, harmony/discord, and journey/stasis imagery among the most prominent baseline metaphors. What do we gain by using the tools of cognitive poetics to reveal the operations of blended spaces in so many African American poems from the start of the tradition and continuing in this period? A belt is a polysemous term with two opposed metaphorical meanings: to connect or to separate two things or ideas, such as the upper and lower halves of the body. Gardner wrote his poem during the Great Depression, when African American Renaissances were taking place in urban centers across America. It was a time of ambivalent tension for African Americans, who felt hope and optimism about better economic, educational, social, and cultural opportunities, but were angry and frustrated that progress was taking such a long time, and disrespect was not fully eradicated. The poem opens with a "scar," which represents the positive value of healing mapped against the negative value of the visible and lasting injury. Similarly, the sore is half-healed, both a positive and a negative state compared to an immediate injury or full restoration to health. The embodied images in line one become metaphors for geographical space in line two: the half-healed scar that is on the body's periphery is on the outskirts and not the heart of the town. Outsiders pass and do not stay as they form negative judgments about this visual blight.

In stanza two, we experience the inverse of the diction and imagery that are rampant in literary-historical descriptions of these first (1910–30s), second (1930s–60s), and third (1960s–80s) so-called renaissance movements or moments: "blossoming," "garden," "flowering," "blooming," "watered," "growth," and "flourishing," as well as musical imagery of "harmony," "choruses," and "unison," are extremely common terminology for these creative, cultural, and social phenomena. Stanza two brings the cacophony of "din" and "noises" together with the unsightly images of "garbage dumps" and "railway tracks." In the blended space, Gardner's poem creates a situation which is both linear and circular: the lasting effects of a negative past are an ineradicable model for both the present and the future. Cultural images are present but inverted: instead of musical harmony and choruses of voices singing together, there is disharmony and racket. Surrounding representations of both human and natural geography are ugly. There are refuse and garbage instead of sky and water. The ruling forces ("reign supreme") are "din and noise," biproducts instead of embodied humans (caring leaders).

In this poem, there is little expansion and maximum compression of source domains: apart from the passers-by, who are transitory, presumably not black, and separated from the "we" perspective of the final line of stanza two, the narratorial point of view is unitary, and the details are narrow, local, and closely related. The viewpoint radiates inward, not outward, and the projected future is bleak instead of presenting vast and open horizons for progress. Rather than harmonious connections, economic balance, and peaceful relationships, this poem conveys a belt that divides and separates, which results in a dystopian environment of ugliness, disharmony, hardship, deprivation, and isolation. As the United States continued its struggle with problems of Civil Rights and fair treatment for African Americans, here is an example of how metaphors and images reflect and influence political, historical, personal, national, inter- and intracultural communication.

To summarize some current commonplaces about the modern period, Arthur P. Davis and Michael W. Peplow serve as examples of critics who refer to the period as the New Negro Renaissance, the earlier – and now later returning – term which appropriately broadens the geographical scope beyond Harlem without diminishing this location as a center of art production and publishing.[7] They date the period from 1910 to 1940, peaking in the 1920s, and present it as an era of "revolt" against the literature of the preceding decades, and a "rebirth" of Dunbar's post-Reconstruction writing. The idea that this period broke with, rejected, or rethought its own lineage is articulated by Sanders and others. The claim is that pre-modern predecessors worked either in the tradition of dialect folk poetry (Dunbar, James Edwin Campbell) or Victorian sentimentality (Harper), both of which left little material for the next generation to work with "in the ongoing cultural war against representation." According to this interpretation, their inheritance of an outmoded literary legacy ill-suited to the more revolutionary climate of their times left the first generation of modern poets on their own to "invent a new poetic language, new forms" by remaking the past for a new era.[8]

Others refer to the Harlem Renaissance as a moment in time and space placed within the larger ideological and cultural context of the New Negro Movement, with slippery senses at different times about who precisely fits the description of a New Negro. Famously, an original "New Negro," Booker T. Washington, was recharacterized in hindsight by more progressive black modernists as an Old Negro for their perceptions of his accommodationist attitudes. Davis and Peplow share the perspective of other critics who consider the modern period as the model and seedbed for the New Black Renaissance of the 1960s and 1970s for their shared emphases on folk materials, the "common" person, Black Nationalism, racial pride, heroes of black history, Pan-Africanism, and social protest.[9]

Jeffrey B. Ferguson places the period during the years from 1914 to 1939, which spans World War I to the start of World War II. Referring to the Harlem Renaissance as "a braiding of history, memory, and myth," Ferguson considers the heart of this period to be the early 1920s to the late 1930s, "when culture came to the forefront of the many-sided debate surrounding African American freedom."[10] Ferguson's portrait of the era locates its foundations in the New Negro Movement of a decade earlier.

---

[7] Arthur P. Davis and Michael W. Peplow, eds., *The New Negro Renaissance: An Anthology* (New York: Holt, Rinehart and Winston, 1975).
[8] Sanders, "African American Folk Roots and Harlem Renaissance Poetry," p. 99.
[9] See, for example, pp. xxix–xxxi in the Introduction to *The New Negro Renaissance*.
[10] Jeffrey B. Ferguson, *The Harlem Renaissance: A Brief History with Documents* (Boston: Bedford/St. Martin's, 2008), p. 1.

He joins other critics in presenting a confluence of aligning forces as the instigating conditions: an internationalist perspective resulting from service by African American troops in World War I, and national shifts such as the Great Migration northward for African Americans, increased individual and institutional racial violence and intolerance, and the emergence of strong leadership, with conflicting ideas for Negro progress, as represented by Washington, Marcus Garvey, and Du Bois.

In *The Cambridge Companion to American Civil Rights Literature*, editor Julie Buckner Armstrong makes a compelling case – which is cohesive with the more expansive thematic and aesthetic views of this book – that the literature of the Great Migration (1910s), the "Red Summer" (1919), the Harlem or New Negro Renaissance (1920s), the Brown v. Board of Education of Topeka, Kansas ruling (1954), the Civil Rights Acts (1957, 1960, 1964), the Freedom Summer (1964), and the Black Power and Black Arts Movements (1960s and 1970s) be viewed in the larger framework of American Civil Rights writing extending from the Emancipation Proclamation (1863) to the early twenty-first century (the killing of Trayvon Martin in 2012).

Several academic studies, including Davis and Peplow's, provide useful chronologies of key events, which help to justify their decisions on their preferred dates and names for the period. With others, Davis and Peplow start the period in 1910 because of such momentous events as the formal start of the National Association for the Advancement of Colored People (NAACP), and Du Bois's appointment as editor of its magazine, *The Crisis*, which was considered essential reading in black households. To mark the end of the period, Davis and Peplow join numerous other critics who choose 1940, which saw the publication of Hughes's *The Big Sea: An Autobiography*, in which he famously looked back to reminisce on the era and wrote that "the Negro vogue ... reached its peak just before the crash of 1929."[11] Among other signal events that they note in 1940 was the death of Marcus Garvey, whose Universal Negro Improvement Association (UNIA) was a crucial force in spreading Black Nationalism and an internationalist perspective. Although Davis and Peplow base their interpretations on a chronological series of factors, Michael A. Chaney provides a more thorough and analytical chronology of key writers, significant events, and publications of the Harlem Renaissance in the

---

[11] Hughes, excerpt from *The Big Sea* titled "When the Negro was in Vogue," in Gates and Smith, eds., *The Norton Anthology*, Vol. 1, p. 1324.

opening pages of *The Cambridge Companion to the Harlem Renaissance*.[12]
Another helpful chronology is found in *The Harlem Renaissance: Hub of
African-American Culture, 1920–1930*, whose title delineates the years of
the movement according to author Steven Watson.[13] A very brief chronology closes *The Harlem Renaissance: A Brief History with Documents*,
edited by Ferguson, which begins with the start of World War I and
ends with the publication in 1939 of "The Negro: 'New' or 'Newer'" in
Opportunity, with Locke's *The New Negro* in 1925 as a near-midpoint.
This volume opens with a concise but useful summary of major figures
and publications of the Harlem Renaissance.[14]

In *The Music of Black Americans*, musicologist Eileen Southern also
looks ahead to embed the Harlem Renaissance in a larger period of
changes taking place from 1920 to 1996. Alternately using the designations of the Black Renaissance and the New Negro Movement, Southern
describes the primary manifestation as literary but with explosive impact
on all art forms, the re-creation of new kinds of theatrical and musical
productions, the breaking down of artistic boundaries, and cross-arts
interchange. Southern accepts James Weldon Johnson's "informal inauguration" of the period in 1917, with the publication of his *Fifty Years
and Other Poems* commemorating the fifty years since the Emancipation
Proclamation. With other scholars, she identifies several major factors as
the initiators of this period: "a new interest in the so-called 'Negro problem'" after World War I, escalating black militancy, the race riots of 1919,
which James Weldon Johnson named the "Red Summer," enhanced
interest from both black and white society in black cultural products,
increasing enthusiasm for Garvey's Back to Africa Movement, the Great
Migration of African Americans from South to North in hopes of greater
freedom and economic opportunities, and a quick succession of books
by authors such as McKay, Toomer, Cullen, and Hughes. For Joan R.
Sherman, this "Renaissance" took place from 1917 to 1928 and ended
with the Depression.[15] Sherman's use of quotation marks around the
word "Renaissance" intentionally problematizes this term considering her
own pathbreaking work in honoring the literary jewels of the nineteenth
century.

---

[12] See Hutchinson, ed., *Cambridge Companion to the Harlem Renaissance*, pp. xi–xx.
[13] Steven Watson, *The Harlem Renaissance: Hub of African-American Culture, 1920–1930* (New York: Pantheon Books, 1995).
[14] See Ferguson, *The Harlem Renaissance*, pp. 188–9 and 30–4.
[15] Sherman, ed., *African-American Poetry: An Anthology*, p. iv.

In the third edition of *The Norton Anthology of African American Literature*, Volume 1, editors Henry Louis Gates, Jr. and Valerie A. Smith acknowledge that some critics decenter the focus of the modern period away from Harlem to emphasize national and international influences and production. But they defend the notion and reality of the Harlem Renaissance, which they call "a cultural flowering" between 1919 and 1940. They identify this time and place as the source of "an outpouring of publications by African Americans that was unprecedented in its variety and scope, so that it clearly qualifies as a moment of renaissance."[16] The editors point to such signal moments and publications as James Weldon Johnson's *Book of American Negro Poetry* (1922), in which Johnson looks to the Irish Renaissance as a model for the emerging generation of more revolutionary African American writers and artists. But they otherwise note the absence of influence of the international "radical modernist strain" on Hughes, Cullen, and the younger writers of the Harlem Renaissance, claiming that only E. A. Robinson and Carl Sandburg had significant impact. They attribute the absence of influence on "some inattention" as well as the claim that the millennial ennui of T. S. Eliot would have little meaning for poets motivated by unbridled optimism in the post-slavery era whose project was fundamentally different.

This is a canonical perspective that bears challenging if we broaden our view beyond Harlem and the segmented vision of an African American poetry canon that must remake itself with every new era and set of challenges. African American poetry's trajectory has been more steadily progressive, cohesive, and innovative than such perspectives allow. A path of internationalism and/or radical modernism does not preclude "influence" by the canonical figures of the mainstream "high modernist" tradition, though such influence is not hard to find. Neither does artistic dialogue or common aesthetics among diverse people living in the same time and place qualify the vaunted burden of "authenticity" or "difference" that has been so consistently placed on African American poets. Many African American poets of the first half of the twentieth century used international perspectives, experiences, and non-canonical resources and materials to dynamically extend and continue the path of radical innovation with no loss of connection to their brilliant predecessors. Thematic and formal radicalism, and international perspectives, which often were used to confront and correct America's limitations and failures, did not escape

[16] Gates and Smith, eds., *Norton Anthology of African American Literature*, Vol. 1, p. 929.

figures such as Cullen (1903–46), Waring Cuney (1906–76), Walter Everette Hawkins (1883/6 –?), Frank Horne (1899–1974), Welborn Victor Jenkins (1879–1960), Fenton Johnson (1888–1958), Helene Johnson, Hughes, McKay (1890–1948), Sexton, Edward S. Silvera (1906–193–?), Toomer (1894–1967), Tolson (1898–1966), and countless others. But there was no need for these innovators and carriers of their own traditions to filter such influences through figures such as Ezra Pound and Eliot, who themselves were not natively "internationalists" and bore their own forms of cultural orthodoxies.

Robert Thomas Kerlin opens his anthology, *Negro Poets and their Poems*, with a chapter called "The Present-Day Negro Heritage of Song," which acknowledges the centrality of music in African American poetry from its beginnings and brings together the oral and written traditions in the same category. The first section under this heading encompasses "The Spirituals" and "The Seculars," which even then he referred to as "Untaught Melodies." The second section under this heading of "Heritage of Song" – note the use of the word "heritage" to suggest a tradition and canon from the outset – is "The Earlier Poetry of Art," which includes Hammon, Horton, Wheatley, and Harper, as well as the surprising inclusion of Dunbar with the "early" poets. In virtually every section of his book, Kerlin includes interesting poets who now are routinely overlooked. Grouped with the "earlier" artistic poets, we find J. Mord Allen, who published his poetry collection in the year of Dunbar's death, 1906. Quite an exciting poet, Allen appears in several collections, including Redmond's *Drumvoices*, but is virtually unknown today. Chapter 2, which Kerlin refers to as "The Present Renaissance of the Negro" – even in the fourth edition published in 1935 – contains only McKay of the usual poets we would expect to find: no Cullen, Toomer, Georgia Douglas Johnson, or Hughes. Instead we find a first-rate array of poets including Corrothers and Fenton Johnson, but also fine poets who now are all but forgotten, such as George Reginald Margetsen and Walter Everette Hawkins. It is not until Chapter 5, under "The New Forms of Poetry," sub-divided into "Free Verse" and "Prose Poems," that we encounter James Weldon Johnson, Du Bois, Hughes, and Cuney, again side by side with the very worthy and wrongly overlooked Silvera, the wonderful Sexton, and the intriguing Andrea Razafkeriefo.

Quite significantly, we find the appearance of "The Poetry of Protest" – a phrase that has mainly been associated in this tradition with the Civil Rights and Black Arts Movements and their aftermath – as early as 1935 in Kerlin. In this section, Kerlin locates Georgia Douglas Johnson and

McKay, alongside the little-known Lucian B. Watkins (1879–1921) and Winston Allen. The configuration of categories and figures in the 1930s was radically different from what it became in the late twentieth century, suggesting alternative ways to imagine the canon and how it might have developed and still could develop. As an example of this common perspective that "protest" is recent and a defining feature of the 1960s onwards, an excellent volume called *Of Poetry & Protest: From Emmett Till to Trayvon Martin*, co-edited by Philip Cushway and Michael Warr, starts with the May 1963 Children's Crusade in Birmingham, Alabama. This volume, spanning the period from the 1960s to 2012, contains an admirable cross-section of literary styles and intergenerational poets from the formally conventional to the quite innovative, including a wonderful selection of poems and reflective essays by Elizabeth Alexander, Amiri Baraka, Wanda Coleman, Rita Dove, Duriel E. Harris, Tyehimba Jess, Douglas Kearney, Yusef Komunyakaa, Haki Madhubuti, Harryette Mullen, Marilyn Nelson, Sterling Plumpp, Ishmael Reed, Ed Roberson, Sonia Sanchez, Tracy K. Smith, Natasha Trethewey, Ronaldo V. Wilson, and Al Young, among others. It is a very positive move to show that the poetics of protest via the contents of resistance, refusal, and self-assertion are manifested in a wide range of styles and forms in this tradition. But the inadvertent message also might be that political or protest poetry is a twentieth century phenomenon which is not imbricated in an entire canon.

The book opens with the lyrics of a song commonly sung during this moment of protest:

> Ain't gonna let nobody
> turn me around,
> Turn me around, turn me around,
> Ain't gonna let nobody
> turn me around; I'm gonna keep on a-walkin',
> keep on a-talkin',
> Marchin' up to freedom land![17]

Although these are the words of one of the oldest antebellum slave songs, contributor Tamara Ginn attributes the lyrics to "Unknown. Public Domain. 1924." The presentation of this song as a post-World War I creation of unknown origins entirely erases its identity, meaning,

---

[17] Philip Cushway and Michael Warr, eds., *Of Poetry & Protest from Emmett Till to Trayvon Martin* (New York: W. W. Norton, 2016), p. 7.

message, and provenance in the African American poetry tradition. The perpetuated use of this venerable slave song during the 1960s and 1970s and after is an accurate example of the "continuity and wholeness" of this tradition as it creatively revitalizes a touchstone of its own heritage to form a global allusion to later moments in time. Yet the vital influence and inventive repurposing of these foundational "protest poems" is made invisible even in so excellent a volume, which is sadly all too frequent.

In *Drumvoices*, Redmond – writing in the 1970s – predicts the pattern of "the long twentieth century" by focusing on the period from 1910 to 1960, essentially presenting a view of extended modernism. Redmond takes the periods he refers to as the Negro Awakening, New Negro Renaissance, and Harlem Renaissance and includes them in the context of an expanded view of the mid-twentieth century – from post-World War I through post World War II. A history of African American poetry must recognize and account for a large and indeterminate body of lost or overlooked voices. The reasons for this exceptionally high number of forgotten and unknown poets have been discussed and explained in Chapters 1, 2, and 3 of this volume. The circumstances were unique of a kidnapped population from largely oral cultures who spoke multiple African languages, and therefore needed to forge linguistically and conceptually original ways to communicate with each other and their English-speaking captors. People in a state of enslavement were widely deprived of literacy, and needed to read, write, and share their words secretly and anonymously for protection and safety. The literate free black population was systemically discriminated against educationally, politically, professionally, and culturally. Their channels of communication with enslaved African Americans were limited, internecine, obstructed, and intermittent, conducted through the system of the underground railroad as well as clandestine publications. Existing negative stereotypes and deprivations by the mainstream white population enabled few and prejudicial opportunities for black writers to publish and disseminate their writing. The standards of changing times, though consistently antagonistic, externally determined the acceptable modes of writing and publication for black writers. Consequently, some black poets were prominent in earlier periods and later fell from sight and cultural memory, as in the case of the formerly renowned Whitfield, and to some extent the well-known, if less famed, examples of Simpson and Alfred Gibbs Campbell. The full details of the origins, authorship, and creative processes of slave songs will remain unknown forever. There are so many serious poets of the nineteenth century who remain under-recognized and underappreciated that Sherman could publish an anthology of their work that refers to them as "invisible poets."

As we move into the twentieth century, we see a formalized or academic canon start to develop largely by the attention brought to literary figures through the phenomenon of the Harlem or Negro Renaissance. But from the origins of the tradition, and increasing dramatically from the mid-nineteenth century through the mid-twentieth century, every anthology and archival collection unearths unfamiliar or little-known names and voices whose presence – whether we think of them as "majors" or "minors," to invoke Dunbar – has the potential to transform our imagination of the canon. This group includes the poets, many of them anonymous, whose writing appeared in newspapers and magazines. Canon formation and critical evaluation are complex and essential issues to consider as they apply to this tradition, but it can be claimed with assurance that this canon has evolved neither organically nor without significant obstruction and impediment on several levels. How has the current canon evolved compared to what earlier anthologies suggest it might have been? Consider *Angles of Ascent*, the excellent anthology edited by Charles Henry Rowell, whose entire section of "modernists" – dated from 1940s to 1960s – consists of Gwendolyn Brooks, Hayden, and Tolson. These selections are admirable choices, certainly, but the limited and chronologically late representation for "modernism" necessarily excludes countless other directions of the field as it unfolds in the remainder of this anthology. Granted there are limitations in the quantity of poems that can be included, and this is the earliest represented period in *A Norton Anthology of Contemporary African American Poetry*.[18] But where have the poems gone from the anthologies edited by Kerlin and Arnold Adoff? When we examine anthologies of early to mid-twentieth century poetry such as *Caroling Dusk, Soulscript, You Better Believe It, Sixes and Sevens, Dices or Black Bones, Black Fire, Natural Process*, and many more, the absence today of poets who were previously being published routinely is noteworthy and deeply worrying, both for the fact and potential reasons, which will be discussed in more detail in the next chapter.

As a work of literary criticism, it is impossible to overestimate the importance of James Weldon Johnson's often-cited Preface to *The Book of American Negro Poetry*, published – by any of the varying standards – in the heart of African American modernism. Perhaps almost as true today

---

[18] Charles Henry Rowell, ed., *Angles of Ascent: A Norton Anthology of Contemporary African American Poetry* (New York and London: W. W. Norton and Co., 2013).

as it was in 1922, Johnson states, "The public, generally speaking, does not know that there are American Negro poets – to supply this lack of information is, alone, a work worthy of somebody's efforts."[19] In curricula at all academic levels, from elementary school through college, classes in American literature and culture typically contain few, if any, poems by African Americans. At best, the topic is raised during Black History Month in February, and limited to a select few "accessible" poems, most often by Maya Angelou (usually "Phenomenal Woman" and "Still I Rise") and Hughes (often examples like "The Negro Speaks of Rivers" and "I, Too"). Johnson considers the absence of knowledge and exposure to be a problem not only for African Americans but for America, because "No people that has produced great literature and art has ever been looked upon by the world as distinctly inferior." To change "the national mental attitude" of the United States towards African Americans and raise their status, Johnson believes the most important thing is "a demonstration of intellectual parity by the Negro through the production of literature and art." For Johnson, African Americans already had produced great poetry in the form of slave songs, but he acknowledges that they have been almost entirely neglected. He also asserts that the greatness of these poems – and other art produced by African Americans – resides in what he calls their "transfusive" quality: the ability to "suck up the national spirit from this soil and create something artistic and original, which, at the same time, possesses the note of universal appeal."[20]

In establishing his own canon, Johnson starts with Wheatley, as discussed in Chapter 2, who he believes has never been given her due while also denying that she was a great poet. We also note that in his discussion of Wheatley, reflecting the subconscious sexist values of his age, Johnson refers to her consistently as "Phillis" while his Preface comments on men by using their surnames, such as "Coleridge-Taylor," "Dumas," "Dunbar," "Hammon," "Pope," and "Gray." Johnson continues his recitation of the African American canon with Hammon, Horton, Harper, James Madison Bell, and Albery Allson Whitman, until reaching Dunbar, "the greatest figure in literature which the colored race in the United States has produced." While Johnson notes the ability of African Americans to adapt and create something great by channeling the spirit of a foreign land, he also points to the racial purity of Dunbar as an argument against any racist belief that a mixture with white blood accounts

[19] Johnson, *Book of Negro Poetry*, p. vii.
[20] Johnson, *Book of Negro Poetry*, pp. vii and xix.

for any excellent achievements in African Americans. In his evaluations of this canon that he articulates, every figure is addressed as an American and within the national context of the United States.

According to his argument, the creation of great poetry and the other arts is sufficient to gain respect, as he makes the important link between cultural esteem and social status. The dilemma presented by Johnson is a conundrum. African Americans will not be denigrated in America if they create great art, but they have created great art that has been largely ignored and they are still regarded by many as inferior. Is the appreciation of art not as objective as Johnson may wish to believe? Is the identity of the creator a more important factor than the quality of what is created? Is evaluation of art ever divorced from consciousness of who produced it, and should it be? These remain key critical questions to consider.

From 1962 to 1975, the Heritage Series of Black Poetry – edited, managed, and published in London by Dutchman Paul Breman – was one of the most important publishing outlets for a diverse and visionary range of African American and African diaspora poets, which was explicitly designed to bring together poetry from the early and later twentieth century. This truly remarkable enterprise published twenty-six chapbooks, an anthology, and seven pamphlets from April 1962 to December 1999.[21] It aimed with astonishing creative – if not financial – success to preserve and unify what Breman called "a crossroads" (invoking blues musician Robert Johnson, of whom Breman was well aware) of black poetry over virtually the entire twentieth century whose existence and correlations threatened to be lost or ignored. For further insight, a previously unpublished interview with editor-publisher Breman appears in the Appendix of this book. Born in Amsterdam in 1931 during the Depression, Breman spent his school years in the Europe of Nazi occupation, an era when much of the continent experienced a state of blues. Searching for music that conveyed the tone of the times, he discovered first blues and jazz, which led him to a lifelong fascination with black poetry. The series was one of the most important publishing ventures in twentieth-century black poetry, and there is a great deal to be learned from the editorial

---

[21] These dates include the period of the publishing house's formal operation (1962–75) and its aftermath of seven related pamphlets produced from December 1993 to December 1999. The seven pamphlets are: 1. *Crap shootin' papa: mama done caught your dice* (December 1993); 2. *The Daily Grind*, Fenton Johnson (December 1994); 3. *Sometimes I Wonder*, Waring Cuney (December 1995); 4. *7 @ 70*, Russell Atkins (December 1996); 5. *Magic Words*, Allen Polite (December 1997); 6. *To Yolande*, Countee Cullen (December 1998); and 7. "Heritage Notes: The '*Without Whom's*'" (December 1999).

perspective, which aimed to reveal and reconnect. Each distinctive volume and pamphlet, every one of which bears further study, focuses on a continuing tradition of originality and roots, "wholeness and continuity."

The roster of featured poets from the United States, Africa, and the Caribbean is a revelation in itself, especially if we recall that most of them were unknown or little known, and had their first or very early publications with the Heritage Series: Hayden, Ray Durem, Calvin C. Hernton, Conrad Kent Rivers, Audre Lorde, George R. Bell, James W. Thompson (Abba Elethea), Willard Moore, James A. Emanuel, Russell Atkins, Raymond Patterson, Percy Johnston, Allen Polite, Charles Anderson, Horne, Bontemps, Lloyd Addison, Dudley Randall (whose equally distinguished, though editorially different, Broadside Press was the United States distributor of the Heritage Series), Reed, Owen Dodson, Clarence Major, Mukhtarr Mustapha, Sebastian Clarke (Amon Saba Saakana), Eseoghene (Lindsay Barrett), Frank John (Nkemka Asika), Cuney, Dolores Kendrick, Ellease Southerland (Ebele Oseye), Ronald L. Fair, and Samuel Allen (Paul Vesey). Many of these poets are still woefully little known and would benefit from further attention and appreciation, though Breman was gratified by the success of figures like Hayden, Lorde, Major, and Reed. Aldon Lynn Nielsen has drawn well-deserved attention to Addison and Johnston, and new studies on Umbra by David Grundy and Jean-Philippe Marcoux will bring more recognition to figures such as Hernton associated with this enterprise. The original title of the series was Heritage: The Poetry of the North American Negro, later becoming The Heritage Series of Black Poetry reflecting its broadened scope – to include African, European, and Caribbean poets – and the changing times. Its advertising campaign in 1969 called it "the world's longest running series dedicated to publishing black poetry." Breman chose "Heritage" for the series title because "the poet is a bridge between past and present, and also between present and future – he uses a heritage and leaves one." With its final extraordinary title published in 1975, *Paul Vesey's Ledger* by Samuel Allen, it is important to recall that this series was published during the time frame – whose fiftieth anniversary was celebrated in 2014–15 – of major milestones in the Civil Rights and Freedom Movements: the Freedom Summer, the March on Selma, the Voting Rights Act, the Freedom Schools, the Civil Rights Act, and the Free Speech Movement.

The Heritage Series offers an exceptionally varied perspective on the full range of African American and African diaspora poetry and poetics, including some of its most innovative and challenging manifestations. As Breman, who had no previous experience or plans in publishing, wrote of his impetus for this venture: "I learned that (Robert) Hayden was preparing a definitive collection of his verse, and heard it did not seem easy to find a publisher... I thought that a crying shame ... I decided I might as well have a go myself." Hayden's *A Ballad of Remembrance* became a central reason for the series as well as its first published title. Many revered poets of the twentieth and twenty-first centuries got their start or made career progress through their publication in this series. In addition to two eventual volumes by Hayden – *The Ballad of Remembrance* and *The Night-Blooming Cereus* – the series included an authentically monumental list of titles: *Personals* by Bontemps (1963), *Haverstraw* by Horne (1963), *Heretofore* by Atkins (1968), *The Still Voice of Harlem* (1968) and *The Wright Poems* (1972) by Rivers, *The Aura & The Umbra* by Lloyd Addison (1970), *Cables to Rage* by Lorde (1970), *catechism of d neoamerican hoodoo church* by Reed (1970), *The Confession Stone* by Dodson (1970), *Love You* by Randall (1970), *Private Line* by Major (1971), *Take No Prisoners* by Durem (1971), *Thorns and Thistles* by Mukhtarr Mustafa (1971), *Light a Fire* by Frank John/Nkemka Asika (1973), *The Conflicting Eye* by Eseoghene/Lindsay Barrett (1973), *Storefront Church* by Cuney (1973), *The Magic Sun Spins* by Ellease Southerland/Ebele Oseye (1974), and *Through the Ceiling* by Dolores Kendrick (1974), among others. The primary goals of this venture were to showcase the writing of Harlem Renaissance poets who had never published a poetry collection (such as Bontemps and Dodson), and new poets to give them a platform from which to take off. Prime examples were the first two volumes in the series, both published in 1962: Hayden's *A Ballad of Remembrance* certainly propelled Hayden's career forward. He won the Grand Prix de la Poésie at the First Festival of Negro Arts in Dakar in 1966. Breman – in the biographical note on the back of *The Night-Blooming Cereus* – credits the tireless promotion of Hughes and "the extraordinary Rosey Pool" for Hayden's success in winning this international prize. The second volume equally set the tone for the quality and aesthetic diversity of what was to follow over the next thirteen years: *Sixes and Sevens*, an anthology of thirteen "new" poets, none of whom had published a full-length poetry collection yet. The poets represented included Hernton, Patterson, Johnston – whose work Breman knew through Dasein – James A. Emanuel (who would go on to become Dudley Randall's best adviser), and Allen Polite, in addition to a number of figures who were to publish full Heritage Series volumes of their own in the future, including Lorde, Atkins, Rivers, and James Thompson.[22]

A transatlantic network of organizations, individuals, and movements closely associated with the series helped to facilitate its success. That included most notably Hughes and Bontemps, who encouraged numerous poets to send their work to Breman. Other groups in close communication with Breman included the poets associated with Umbra, Free Lance, OBAC (Organization of Black American Culture), a Chicago-based contingent of poets (Ronald Fair, Rivers), Dasein (Johnston, Dolores Kendrick), and Broadside Press (Breman referred to Randall, as well as Pool, as his "without whoms"). Some of the closest international connections included poets affiliated with the Caribbean Artists Movement (such as Kamau Brathwaite and Linton Kwesi Johnson, who appeared in Breman's Penguin anthology) and London-based figures involved in theatre and the arts such as Amon Saba Saakana, Lindsay Barrett, and Frank John.

The aesthetic terrain established by this publishing house – started of necessity, according to Breman – provides a revealing and expansive portrait of the links and trajectories of African American and African diasporic poetry and poetics from as early as the 1940s to the present that still are not fully recognized. Much of the work that was published in this series in the 1960s and 1970s was written a decade or more earlier. Although Hayden had published *Heart-Shape in the Dust* in 1940, followed by *Figure of Time* in 1955, his A *Ballad of Remembrance* – launching the Heritage Series in 1962, but mainly containing poems written in the fifties – was a larger collection of more recent work, and contains many of the most famous poems of his career. It is staggering to realize that the first collection in the Heritage Series included for the first time in book form Hayden's poems "Homage to the Empress of the Blues," "Middle Passage," "O Daedalus, Fly Away Home," "The Ballad of Nat Turner," and two famed sonnets, "Frederick Douglass" and "Those Winter Sundays." Breman said that "Those Winter Sundays" was his

---

[22] The Dasein Literary Society was an informal group of stylistically diverse black writers based in Washington, DC from the late 1950s to the early 1960s. Originally based at Howard University, the name of the group and its quarterly journal comes from the term used by philosopher Martin Heidegger to refer to a mode of being in the world that is specifically human. Some of the key and associated figures include Percy Johnston, Walter De Legall, Lance Jeffers, and Dolores Kendrick. For more information, see the well-detailed history and literary analysis provided by Aldon Lynn Nielsen in *Black Chant: Languages of African-American Postmodernism* (Cambridge: Cambridge University Press, 1997), especially pp. 62–77.

favorite poem in the book, and wondered in an interview forty years later if it had become well known, which I assured him it had. *The Ballad of Remembrance* also became the core of Hayden's *Selected Poems* in 1966 by October House, his first so-called "commercial publisher."

With the second edition of Volume 4, *Personals* by Bontemps, the Heritage Series volumes took on the distinctive new look with the striking Frits Stoepman design now recognized by book aficionados who are familiar with this series: the portrait front covers, back cover biographies, Gill Sans Bold font, Basingwerk Parchment, and PB monogram logo on front left and back right covers. Breman traded Stoepman three books on erotic French cinema for the logo. Starting with Volume 4, a few issues also contained introductions or essays. A prime example is Volume 4, which Bontemps approached Breman to publish. It contains Bontemps's famed poems "Southern Mansion" and "Nocturne at Bethesda," plus a quite valuable memoir about Harlem of the 1920s versus the 1940s from the vantage point of 1963, which is discussed in this book.

The first four volumes appeared in 1962–3, followed by a four-year hiatus when the press ran out of funds. In 1966, Breman made his first trip to the United States – in part to attend the ceremony in New York where Hayden received the Dakar Poetry Prize from Léopold Sédar Senghor. He traveled the country to meet many of the key Heritage Series poets: Mari Evans, Rivers, Hayden, and Atkins. He said that this trip was directly responsible for the revival of the Heritage Series. The second incarnation of the series was fueled by Breman's fresh energy after this lengthy United States trip but also by his arrangement with Randall and Broadside Press, coming shortly afterwards, which became the Heritage Series's US distributor. As Breman said, Broadside was set up to reach the right audience while the Heritage Series was not: that enabled Breman to at least recoup publishing costs, but also meant that when Broadside paused, it was the end of Heritage. The history of Broadside Press is of immense importance to the legacy of African American poetry editing and publishing. *Wrestling with the Muse: Dudley Randall and the Broadside Press* by Melba Joyce Boyd is the definitive treatment of this topic. With extensive bibliographical information, it is essential reading for anyone interested in the tremendous contribution made by Randall and this press.

To fulfill its mission of building bridges across eras, the Heritage Series has a subtle pattern of presenting work from an earlier era juxtaposed with work of a later era in the same volume. For example, the introduction to Bontemps's *Personals* contains poems written twenty years and more before this volume was published. As noted, the volume also contains a very important introduction by Bontemps discussing the Harlem Renaissance, the New Negro, and changes to Harlem during the period of World War II. Here we have a memoir of Harlem in 1924 compared with Harlem in 1942 in a book published in 1960, an era on the brink of the "second Renaissance." Or consider Durem's extraordinary volume, *Take No Prisoners*. These poems have been credited as precursors to the Black Power Movement – but how does our perspective of history change by realizing that these poems were mainly written between 1950 and 1951, and recognizing the trajectory that they form with "A Decoration for the President," which appears in the same volume and was written in 1961? Many other volumes in the series contain much earlier work, though the books appeared in the 1960s and 1970s. Part of Breman's mission was to fill in a history – this was not all new writing, though most of it had never appeared in print or only in magazines.

To point out a few highlights that characterize the value of this series, the second Rivers volume, *The Wright Poems,* with an introduction by Ronald Fair, and the Durem volume *Take No Prisoners* both were published posthumously. Just as he did with a Fenton Johnson Heritage Pamphlet, it was a priority for Breman to bring poetry to light by those who had passed away and might be forgotten without such attention. He wanted to provide a platform to new writers but also had a recovery motive to preserve work by important writers who had no future, except in additional uncollected materials. Another exceptional volume is Atkins's Volume 7, published in 1968, *Heretofore*, which also contains some of his most important poems, including "Night and a Distant Church," "Trainyard at Night," and "The Seventh Circle (Poem in radio format)." In a significant description, Atkins was presented as having produced an original and formidable body of poetry and poetics ("the first retrospective exhibition"), which explicitly correlates technique with innovation. The book states that Atkins had published four previous chapbooks but "the present collection of his work arranged largely in chronological order affords the first retrospective exhibition of Atkins as a restless experimentalist with a very high regard for craftsmanship." Atkins was described in the Heritage Series advertising as the "controversial poet who is also editor of the long-lived Free Lance Magazine." This is a tradition whose major practitioners often have been disregarded for the magnitude of their own poetic opus and editorial leadership in publishing black writing. Technical skill too often has been associated with Anglo-American conventions while experimentalism is pejoratively connected to incompetency or strangeness. In this context, the presentation of Atkins has resounding meaning. Thanks to their dedicated and timely work in recovery, collection, preservation, and dissemination, Atkins's work should be gaining well-deserved wider appreciation and recognition through the marvelous efforts of Kevin Prufer and Michael Dumanis.[23]

The Aura and the Umbra by Addison underscores Breman's close connection to poets affiliated with Umbra – the group and the magazine – which includes Hernton's appearance in *Sixes and Sevens*, Addison's *The Aura and the Umbra*, Reed's *catechism of d neoamerican hoodoo church*, Patterson's *Riot Rimes* (not published, though scheduled as Heritage Series 7) and appearance in *Sixes and Sevens*, and Durem's *Take No Prisoners*. The inclusion of Addison in the series also shows Breman's remarkably diverse taste as an editor – with Atkins, Polite, Hernton, Reed, and others, the avant-garde tradition is well represented, as is the surrealism of Negritude, with *Thorns and Thistles* by Mukhtarr Mustafa. The group and magazine Umbra of course took their name from the central poem in Addison's Heritage Series book. Also "Black in search of beauty" appears here for first time in print. This volume represents ten years of Addison's writing. It is described in a 1969 advertisement as the volume "which gave a name to the legendary New York writers workshop."

Two other Umbra-related figures are James W. Thompson and Durem. Thompson's Heritage volume is *First Fire: Poems 1957–1960*. His biography in the book says: "He was to have edited the third issue of 'Umbra' after the original editors split up over Ray Durem's paper assassination of president John Kennedy: it is typical of the paranoid situation around Thompson that he appears as 'editor emeritus' only on the rare coloured copies of the resultant 'Umbra anthology 1967–1968' to disappear without a trace on the uncoloured trade edition." Durem's "paper assassination" of Kennedy took the form of his poem, "A Decoration for the President," which was published in his Heritage Series volume, *Take No Prisoners*. His biography in this volume says: "Other work had been accepted for publication in Umbra 2, the New York magazine run by Hernton, Dent and David Henderson, but one of the pieces selected would lead to a rift in the editorial board: 'A decoration for the President' was thought unsuitable in the wake of the Kennedy assassination and consequently appears here for the first time." Durem was published in

[23] See, for example, Prufer and Dumanis, eds., *On the Life and Work of an American Master* (Missouri: Pleiades Press, 2013).

Umbra 2 and the Umbra Anthology of 1967. His poems in *Take No Prisoners* mostly date from 1950–8, and he died in 1963. The Heritage Series published the first poetry collection by Umbra figure Reed, which Breman discusses:

> Ishmael Reed's *catechism* is the only book in the Heritage Series that sprang fully-grown through my letterbox, one morning very early in 1969. Ron Fair or Clarence Major must have suggested that I might be interested – and from the minute I opened the envelope and read the contents it was quite clear that here was the next book, and a very remarkable one at that.[24]

Catechism of d neoamerican hoodoo church includes some of Reed's indisputable classics: "I am a cowboy in the boat of ra," "black power poem," "Badman of the guest professor," and "Dualism in ralph ellison's invisible man."

Hughes had a major role as well in the evolution of the Heritage Series, and his sometimes underappreciated encouragement of diverse experimental poetry brought many important writers to Breman's attention. Breman and Hughes began corresponding in 1954 and first met in 1960. Hughes was responsible for Breman's contact with Bontemps, Durem, and Polite, among others. Another important figure is Casper LeRoy Jordan, who was the Wilberforce University librarian when Rivers studied there, and got Rivers involved in Free Lance, which published three mimeographed pamphlets of his poetry. Rivers was a founder of OBAC in Chicago, with Fair, David Llorens, and Gerald McWorter. His posthumous collection *The Wright Poems* pays homage to precursor and literary role model Richard Wright, forging internal connections within the series as Breman had hoped (further extended by Fair's Introduction) – with the pathos of a young deceased struggling poet's tribute to the spirit and inspiration of his literary hero, who had died in 1960. Rivers would be virtually unknown and not well represented if not for small presses such as Heritage from London and Free Lance from Cleveland. This beautiful collection contains facsimiles of the manuscripts of the poems "Night Letter from Paris" (see Figure 2 on p.155) and "Postscript to a Poem," together with a letter to Breman from Rivers about his first Heritage Series collection, *The Still Voice of Harlem* (see Figure 4 on pp. 182–6). The letter was written one month before the poet's death – which took place three weeks before the publication of *The Wright Poems*.

[24] Ramey, *The Heritage Series of Black Poetry*, p. 144.

The Night-Blooming Cereus, Volume 20, published in April 1972, was Hayden's second Heritage Series volume. It was a special number which marked the tenth anniversary of the Heritage Series which started fittingly in 1962 with the publication of *A Ballad of Remembrance*. Eseoghene, born in Jamaica as Lindsay Barrett, also published his first poetry collection in the Heritage Series: *The Conflicting Eye*, published in 1973, was Volume 21. Volumes by Sakaana and John exemplify the Caribbean presence in the Heritage Series, in addition to African Muktarr Mustapha. Through this expansion of the Heritage Series to include poets from the black diaspora, as well as representatives of Pan-African consciousness, we can also recognize the influence of Negritude through the work of Samuel Allen and the Pan-African vision of Ellease Southerland/Ebele Oseye. The representation in the Heritage Series is not merely geographical or even national, but also stylistic: John, originally from Trinidad, and later relocating to London and then New York, drew on oral and chant traditions used for revolutionary purposes: "to put me right ... to help put other black people right." The Heritage Series incorporates the folk tradition of African American music and its literary impact represented in the blues, ballads, ragtime, and gospel poems of Cuney. We find the earliest soundings of the Black Arts Movement and its revolutionary consciousness in Durem. We find the strong surrealistic influence of Negritude in Mustapha. We find Pan-African visionary representation in the work of Southerland/Oseye. We find the slave song tradition in Kendrick. We find the avant-garde represented in Addison, Reed, and Atkins. We find representatives of Umbra, Dasein, and Free Lance. More great poems first published in the Heritage Series include "No Images" by Cuney, "For James" by Frank Horne, "Martha" by Lorde, "Those Winter Sundays," "Middle Passage" and a raft of others by Hayden, and an equally important array of examples by Addison and Atkins. We even find the appearance of the notorious poem "A Decoration for the President" by Durem.

In a promotional pamphlet advertising "12 years of published black poetry" for the Heritage Series, numerous quotations appear with quite a mixture of sentiments and attitudes, which probably relate to the personality, nationality, and race of Breman rather than the contents of the series, which were broadly admired. One such endorsement from Linton Kwesi Johnson bears mention: "It is a very useful and readable collection of poems, not because of its editor but in spite of him" (*Race Today*). Here is the assessment by Redmond in *Drumvoices*: "Nevertheless (alas!), one wonders where these black poets might have gotten published

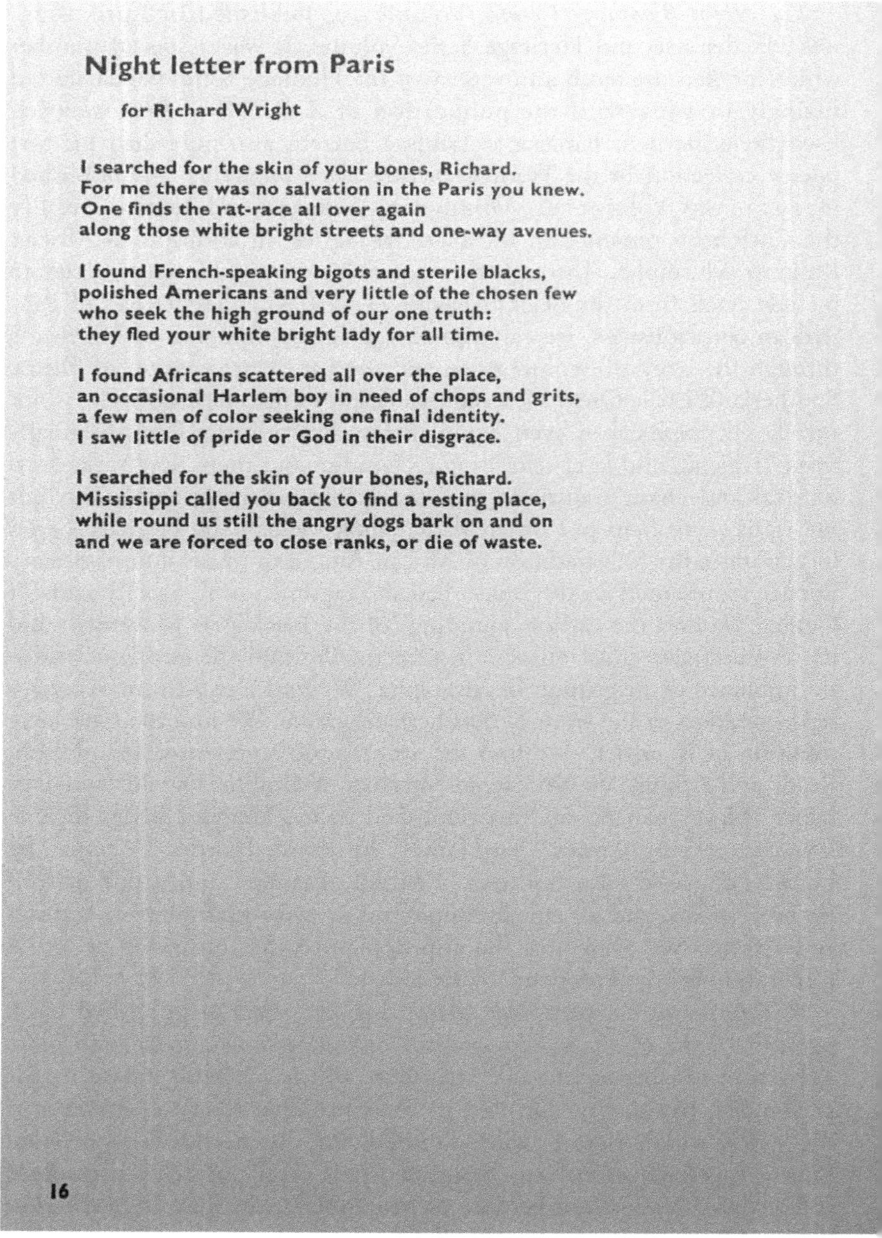

Night letter from Paris

for Richard Wright

I searched for the skin of your bones, Richard.
For me there was no salvation in the Paris you knew.
One finds the rat-race all over again
along those white bright streets and one-way avenues.

I found French-speaking bigots and sterile blacks,
polished Americans and very little of the chosen few
who seek the high ground of our one truth:
they fled your white bright lady for all time.

I found Africans scattered all over the place,
an occasional Harlem boy in need of chops and grits,
a few men of color seeking one final identity.
I saw little of pride or God in their disgrace.

I searched for the skin of your bones, Richard.
Mississippi called you back to find a resting place,
while round us still the angry dogs bark on and on
and we are forced to close ranks, or die of waste.

16

Figure 2   "Night Letter from Paris" by Conrad Kent Rivers

I searched for the skin of your bones, Richard;
For me there was no salvation in the Paris you knew
One finds the rat-race all over again
Along those white bright streets and one-way avenues.

I found French speaking bigots and sterile blacks
Polished Americans afraid to look back,
I found Africans indifferent to my American clothes
So went the way the true expatriate goes

Alone

17

if such 'necessary diseases' as Bremen [sic] did not exist," and "In addition to such 'suspicion,' felt also by black poets, there is great resentment of Bremen's [sic] fast-draw critical evaluations of the poetry – which are often caustic, ridiculous and narrow, and reflect a lack of the broader concerns of black poetry."

Several Heritage Series authors were interviewed for retrospective comments on the enterprise which appear in *The Heritage Series of Black Poetry, 1962–1975: A Research Compendium* edited by Ramey in consultation with Breman. Major wrote, "Paul's range seemed broader than say Jones's or Randall's at Broadside. Broader than that of editors publishing anthologies and books of African American poetry in the 1960s and 1970s. At least he wasn't insisting that all the poems be works of protest."[25] Sakaana reflected, "I was astonished by the wide variety of writers he published, from the sublime to the moderate, from the nationalist to the humanist, from the revolutionary to the conventionalist." Fair commented on "his passion for Black poetry resulting in his creating the Heritage Series, through which many of our best poets got their first important international exposure." Kendrick wrote, "Nothing can diminish the contribution that Paul Breman has made. He was out there by himself, publishing this important African American poetry. This man has made one of the finest contributions to African-American literature on either side of the Atlantic. He wanted to get a broader audience for this poetry, not attention for himself." Here are the words of Sonia Sanchez:

> The Heritage books were done quite well and were very important work. I was exposed to Mari Evans, Robert Hayden and Audre Lorde through their Heritage books. Black writing had been consciously ignored in this country. Paul Breman showed the range of black writing in this country. I think Breman wanted to show that the African American tradition was not one thing or the other – but it was many things. The Heritage Series was showing the wide range of black writing in America. I think this recognition is long overdue.

I asked for a retrospective comment from Breman too, who looked back at the Series in 2006 for the first time in thirty years. Breman concluded in a personal letter, "There is a godawful lot of very good stuff here – and very little crap." I agree, and that is no small achievement.

---

[25] See Ramey, *The Heritage Series of Black Poetry*, pp. 170, 175, 183, 174 and 171.

Breman deserves resounding posthumous praise for broadening perceptions by deliberately seeking out what could represent the full aesthetic gamut of black poetry – an especially bold mission and vision in the early to mid-twentieth century. Whether or not it has received proper credit, the impact of this remarkable enterprise which formally took place during a thirteen-year period has been immense. As only one of many examples, this series has been a major inspiration to giovanni singleton in her own enterprise of editing and publishing *nocturnes (re)view*. It is a unique achievement which remains insufficiently recognized for its role in offering confidence and opportunities to many African American and African diaspora poets struggling with the question of whether they deserve to consider themselves poets. The answer speaks for itself.

In examining enterprises like the Heritage Series and other heroic publishing ventures, it is time to call special attention to several figures with small *oeuvres* but distinctive voices that illuminate dominant patterns of the earliest periods of African American poetry and serve as important precursors for those who would follow. The definition of "minor poets" should be questioned when applied to figures like Fenton Johnson, J. Mord Allen, Helene Johnson, and Welborn Victor Jenkins (1879–1960), whose output was relatively small. *This Waiting for Love*, edited by Verner D. Mitchell, is an important collection of the poetry of Helene Johnson, with a revelatory introduction about this famously private poet. Much more study and research should be possible with a full overview of her work now available. Cuney also is often put into the marginalized category because he published only two books in his lifetime, but his actual literary output was prolific, much of which is in the personal archive of Breman, now located at two major locations: Special Collections at Williams College and the Vivian G. Harsh Research Collection of Afro-American History and Literature in the Chicago Public Library. Cuney's place in posterity might look altogether different if more of his work were made available. In correspondence dating from 1952, Breman would often receive three to four letters a week from Cuney, each containing six or seven poems. Breman, who edited and translated Cuney's first poetry collection, *Puzzles* (1960), held a collection of approximately four hundred poems by Cuney, almost all unpublished, apart from the few that have been anthologized and those in Cuney's only English poetry collection, *Storefront Church*, Volume 23 in the Heritage Series. Before the untimely deaths of both Breman and Lorenzo Thomas, Thomas and I had been given permission by Breman to access the Waring Cuney materials remaining in his home, where they were housed until being acquired by Williams College posthumously. Thomas and I both thought Cuney was underrated and overlooked and planned to co-edit a selection of his poems in hopes of encouraging more attention and appreciation for his contribution and place in the canon. This project of recuperation and dissemination remains an undertaking that could be of extraordinary benefit to properly establish Cuney's reputation and augment the canon.

Similar to Cuney and Helene Johnson, Fenton Johnson has never entirely disappeared from literary awareness, but all three are typically represented in anthologies by a poem or two, and the scope of their literary oeuvre is not well known. Fenton Johnson's critical attention and acclaim also are not where they should be for one of the most avant-garde and gifted African American poets of the twentieth century. As early as 1962, Breman considered that Fenton Johnson and Horton were two poets who "badly need collected editions."[26] Breman himself attempted to rectify the situation. Breman, who considered Fenton Johnson as "one of the great forerunners" of the sixties generation, had been told by Hughes that Bontemps possessed unpublished poems by Fenton Johnson, who had died in 1958. When Breman wrote to inquire, Bontemps responded that he did have "a number" of Fenton Johnson's poems, which were "left by Fenton with Jack Conroy who in turn gave them to Fisk University," where they remain. The rest of Fenton Johnson's work was reported to have been destroyed in a cellar flood. It was agreed that Bontemps would edit and write the introduction for "42 WPA Poems" for the Heritage Series, and Breman would publish *The Daily Grind* as Volume 4 of the Heritage Series. This could have made a major difference to Johnson's prominence as an important modernist influence on the 1960s generation. But as Breman recounts, "on re-reading we [Bontemps and Breman] both came to the conclusion that publishing them all would actually not be too kind to their author. 'I find myself agreeing with you about Fenton Johnson's poetry,' wrote Arna in April 1963 – 'perhaps it is just as well to let Fenton rest in peace.'"[27] With all of the principals now gone, it is tantalizing to imagine those poems. In fact, the quantity of lost or missing African American poems throughout the history of the tradition is staggering and tragic. Any project of recuperation is urgent and does justice to history and literature.

---

[26] Paul Breman, ed., *Sixes and Sevens: An Anthology of New Poetry* (London: Paul Breman, 1962), p. 7.
[27] Breman, *Sixes and Sevens*, pp. 134–5.

One of the main purposes of the Heritage Series conceptually reinforces the critical perspective of this chapter: the series was intended to focus on Harlem Renaissance forebears who had never published a poetry collection and link them in a lineage with the then contemporary poets of the 1960s and 1970s and future generations. At its inception, it was not known how long the series would last, but Breman was disappointed when it ended in 1975. When the decision was made not to proceed in publishing Johnson's uncollected work, there was a space in the schedule. Breman decided to take Bontemps up on his 1959 suggestion, "When you are thinking about older poets, remember one by the name of Arna Bontemps whose things have enjoyed widely scattered publication but have never been brought together."[28] And so, Volume 4 was dedicated to another precursor, whose "scattered publication" is extensive in a long literary career and whose accomplishments as a poet would be yet another valuable research subject.

There is now increasing and well-deserved attention being paid to Fenton Johnson, as indicated by his 2016 induction into the Chicago Literary Hall of Fame.[29] It is of tremendous benefit to his undervalued reputation, and yet another indication of the importance of digital humanities to African American poetry, that all of Johnson's published books now are accessible as free digital downloads. One of the finest academic treatments of Fenton Johnson is by the extraordinary poet-critic, the late Lorenzo Thomas. It appears as chapter 1 of Thomas's *Extraordinary Measures: Afrocentric Modernism and Twentieth-Century American Poetry* and should be the starting point for all who are interested in this under-lauded poet. During his lifetime, similarly to Whitfield, Fenton Johnson had an unusually high level of acclaim across racial lines for a black poet writing in the first two decades of the twentieth century. The most active, and relatively brief, period of his literary productivity was from 1913 to 1920, but he may well have continued writing without publication, which makes the loss of his materials particularly tragic. His most famous poems appeared in the day's most nationally and internationally prestigious literary magazines, which were not exclusively or at all associated with African American writing. His poems appeared several times in Harriet Monroe's renowned magazine *Poetry*, and he was the only black poet ever to appear in Alfred Kreymborg's *Others*, ironic for a journal whose purpose was to provide

[28] Ramey, *The Heritage Series of Black Poetry*, p. 135.
[29] https://chicagoliteraryhof.org/inductees/profile/fenton-johnson (last accessed August 19, 2018).

a forum for writers excluded by the mainstream. We see in Fenton Johnson's work yet another example – as with Alfred Gibbs Campbell, slave songs, Whitfield, Simpson, Corrothers, Helene Johnson, and so many others in this tradition – of non-canonical poets who used African American culture for preserving and innovating their visions of African American traditions. We also see the ambivalent critical reception afforded to his poetry, which by now is a familiar echo of patterns we have seen since the start of the tradition.

In the middle of the twentieth century, a relatively wide selection of Fenton Johnson's poems appeared in major anthologies: five poems apiece appear in *The New Cavalcade* and *American Negro Poetry*, edited by Fenton Johnson's friend and eventual literary executor, Bontemps. In recent decades, Fenton Johnson continues to be widely anthologized, but his representation has dwindled to one or two poems in African American anthologies, most often "The Scarlet Woman" and "Tired," as in *The Norton Anthology of African American Literature*, but his work rarely appears outside the context of black poetry. This situation is especially ironic considering Johnson's appearance in *Poetry* and *Others*, two little magazines associated with the new poetry of modernism, though in the case of *Poetry*, there was an occasional strain of ethnophilia in Monroe's selections.

By the time he self-published his second collection of verse, Fenton Johnson confidently billed himself on the title page as "Author of 'A Little Dreaming,'" his first self-published volume. The Foreword consists of two endorsements, which lay out clearly the dilemma that Fenton Johnson inherited from one of his literary idols, Dunbar. As we see from Fenton Johnson, not everyone in the first post-Dunbar generation rejected him but all were writing in some way in reaction to his looming example. *Literary World* (London) commented: "Mr. Johnson is a young colored poet of America; some of his verse is in formal cultivated English, some in the corrupted language of the American negro. The latter rings true; it expresses with singular intensity an [sic] sorrows of a subject race" (April 2, 1914). As we have seen with slave songs, as well as with Dunbar, "a jingle in a broken tongue" that could be denigrated as substandard was accepted as the "true" and preferred mode of communication for African American poets. This "endorsement" echoes William Dean Howells's assessment of Dunbar. The comparison with Dunbar, America's most famous African American poet, was made explicit by the racist second blurb, from *American Review of Reviews* (January 1914). Fenton Johnson's poems are described as an expression of untutored naiveté connected to the same prejudiced judgments of Dunbar and slave songs: "a natural, spontaneous lyricism with the same distinguishing racial qualities that characterize the work of Paul Laurence Dunbar. Many of the lines are melodious with the primitive, plaintive reediness of the Negro 'Spirituals' of slave days. The chant-like form is effectively used, as in his lament for Dunbar."

These are especially telling comments in light of the opening poem of the collection, "Prelude," which deserves to be far better known for carrying on the problem voiced a decade earlier in Dunbar's "The Poet" (1903):

> He sang of love when the earth was young,
> And Love, itself, was in his lays.
> But ah, the world, it turned to praise
> A jingle in a broken tongue.

In Fenton Johnson's "Prelude," four iambic pentameter stanzas of varying numbers of lines open with a three-line preamble that sets the romantic scene and establishes the situation of "the musing dreamer" who "ponders ere the birth of dusk." The second stanza hymns the English literary tradition, "the gift of Shakespeare and the heritage / Of Tennyson," including "The music of the songs the lusty sang" in taverns. In spite of this passion for the sounds of English verse nursed in him since childhood, the speaker is told in the second stanza, "O Man of Dusk, / Give us thy songs in broken Afric tongue, – / [...] Be thou as Burns or Dunbar was." And, in fact, many of the poems that follow are solidly in the Dunbar tradition, some echoing Dunbar's post-Romantic ballads, and others his vernacular poems set in plantation culture.

In his collection of critical essays, *The New Sentence* (1989), poet-critic Ron Silliman, himself associated with the L=A=N=G=U=A=G=E Poetry Movement, points to Johnson's poem "The Minister" as a precursor to the "prose poem with a clear, if simple, sentence: paragraph relation."[30] Silliman, who is well informed about African American (and other) poetry, was especially enthralled by this poem as the "first instance in English of a prose poem which calls attention to a discursive or poetic effect."[31] In *Negro Poetry and Drama*, Sterling A. Brown called Fenton Johnson's poems "striking departures in Negro poetry," but are

---

[30] Ron Silliman, "The New Sentence," in *The New Sentence* (New York: Roof Books, 1989), pp. 63–93.
[31] "Fenton Johnson," Chicago Literary Hall of Fame (last accessed October 5, 2017).

they? How would they appear if we continue our task of reimagining the canon by embracing innovation as an inherent and self-referencing feature of this tradition, and discovering how this process of signifying on the past leads to a chain of fresh poems that consistently carry on elements of the tradition?

Visions of the Dusk contains a section called "Negro Spirituals" consisting of ten poems, but the whole collection is infused with themes and devices that are obviously working in the tradition of slave songs, including a poem called "Singing Hallelujia (A Negro Spiritual)." This poem reflects both the structure and themes of many slave songs. Fenton Johnson's early poems could easily be read as youthful experiments with a variety of customary influences of the era, from post-Romantic nature poems ("The Lonely Piper") to post-Dunbar vernacular poems of plantation life ("De Ol' Home"), before his abrupt departure into "new" realms of the "new modern lyric" and "New Negro" movement. But on closer examination, the continuities that lay the groundwork for the truly great poems written about a decade later become more evident. The jarring juxtapositions found in *A Little Dreaming* contain the variety of experiments in voice, style, and period that might be expected from a young developing poet in the World War I years. But the additional pressures placed on a young black poet, raised in educational and economic privilege in the northern metropolis of Chicago, become clear, based on the extremity of variety. A Round Table Romantic fantasy, "Launcelot's Defiance" ("My liege the King, why burns the flame of wrath / Upon thy cheek? Is it for Guinevere?"), is immediately followed by a dialect poem set on an antebellum plantation, "Uncle Isham Lies a-Dyin'" ("Oh, de dahk an' dreahy night am camein', / Thru de cabin do' de night camein'"). But then, looking back to Wheatley, we see the racial reference points enter subtly into conventional form to meld the Anglo-American tradition with African American tropes of images of Africa, search for family and heritage, and the importance of land and place, as in "The Lover's Soliloquy":

> I
>
> Love's charm belongs to every age and clime;
> To every sep'rate man the burning flame
> Comes once or twice or thrice, as wills the God.
> In Ethiop, beneath the rose-dipped sun,
> My fathers wooed their dusky paramours,
> As you and I, in this, our latter day;
> And where the silver-breast Euphrates lies,

A mirror for the milk-white moon to shine,
Our common parent sighed for Mother Eve.
As you and I, in this, our latter day.

II

Without the passion love, no sun would glow,
No golden moon would grace the summer eve,
The golden-rod would cease to charm the eye;
The gilded rose would wither ere its day,
And all the general universe be black;
For when within thy heart thou know'st that Love
Hath wrought his miracle, thou art a God,
And all that is of earth is slave to thee.

There is tremendous ingenuity in this poem that effortlessly establishes a black diasporic perspective in a modernized conventional form. The soliloquy, evoking a modern sonnet wed to a dramatic monologue, employs iambic pentameter with an understated and irregular rhyme scheme to unleash a metaphysical conceit based on racial signifiers, Africa as the site of an imagined past, and African American history. Section I ponders the existence of love in all times and places as the speaker is thrown back mnemohistorically in line four to Africa where the ancestors, who made the life of the speaker possible, sought their lovers who would guarantee the future of this family.[32] Darkness is privileged as the focal point of section I: the "dusky paramours" are center stage against the backdrop of light as "the silver-breast Euphrates" mirrors the "milk-white moon." In section II, silver transforms into the darker burnished gold as we encounter four glittering lines of sensuous pleasures based on images of gold associated with love. But these antithetical images are presented as hypothetical negatives or absences: without love, there would be no golden glow and the whole universe would be black, suggesting the primordial chaos out of which the heavens and earth and mankind were created in Genesis. The ingenious metaphysical turn takes place in the last three lines, when we are told that one who experiences love becomes a divine ruler who enslaves the whole world. The strong and positive image of blackness as the lover in section I is echoed in section II with the reference to slavery in its obvious relevance, but here the black speaker becomes the master, a God, over an enslaved world through the power of love.

---

[32] More than the preservation of facts, mnemohistory refers to the way history is remembered, and how collective memory defines a culture in the present. This concept has great usefulness and applicability to African American culture and other diasporic populations.

A closer look reveals startling originality that foreshadows the more famous poems that represent the pinnacle of his literary oeuvre. It may be correct to see Fenton Johnson as a bridge between eras but is more constructive to view him – as do several critics – as a poet ahead of his time pointing the way to the future. We see it in *Visions of the Dusk* in "The Creed of the Slave," a vernacular poem that appears to reflect the slave's acceptance of his/her status in awaiting deliverance to "freedom" in the Christian afterlife, which fulfills the stereotype that many still hold about the operations of slave songs:

THE CREED OF THE SLAVE
1.

Ah lubs de worl'. – Kain't he'p it, dat's mah way.
Futh'mo' Ah lubs de night, Ah lubs de day,
Ah lubs de suff'rin' crittuhs dat Gawd made,
De li'l 'uns playin' 'near de locus' shade,
Ah lubs de shadduhs by de gret big road,
Ah lubs to tote wid me de hebby load
Thoo'all de live long night an' thoo' de day.
Ah lubs de worl'. – Kain't he'p it, dat's mah way.
2.

Go crack yo' whups, an' break dis flesh o' mine,
Ah ain't a-gwine tuh, leave dis love behin';
Ah wu'k an' bleed fu' dose dat hu't me mos',
But in de mawnin' w'en Ah am a ghos'
Ah pray de Lawd dat you kin come up daih
An' play wid me erpon de golden staih.
Ah lubs you all, po' suff'rin' clay; –
Ah lubs de worl'. – Kain't he'p it, dat's mah way.

The clever double-voicing, and ironic tone of self-possessed defiance enrobed in a faux posture of simple acceptance, demonstrates Johnson's repurposing of slave songs for revolutionary means. The irony and resistance that often are subtly present in slave songs are in evidence here, which demonstrates the operational power of the tradition's origins. The same themes, styles, and tones will later emerge in better-known poems such as "The Barber" and "Aunt Hannah Jackson," whose tones and closures are also equivocal, and very problematical to gauge. A revolutionary figure who dreamed of harmonious communication between the races, Johnson also displayed the black pride that is so strongly associated with the 1960s and 1970s. As editor of the monthly magazine with its modest subtitle, *The Favorite Magazine: The World's Greatest Monthly* (August 1918, 1:1 – January 1920, 10:1), Johnson included three or four pages of poetry per issue, which he called "the first and only weekly magazine published by and for colored people." This was the organ used to articulate and promote Johnson's vision of the Reconciliation Movement, and in its pages appeared poems by Will Sexton ("A Visit to State Street" and "Chiseled Gems"), as well as Moses Jordan, H. Georgiana Whyte, Frank M. Livingstone, Timothy Thomas Fortune (T. Thomas Fortune), Azalia E. Martin, Silas X. Floyd, and of course, Johnson himself. As an indication of the progress afforded by increased awareness and access to resources, digitization has provided a wealth of modern literary magazines, where many of the most avant-garde African American poems were published, since full-length collections, even in the 1960s and 1970s, remained a relative rarity.

Helene Johnson also should now receive more interest and respect thanks to Verner D. Mitchell's excellent editorial work. It is particularly helpful that *This Waiting for Love* provides the precise date and place of each poem's first publication, which enables us to track her development more readily. In addition to the complete body of her poems, this volume features an invaluable closing section of letters both to and from Helene Johnson, which offers vivid descriptions of what it was like to be one of the youngest Harlem Renaissance poets. Through their letters to Helene Johnson, we also gain richly nuanced perspectives of her intimates Thurman, Zora Neale Hurston, Cullen, and Johnson's cousin, Dorothy West. Helene Johnson produced many intriguing and original poems where the voice and dictional control are modulated with great subtlety and skill. Only a few of her poems are well known, but her other work deserves much wider recognition. The most frequent to be anthologized are "Poem" and "Bottled: New York" (which appears under the title "Bottled" in *This Waiting for Love*) with their brilliant and quite shocking shifts of register and diction, as well as "Sonnet to a Negro in Harlem," whose tonal complexity is deft and mysterious. "Magula" is sometimes anthologized, but Mitchell shares poems that are not well known and some gems that are previously unpublished.[33] "A Southern Road," "Regalia," "Mother," and "I Am Not Proud" are just a few examples of writing that indicate a poet who currently is greatly undervalued. The complete poem of "I Am Not Proud" reflects the lyric compression

---

[33] "Magula" is the poet's spelling of the title, though the poem appears as "Magalu" in *Shadowed Dreams: Women's Poetry of the Harlem Renaissance*, edited by Maureen Honey, and *The Poetry of Black America*, edited by Arnold Adoff.

of imagism and objectivism and looks ahead to the anthemic proclama-
tions of the era to follow:

> I am not proud that I am bold
> Or proud that I am black
> Color was given me as a gage
> And boldness came with that.

If we are looking for indications in this period of poets who inventively extend and repurpose the origins of the tradition, both Fenton
Johnson and Helene Johnson provide excellent modernist examples.
"Goin' No'th" by Helene Johnson is a previously unpublished (and
undated) poem, though its positioning in this chronologically organized collection probably dates it at about 1935. At this time, it was not
common for poets to use vernacular (though not unique, as with James
Weldon Johnson's famous poem "The Creation"). The durability of
vernacular diction is presented here in a poem that palpably updates
the early exploratory mode of Corrothers and Dunbar. Preserving the
oral tradition via both slave songs and traditional tales, this is a trickster poem that charms readers in faux-folk mode, which echoes the sly
double-voicing of Dunbar's "An Ante-bellum Sermon." In this narratively
driven lyric, a Southern character is joining the Great Migration "to
make somethin' of hisself": "It was goin' be easy findin' work up no'th /
Where you could pick money off de streets." He is reassured by carrying
with him in one pocket the small Bible given to him by his pappy: "He
was goin' need dat, alright. Ev'y man had to have de / Word of God wid
him when he was travellin' or he wouldn't / Have no luck." The other
pocket contains his wallet. When he boards the train, he hears a thump,
and is afraid that he has lost his wallet. He is relieved to discover that he
still has his wallet but has "only" lost his Bible given to him by his pappy.
The suggestion is that, as for so many African Americans moving North
without family ties and with unrealizable expectations, this character
will have no luck. This poem cleverly hides its social commentary about
religion, migration, and the devaluing of tradition and family bonds in
the modern era. It does so by using the updated literary tools of the past,
which is fully revealed with the conclusion and the repetition of "no'th"
(embedding the negation of "no") in the rhythm of the train, evoking the
underground railroad, and the plantation imagery of slave culture:

> 'Course he'd buy another Bible directly he got no'th.
> No'th. Goin' No'th. No'th at las', Lord.

"Goodbye, mammy, at de cabin do;
Goin' no'th, won't see you no mo'."

Good tune to dat song alright. But de words
Was jes' a mess of lies. [34]

The extended period from approximately 1910 to 1940 can be viewed as an avant-garde movement, supported by Bontemps's recollections about the self-awareness of group identity, sense of a significant mission, and the radical (and changing) diversity and critical arguments that bonded and divided key participants. Here we are dealing with the issues that arose both later and earlier regarding the mapping of race over practices considered to be innovative. Yet this era was without question a moment, movement, or grouping of writers both connecting and disconnecting with each other as they engaged in the process of rejecting the past to create new modes of expression to best suit the present. We also have allusions and citations to the past, which was itself an avant-garde practice in the context of a perceived heavily assimilationist history for this genre going back to its origins.

"O Daedalus, Fly Away Home" by Hayden is a canonical poem yet reads as a deceptively innovative work if repositioned in the context of slave songs and their hidden oppositionality. This poem operates as a veritable modern slave song, similarly to the cited poems by Fenton Johnson and Atkins. This poem is replete with diction of slave songs ("Fly away home"), references to African origins ("Do you remember Africa?"), diasporic diction ("Night is juba"), diasporic survivals such as the invocation of ancestors as spirit guides who are able to transcend Cartesian physics ("My gran, he flew back to Africa, / just spread his arms and / flew away home"), and commonplaces of plantation culture ("Pretty Malindy, dance with me"), including references to music ("coonskin drum and jubilee banjo").[35] Slave songs' call-and-response structure is reproduced in the alternation of verses and italicized refrains from slave songs, all playing on phrasal variants of "fly away." It uses such baseline phrases and ideas from the slave songs as "O cleave the air," with "cleave" in its polysemous sense of divide and cling. The imagery of "wings" and "fly away home" brings together the classical myth of Icarus

---

[34] Verner D. Mitchell, ed., *This Waiting for Love: Helene Johnson: Poet of the Harlem Renaissance* (Amherst: University of Massachusetts Press, 2000), pp. 63–6.
[35] The phrases in quotation marks all come from Hayden's poem, "O Daedalus, Fly Away Home."

and Daedalus with the equally classical imagery of slave songs in African American culture.

With the heyday of the Harlem Renaissance in the 1920s, and the drama of the Civil Rights Movement from about 1960 to 1975, mid-century African American writers have long been left in the position of "poets between worlds," in the well-known description by R. Baxter Miller. While the view is understandable that poets in the mid-twentieth century world faced circumstances that differed in nature from the eras that preceded and followed, it is equally apt – perhaps even more so – to view them as poets connecting worlds. Many Negro Renaissance poets were actively writing in the 1940s and later, and it is more critically justifiable to view their projects as extended endeavors. It also becomes clear through this perspective that African American poetry has not been a stop–start process of endless reinventions for new eras, but a continuous path asserting itself, building on itself, and using modes of creativity to make its poetic legacy consistently meaningful, applicable, and reflective of the current moment. Close examination shows that some of the most extraordinary poets produced major work during a time that cannot be chronologically or stylistically affiliated with the Harlem Renaissance or the Black Arts Movement, although they may have links to both. The aesthetic sensibilities of poets born around the time of World War I were heavily influenced by the Harlem Renaissance but had major impact on the Black Arts Movement. After World War II, disenfranchisement and alienation reached boiling points, and were in precarious tension with pressures to assimilate and accommodate. Early anthemic poetry by figures such as Durem ("Take No Prisoners") and Patterson ("Black All Day") helped set the tone for the Black Arts and Black Power Movements to follow. They were preceded by Will Sexton's equally powerful but relatively and undeservedly obscure modernist poem, "The Bomb Thrower:"

> Down with everything black!
> Down with law and order!
> Up with the red flag!
> Up with the white South!
> I am America's evil genius.

This mid-century period also saw the emergence of two particularly important female voices, Margaret Walker and Gwendolyn Brooks. Poetry of the era displayed a continued expansion of formal possibilities and variety, from prose poems to sonnets to late modernist innovations signaling the coming explosion of twenty-first century experimentalism.

In another problem with conventional periodization, the first so-called Renaissance was traditionally positioned in about a twenty-year period from roughly 1910 to 1929. With the drama of the so-called second Renaissance in the 1960s and 1970s, there has been curious disregard for the unnamed chasm in mid-century, which includes the 1930s to the 1950s, although substantial important poetry was produced during this time connected to both the earlier and later moments. In calling for more attention to be paid to the "wholeness and continuity" of the African American poetry tradition, Stephen Henderson asks for the forging of more extensive and inventive intra-literary dialogue to avoid impressions of isolation, especially in relation to what he terms "*saturation*," a sign or condition of "black awareness." As Henderson puts it in an issue that still perpetuates, "the problem of relating the structure of a Phillis Wheatley couplet to a Ted Joans rap has, to my knowledge, been eschewed."[36] Now these correlations and the opening and close of the twentieth century are being reconciled through an expanding body of scholarship. R. Baxter Miller's *Black American Poets Between Worlds, 1940–1960* (1986) is one of the first essay collections to examine this critical lacuna. Among the many highlights are essays by Richard K. Barksdale on Margaret Walker, and Miller on Dudley Randall. It contains a fine essay on Margaret Esse Danner by Erlene Stetson. Stetson describes the poet as "an ironist and imagist," compares her to the also under-appreciated Helene Johnson, and distills her concerns as "invention, civilization, and art."[37] Danner is another highly original and overlooked poet. Her post-imagist attention to vivid sensory description, thoughtfully developed sense of a propositional poetics, and lapidary and sophisticated attention to sound and diction, as well as her construction of her own portrait of a relationship with Africa and her historically pivotal friendships with such figures as Randall, Haki Madhubuti, and Hoyt Fuller, qualify her for more attention and respect.

African American poetry produced during the 1930s has been a long-neglected area. *Anthems, Sonnets and Chants: Recovering the African American Poetry of the 1930s* by Jon Woodson offers fresh perspectives of established figures while introducing lesser known poets whose writing would augment the canon fruitfully. Woodson proves that major work

---

[36] Henderson, *Understanding the New Black Poetry*, p. 68.
[37] Erlene Stetson, "Dialectic Voices in the Poetry of Margaret Esse Danner," in R. Baxter Miller, ed., *Black American Poets Between Worlds, 1940–1960* (Knoxville: University of Tennessee Press, 1986), pp. 93–103; pp. 93 and 98.

was produced during this period by poets who were productive earlier and/or later and serve as links between the Harlem Renaissance and the Black Arts Movement. As Woodson shows, the 1930s displayed a perhaps unprecedented expansion of formal variety, from long lyric sequences to sonnets to modernist innovations signaling the future evolution of surrealist and postmodern experimentalism. While Hughes is shown to continue his steady output of creativity, this also was a period of significant poetic productivity for Richard Wright, who is better known as a novelist. Woodson's book performs a great service by recuperating important writing which shows the consistent pace of productivity in twentieth-century African American poetry resulting in a richer understanding of its evolutions and influences as a canon and tradition. In the Introduction, Woodson states his critical premise: "Literary recovery is a response to some mode of marginalization" and identifies three factors that marginalized 1930s African American poetry: "racism, history, and ideology."[38] I concur with Woodson's explanation that the periodization historically used for African American writing has isolated it into different and separate categories from "white writing" ("Harlem Renaissance" versus "modernism," for example). As a result, writing that failed to fit the standard was excluded from the canon.

Chapter 1 of *Anthems, Sonnets and Chants* places three long poems that Woodson persuasively classifies as African American Jeremiads in the context of the Stock Market Crash of 1929 and the Depression: one each by Dodson, Richard Wright, and Jenkins. In chapter 2, Woodson continues the pattern of offering fresh perspectives on well-known poets such as Tolson, Dodson, McKay, and Hughes, and insightful introductions to lesser known figures worthy of greater recognition including J. G. St. Clair Drake, Marcus Christian, and Mary T. Rauth. Woodson expertly connects "Existential Crisis" to the sonnet as a cultural paradigm (p. 75). He argues that this revered form became a mode of self-fashioning by African Americans in the 1930s to create "an extended multiauthored sonnet sequence" as a "Sonnet Pantext" of the 1930s (p. 89). This chapter also applies and extends Woodson's research on the influence of G. I. Gurdjieff on African American Harlem Renaissance poets including Toomer, Tolson, and McKay, which picks up this theme from his highly regarded book, *To Make a New Race: Gurdjieff, Toomer, and the Harlem*

---

[38] Jon Woodson, *Anthems, Sonnets, and Chants: Recovering the African American Poetry of the 1930s* (Columbus: The Ohio State University Press, 2011), p. 1. Subsequent page references are given in parentheses in the text.

Renaissance. African American poetry on the Italo-Ethiopian War forms the final historical moment and chapter of the book. Here Woodson provides extended commentary on Hughes's poetic address of the war, while discussing the use of this topic by fascinating and lesser known poets: Christian, P. J. White, J. Harvey L. Baxter, and Rufus Gibson.

By 1945, more than a million African Americans had served with distinction in World War II in segregated units of the United States military, an astonishing escalation from the few African American soldiers and officers enlisted in 1941. It is a widely acknowledged irony that the fight for Civil Rights continued on the home front while these soldiers risked their lives to represent their country abroad. This dichotomy is represented in Brooks's poem "Negro Hero" (1945), whose title interrogates what it means to be a hero as an African American. The poem is a long-lined, declamatory, dramatic monologue written from the perspective of an African American soldier who served abroad in combat. It opens with the famous line, "I had to kick their law into their teeth in order to save them." The speaker explains how he was extolled for his success in battle, both in "the Caucasian dailies / As well as the Negro weeklies." This is a subtle commentary on the raced-based economic and informational disparities between those two worlds of publishing and readers. Double voicing is apparent in an ironic parenthetical aside, which is whispered editorially under the breath, as if to a different audience. These lines close the second stanza of this historically based persona poem: "(They are not concerned that it was hardly The Enemy / my fight was against / But them.)" Although the speaker is viewed by white society as heroic for fighting a foreign enemy to uphold democracy, the tone suggests that his true heroism lies in the fight against the real enemy, American racism.

Extending the practices of racial separation in civilian life, the United States Armed Forces did not adopt a policy of integration until 1948. While serving in Europe and the South Pacific, African Americans in the military were exposed to international standards and influences, while also spreading African American culture and arts. The prominence of African Americans honorably representing the United States in World War II, and the ensuing cultural exchange, helped trigger the explosion of African American poetry starting in the mid 1940s. At the same time, pernicious discrimination created narrow perceptions of the genre and its creators, and limited the opportunities to disseminate this vibrant and incisive new poetry. The mid-twentieth century's landmark African American literature anthology was *The Negro Caravan*, originally

published in 1941, which summarized the situation of the time suc-
cinctly: "Negro poets have concentrated upon protest poetry more than
upon poetry of interpretation and illumination, but Negro poets have
often had more to protest than others." Over the next thirty years, as
"Negro Poets" became known as "Black Poets," progress was made to
reflect hard-won rights. But in spite of steps forward, there remained
a lack of understanding and appreciation of the full scope, variety, and
unique value of African American poetry.

Extensive historical material addresses the tumultuous sociopolitical context of the post-World War II years in the struggle for equality
for all Americans, and the slow dismantling of Jim Crow legislation.
African American poetry of this period certainly reflects the lingering
evils of bigotry, the power and agony of the Civil Rights Movement,
the fight for educational and employment parity, and the demand for
freedom and equal opportunity for all citizens. Progress was slow and
inconsistent, but steady, as indicated by some milestones among many
that could be noted. In 1950, Brooks became the first African American
to win the Pulitzer Prize, for *Annie Allen*. That same year, the literary
journal *Free Lance*, which Rivers called "the oldest black-bossed magazine around," was founded by Atkins. This was the era of the landmark
Brown v. Board of Education decision (1954), where the Supreme Court
abolished the policy of segregated schools providing "separate but equal"
education. One year later, a fourteen-year old African American boy
called Emmett Till, accused of whistling at a white woman, was brutally
murdered in Mississippi. In 1955, Rosa Parks refused to relinquish her
bus seat to a white woman in Montgomery, Alabama. In 1962, Breman,
as a young Dutchman in London, started the Heritage Series, the first
press dedicated to publishing black poetry. Civil Rights activist Medgar
Evers was assassinated in 1963. The Freedom Summer took place in
1964, the same year that three young Civil Rights workers – James
Chaney, Andrew Goodman, and Michael Schwerner – were murdered in
Mississippi. In 1965, *The Autobiography of Malcolm X* was published, and
Malcolm X was assassinated the same year. In 1966, Hayden's *A Ballad
of Remembrance*, the first volume in the Heritage Series, won first prize
at the First World Festival of Negro Arts in Dakar, Senegal. The studio
album *A Love Supreme* by John Coltrane was released in 1965, the same
year as the Watts Riots in Los Angeles. Martin Luther King, Jr. was assassinated in 1968. From 1976 to 1978, Hayden served as the first African
American Librarian of Congress, the post that later became the United
States Poet Laureate.

Other important contributions to incorporate this "middle period" into a larger perspective include Lorenzo Thomas's chapters on Margaret Walker and Tolson in *Extraordinary Measures*, the important thread of early and later postmodern attention interwoven throughout Nielsen's *Black Chant*, Maryemma Graham's writings on Margaret Walker, Arnold Rampersad's classic two-volume biography of Langston Hughes, the ongoing insightful analyses of Richard Wright by Jerry W. Ward, Jr., and several outstanding electronic resources such as the History of Black Writing Project at Kansas University.[39] Woodson has performed brilliant acts of literary recovery in response to the marginalization of valuable mid-century poetic voices. He also has edited and written an outstanding introductory essay for *Cries in the Wilderness*, a much-needed anthology of 1930s black poetry that connects these poets to the earlier and later periods. This book will be digitally hosted, with open international access, by the Hunan Normal University Press and its *Foreign Languages and Cultures* (Hunan Normal University). A superb act of restoration, this much-needed anthology represents thirty-five poets, making it clear that some of the best-known twentieth-century African American poets were producing important overlooked poems in the 'teens through the 1950s and even later: Hughes, Wright, Walker, Tolson, Georgia Douglas Johnson, Hayden, Dodson, Frank Marshall Davis, Brown, Cullen, and Gwendolyn Bennett. One of the great benefits of Woodson's scholarship is to perform precisely the intellectual task called for by Henderson by placing some of the best-known poets in this tradition in dialogue with little to virtually unknown figures in hopes of moving the "invisible poets," as Sherman put it, from the margins to the canon. Some intriguing voices have been recovered, such as Benjamin Franklin Gardner, David Cannon, Paul Alexander, Christian, Mae V. Cowdery, Lawrence Gellert, Gladys Casely Hayford, Helen Aurelia Johnson, and Isabelle H. Munroe.

The 1960s to the 1980s have been regarded as a bellwether period for touchstone anthologies and literary criticism in this field. A few key examples include Jones's (Baraka) *The Blues People: Negro Music in White America* (1963), Hoyt Fuller's essay "Towards a Black Aesthetic" (1968), Henderson's *Understanding the New Black Poetry: Black Speech and Black Music as Poetic References* (1973), and Houston A. Baker, Jr.'s *Afro-American Poetics: Revisions of Harlem and the Black Aesthetic* (1988).

---

[39] http://projecthbw.blogspot.com (last accessed August 20, 2018).

American Negro Poetry, edited by Bontemps (1974 revised edition) and *The Poetry of Black America*, edited by Adoff (1973) are exceptional anthologies that cover both African American modernism and the 1960s and 1970s. Both collections are filled with examples of poets and poems that call for further attention. Some of the many important anthologies on the 1960s and 1970s are *Dices or Black Bones: Black Voices of the Seventies*, edited by Adam David Miller (1970), *Natural Process: An Anthology of New Black Poetry*, edited by Ted Wilentz and Tom Weatherly (1970), *Black Fire: An Anthology of Afro-American Writing*, edited by Baraka and Larry Neal (1968), and *Soulscript*, edited by June Jordan (1970). The critical and primary literature on 1900–70 is voluminous on the conventionally canonical figures, poems, and critical approaches. An excellent starting point for the earlier period is the guide to further reading in *The Cambridge Companion to the Harlem Renaissance*, edited by George Hutchinson, and the selected bibliography in *The Norton Anthology of African American Literature*, volume 2, third edition, edited by Gates and Smith. Mid-century through the 1970s resources may be found in the *Norton Anthology* and the guide to further reading in *The Cambridge Companion to American Civil Rights Literature*, edited by Julie Buckner Armstrong.

A valuable recent study of this period is *The Black Arts Enterprise and the Production of African American Poetry* by Howard Rambsy II. He joins the ranks of critics and poet-critics who have produced a wealth of important works during and about this period, including Hoyt Fuller, Baraka/Jones, Nielsen, Lee/Madhubuti, Maulana Karenga, Neal, Kalamu ya Salaam, Melba Joyce Boyd, and Carolyn Rodgers, among others. Rambsy argues that the nuances and operations of this politically charged and aesthetically vibrant era still call for more in-depth study for both its cohesions and its diversity. By choosing the angle that he does – addressing the black-owned outlets of culture, commerce, and control – Rambsy brings together creative and critical resources to show how the coordination of business and art resulted in the movement's success and lasting impact. The range of forms and venues thoroughly and thoughtfully discussed includes black anthologies, polemics, recordings, music, art galleries, performance spaces, presses, magazines, reviews, criticism, visual images, and even the street itself. Rambsy's aim is to highlight "the material production of black poetry and its distinct socialization."[40] The terms

---

[40] Howard Rambsy II, *The Black Arts Enterprise and the Production of African American Poetry* (Ann Arbor: University of Michigan Press, 2013), p. 7.

"enterprise" and "production" in the title are chosen to be ideologically meaningful for the era. The Black Arts Movement did indeed come to represent an enterprise of dynamic production, which Rambsy details by focusing on the explosion of participation in the literary culture of this period. He offers a thorough overview of the activist dimension of this movement in generating black periodicals, poetry anthologies, presses, recordings, essays, editorials, and reviews in the development and promotion of a black aesthetics – in other words, getting the word out while controlling its content and ideology. The book's six chapters cover a range of essential themes in the poetry of the Black Arts Movement, which create a common thread in spite of divergences: a tone of militancy, engagement with jazz, the elegizing of Malcolm X, self-determination, collaboration and group cohesion as a value, and poetry as a form of activism which propelled and directed the entire Black Arts Movement. One of the book's highlights is a section called "Elegizing Malcolm X" in a chapter called "All Aboard the Malcolm-Coltrane Express." Rambsy adds to the discourse while building on acknowledged foundations provided by prior works, including *For Malcolm* by Dudley Randall and Margaret Burroughs. As Rambsy puts it, "in African American discourse, the only martyr celebrated more frequently than Martin Luther King, Jr. and Malcolm X is Jesus Christ."[41] Rambsy provides a comprehensive and illuminating overview of the omnipresence of Malcolm X in publications of the Black Arts Movement, including poems and other writings by poets such as Jayne Cortez, Rodgers, Neal, and Baraka. This chapter also addresses the impact of Coltrane on poetry, echoing Jones's attention paid to the virtually obligatory "Coltrane poem."

Three of many poets who are closely associated with the jazz tradition have been woefully overlooked. Though often anthologized for a very few poems among many wonderful possibilities, the truly unique poet, thinker, artist, and musician Ted Joans (1928–2003) deserves far more attention. Described by many, including longtime friend Diane di Prima, as "one of a kind," his poetry reflects an authentically cross-media aesthetic sensibility of avant-garde practice in painting, poetry, and music. As accurately predicted by di Prima, "his work is going to become more and more important as time goes on." An excellent starting point is the beautifully maintained website dedicated to Joans's full range of interests, ideas, and creations.[42] The great A. B. Spellman (born

---

[41] Rambsy, *Black Arts*, p. 103.
[42] www.tedjoans.com (last accessed August 20, 2018).

in 1935) – whose recent work in poetry and drama are the best he has written – would be a superb subject for an in-depth study, and it is only a matter of time before he receives the critical attention to which he is due. There is an impressive trajectory from his powerful body of early poetry, as well as his classic writings on jazz, to his present output. Spellman's writing has now evolved into a self-proclaimed "slow" and mature voice on subjects in history, philosophy, the many varieties of love, and the continuous melding of the visual and musical that make his writing indispensable to the canon. Calvin C. Hernton (1932–2001) is yet another woefully underappreciated poet: the breadth, originality, and sophistication of his oral and textual sensibilities entitle him to far more recognition of his own work and not isolated to the context of his founding and central role in Umbra. It is to the credit of his longtime friend and colleague Ishmael Reed to have been Hernton's most active promoter and publisher, including producing the beautifully lyrical and poignant collection at the end of Hernton's life, *The Red Crab Gang and Black River Poems* (1999). *The Coming of Chronos to the House of Nightsong: an Epical Narrative of the South* (1964), which Breman always regretted not publishing in the Heritage Series, belongs back in print as another overlooked full-length poetry collection in the African American poetry tradition. Frequently read aloud in its totality by Hernton as an unforgettable dramatic performance, this book deserves to enter the canon as a major literary achievement.

Conrad Kent Rivers (1933–68) is another fascinating figure, far too little known and under-recognized, whose great promise was cut off by a tragically early death. He is one of only two poets in the Heritage Series to be represented by two books; the other is Robert Hayden, for whom the series was founded in the first place. In addition to his Heritage Series books, Rivers is the author of three mimeographed poetry pamphlets "under the auspices of The Free Lance:" *Perchance to Dream, Othello* (1959), *These Black Bodies and this Sunburnt Face* (1962), and *Dusk at Selma* (1965). A selection of his poems introduced by a "Statement" appears in *Sixes and Sevens* (Volume 2 of the Heritage Series, 1962), and his work appeared widely in some of the most experimental little magazines of the day, including *Negro Digest, Umbra, The Antioch Review*, and *Free Lance*, produced by Atkins and Casper LeRoy Jordan. Linked in literary influence and friendship to Hughes and Wright, Rivers left an important body of overlooked writing, with the likelihood that more remains to be discovered. According to Breman, on the back cover of *The Wright Poems*, Volume 18 in the Heritage Series, Rivers also had written "stories and other fiction" and "dramatic work which includes a play on the life of Paul Laurence Dunbar." Living in Chicago and involved in the discussion group that led to the Organization of Black American Culture (OBAC), Rivers is the author of two chapbooks: *The Still Voice of Harlem* (1968), Volume 5 in the Heritage Series, and the posthumously published *The Wright Poems* (1972), with introduction by Ronald L. Fair, Volume 18 in the Heritage Series. Rivers is often anthologized for the opening and title poem of his first book, "The Still Voice of Harlem," which is a brief and lovely, if conventional, lyric evoking the spirit of the age in four stanzas spoken by the beckoning voice of Harlem. The first stanza is an invitation addressing those who would come to Harlem: "Come to me broken dreams and all..." followed by a second stanza urging a young Harlem-bound artist to "weep not" for parents left behind, because we are told in the third stanza "I am the hope / and tomorrow / of your unborn." The closing couplet comprising stanza four expresses the interconnectedness of Harlem and the creative spirit of its young artists: "Truly, when there is no more of me / there shall be no more of you..." Other poems in this beautiful first collection are dedicated to African American literary exemplars and themes, indicative of the development of a self-referencing canon: James Baldwin, an epistolary poem to Richard Wright, Hoyt Fuller ("In Defense of Black Poets"), a poem for Africa, and the poem for Harlem. In *The Poetry of Black America*, poems to Du Bois and Malcolm X appear. Rivers also wrote poems citing Wordsworth and Hemingway, demonstrating his engagement with the British and American canons. This volume also contains a poem called "Watts," which is sometimes anthologized. When Rivers is considered critically, it is generally as a thoughtful and careful stylist with some unexpected twists. He is not generally regarded as particularly involved or invested in the organized politics or rhetoric of the Black Arts Movement or known for being especially experimental. Here is Breman's assessment of Rivers's poetics:

> Rivers was a writer with a great deal to say, on an interesting quest for ways in which to say it. One of the recurring themes in his work is the question of the black writer's position and responsibility, and his ambiguous relations with his dual audience ... Over the years he became more and more interested in reworking, honing, in the *craft* of writing poetry ... Conrad actually had something to say. He felt that this gift – if that is what it is – entailed great responsibilities, and should be used to a purpose.[43]

---

[43] Ramey, *The Heritage Series of Black Poetry*, p. 151.

But here are the self-assessments by Rivers. In the Statement preceding his poems in the Heritage Series (Volume 2) anthology, *Sixes and Sevens* (1962), Rivers wrote, "Praise Bessie and Dinah and Billie: I listened to the sorrow. Praise Miles and Jimmy Baldwin and Ralph Ellison: I glimpsed myself in newer and more experimental forms."[44] Here the poet affiliates himself with both the blues and materials of tradition (including the play he is reported to have written on Dunbar) and the experimentalism of the future, showing precisely that duality exemplified in so many marginalized poets in this tradition. In the same Statement, he also wrote, "I am tired of being mis-represented. No white man can dare write my story for me ... it is for me to do." When his work is examined more closely, it displays itself to be original, varied, and searching, and positions Rivers in a far more bold, revolutionary, and self-assertive light than he is often classified. In examining "Watts," we can see how perceptions may be mistaken about Rivers as well as other poets in the tradition by applying strict categories of theme, style, or intent:

> Must I shoot the
> white man dead
> to free the nigger
> in his head?[45]

This poem consists of a single sentence question, which could easily serve as a mantra for the revolutionary rhetoric of Black Power, and might well be attributed to someone like Madhubuti or Durem if we did not know otherwise. The poem shows the conceptual, almost metaphysical, concerns of Rivers, but in a very unaccustomed style, suggesting levels of innovation that are not necessarily associated with him. The critical assessment becomes even more intriguing if we look closely at other poems from the same volume, such as "Four Sheets to the Wind (and a one-way ticket to France)." The decentered self-position and series of quasi-non-sequiturs on varied topics and in different voices and registers display some of the sensibilities of the New York School and a strong sense of theatrical performance with lines like "When Selassie went before his peers and Dillinger goofed / I read in two languages, not really caring which one belonged to me."[46] Such a line also invokes the cultural

---

[44] Rivers, "Statement," in Breman, *Sixes and Sevens*, p. 30.
[45] Arnold Adoff, ed., *The Poetry of Black America: Anthology of the 20th Century* (New York: HarperCollins, 1973), p. 233.
[46] Adoff, ed., *The Poetry of Black America*, p. 234–5.

duality of double consciousness, and the pulls of the oral and inscribed traditions.

The situation becomes even more interesting and complex if we look at two very important pieces of Rivers's writing published in his second collection, *The Wright Poems*. "A Mourning Letter from Paris (for Richard Wright)" is the sole poem in *The Still Voice of Harlem* dedicated to Rivers's literary idol (along with Hughes and Rivers's uncle, the playwright Ray McIver). In the Introduction to *The Wright Poems*, Fair recalls what Rivers said about Wright: "Years ago, in Chicago, Conrad turned to me and said 'He was a god, man. He really was a god.'"[47] This single dedicated poem is placed within its properly expanded and elaborated context by being reprinted in *The Wright Poems*, but we now discover multiple iterations of poems under the same title in a surprisingly postmodern gesture. In a combination of one-directional dialogue and tribute evoking brief lyrical dramatic monologues, there are two different poems called "To Richard Wright" and a poem called "For Richard Wright." The collection contains two versions of "A Mourning Letter" (see Figure 3). There is the version that appears in *The Still Voice of Harlem*, which Breman's editorial note calls "the final version, completed shortly before Conrad's death." The volume also contains a different, and far more innovative, version of the same poem which Breman's note identifies as "a further reworking of the same material, done in Chicago after the poet's return; never published in this form."[48]

Rivers's deep connection to representing racial consciousness and his increasing interest in experimentalism are shown vividly in his fascinating "Postscript to a Poem," which is reproduced in Figure 4 from a manuscript in *The Wright Poems* accompanied by Rivers's letter to Breman and the "finished" version, "Postscript," edited by Breman.

Breman had a tendency to edit poems by some of the authors he published, while others he left alone. As a publisher he had high respect among those he published; as an editor of poetry, perhaps not so much. Breman himself wrote about how he and Durem nearly came to blows over Breman's unwanted editing, which was undertaken for 'improvement' and to save Durem's literary reputation from bad writing, in Breman's mind. In correspondence to Rosey Pool, now housed in the Moorland-Spingarn Research Center at Howard University, Hayden too

[47] Conrad Kent Rivers, *The Wright Poems*, introduced by Ronald Fair (London: Paul Breman, 1972), p. 4.

[48] Conrad Kent Rivers, *The Still Voice of Harlem* (London: Paul Breman, 1968), pp. 19 and 18.

A mourning letter from Paris

for Richard Wright

All night I walked among your spirits, Richard.
The Paris you knew is most politely dead,
one finds the rat-race all over your beloved Europe.

I found French-speaking bigots and sterile blacks,
polished Americans pretending not to look homeward
where the high ground smells of our quick death,
and new black echoes emerge across the continents,
seek us out in headlines, stares, and along the tourist routes.

I found cokes and pre-war pianos
and bright African lads forgetting their ancestral robes,
while culture-wearing Americans watched the stark reality
of mass integration, not as they supposed.

For here one finds a groove, adapts, then lingers
and stays away from the Champs district where the garçons
come and go counting old-fashioned American dough.

I could not find freedom here, Richard.
Of course the answer becomes in time a mental thing.
In Rome I saw the hand of Michelangelo
which quieted the desperation of the crowded Seine.

And so my good dead friend of words and bitter truth
for me the road to Paris leads back home.
I leave the nightmare of individuality somewhere between
the black and white of being born and surrendered.

I look again toward the cancer of our soul,
long evenings of mute indifference and quasi pain.
One gets to know and feel Harlem's honeyed voice
bringing her dead back to life again.

18

Figure 3   The two versions of "A Mourning Letter from Paris for Richard Wright" by
Conrad Kent Rivers

A mourning letter from Paris

for Richard Wright

All night I walked among your spirits, Richard:
the Paris you adored is most politely dead.

I found French-speaking bigots and some sterile blacks,
bright African boys forgetting their ancestral robes,
a few men of color seeking the same French girl.

Polished Americans watched the stark reality
of mass integration, pretending not to look homeward
where the high ground smelled of their daughters' death.

I searched for the skin of your bones, Richard.
Mississippi called you back to her genuine hard clay,
but here one finds a groove, adapts, then lingers on.

For me, my good dead friend of searing words
and thirsty truth, the road to Paris leads back home:
one gets to miss the stir of Harlem's honeyed voice

or one forgets the joy to which we were born.

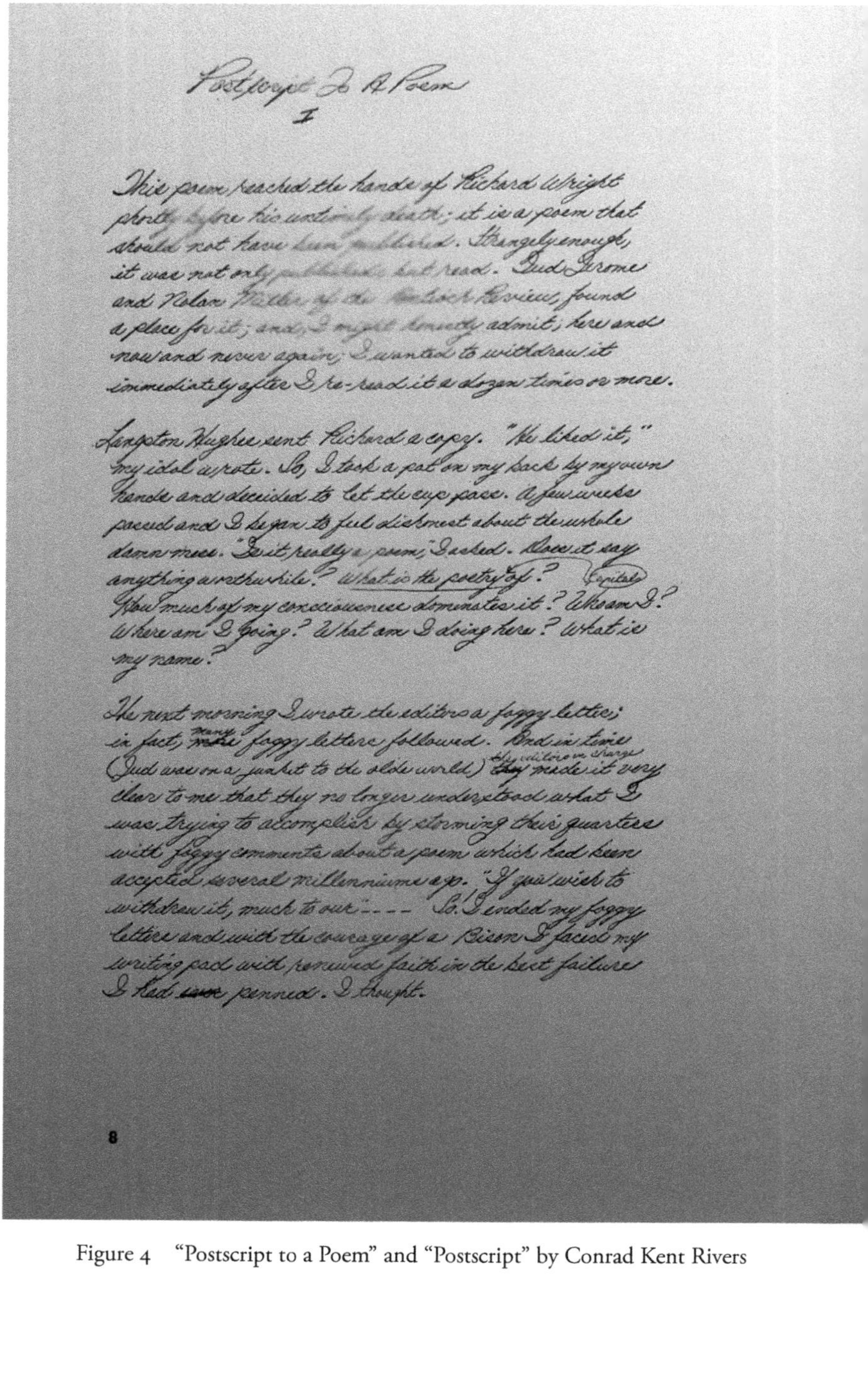

Postscript To A Poem

I

This poem reached the hands of Richard Wright shortly before his untimely death; it is a poem that should not have been published. Strangely enough, it was not only published, but read. Bud Jerome and Nolan Miller of the Antioch Review, found a place for it; and, I might honestly admit, here and now and never again, I wanted to withdraw it immediately after I re-read it a dozen times or more.

Langston Hughes sent Richard a copy. "He liked it," my idol wrote. So, I took a pat on my back by my own hands and decided to let the cup pass. A few weeks passed and I began to feel dishonest about the whole damn mess. "Is it really a poem," I asked. Does it say anything worthwhile? What is the poetry of? (capitals) How much of my consciousness dominates it? Who am I? Where am I going? What am I doing here? What is my name?

The next morning I wrote the editors a foggy letter; in fact, ~~more~~ many foggy letters followed. And in time (Bud was on a junket to the olde world) ~~they~~ the editors in charge made it very clear to me that they no longer understood what I was trying to accomplish by storming their quarters with foggy comments about a poem which had been accepted several millenniums ago. "If you wish to withdraw it, much to our----" So! I ended my foggy letters and with the courage of a Bison I faced my writing pad with renewed faith in the best failure I had ~~ever~~ penned. I thought.

8

Figure 4 "Postscript to a Poem" and "Postscript" by Conrad Kent Rivers

II

Karl Shapiro is the finest critic just around, I thought. I'll send him a copy and get the truth. Of course I never got his copy in the mail. No, I read the to Mrs. Tucker; we were friends employed for the same organization. She was a former English teacher and knew her stuff. I was living and dying and dreaming in Harlem at the time. Two days after I gave her a copy to study and read — she lost it. I gave her another worn copy. I can't recall her exact words to me, but I do recall her mentioning e.e. Cummings or someone in that umbra.

I gave my aunt Lucille a copy to read; I think it embarrassed her. My mother shouted "Oh, Conrad!" My brother wasn't around, I am sure he would have called it as he felt, saw, and heard, assuming of course, that these senses functioned during his analyses.

I never found the borderline between prose and poetry. Richard never found it either. Therefore, it must not exist. His works centered on Race. The people of our streets and the critics of any race, dislike the use of the ugly. I found no insincerity in Richard's work. Freud, yes! Richard's positivistic stand bordered on fanaticism. Some of his critics and to my knowledge, many of his friends, labeled him a fanatic.

9

And like all great men who dare to prognosticate;
his vision foreshadowed his prophecy, and he was
without honor in his land. To my mind Richard
was the first American author to examine the Negro
people in such easy and unoccupied language that
all who read him in earnest, knew exactly what he was
writing about, perhaps many had lived through the ugly
and beautiful found in his words. Certainly every
symbol carried a different interpretation for every
individual (?) set of eyes. But if the reader caught a
glimpse of the "neurosis," if the neglect of our American
society towards its black brothers was visualized and
just briefly conceptualized, something was gained.
Richard wrote the truth. The truth will write about
him. It shall do him honor when you and I are
blank pages. His mystique shall linger. And all
who dare to follow — cannot. It is no longer possible
to blaze his trails. It is one thing to place a pen in
your hands, move through Harlem — on to Chicago —
alas! Paris .... the soft lights of Rome.; but by letting
the place of occupancy live in the pen. Richard was not a
magician; his feat remains to be duplicated.

I only met Richard Wright the poet — ... I never knew
Richard Wright the man. His language took me on a
journey. His truth showed me how ignorant and ugly
and beautiful I AM. His prophecy told me that soon I
would be dead ----- unless? His truth told me
that the American Negro did not buy the biggest car,
nor wear the bright colored ornaments to be seen or
heard —— no! ---- it was something else altogether
different. Our SPIRIT was involved. To be hated
is not to be loved by those who dare to hate.

10

II

The absence of love indicates the presence of hate. We hate what we fear and do not understand. We teach our children to hate. They teach it in turn —— hate can become amoral. We are going crazy and no one really cares and few honestly know. Look at our streets! Look! I dare you! Look into our average homes — not lower middle. Look! Look! Listen! Forget about your front page heroes. All the men are dead. Forget about your century of progress! all the men are dead — and what is fairer to the dead, than for the living to be unalive. Walk into an alley near a bar in an all non-integrated neighborhood — tell me what you hear. If you have any culture don't expect to believe what you see. And don't give me that snow job about Lena Horne and the rest —— nice people! But they DON'T live around here anymore. I do. We do —— —

I never knew Richard Wright the MAN. I mourn for the poet. It was too soon. God! Jehovah! Whatever name you use — it was too soon. Where shall we find another man? We're only last two: Dunbar and Richard.

I dislike this poem very much! I shall not re-publish it again. There is little truth in it ——. The language does not take us on a journey; it does not allow us to see, to hear, to feel, to know, to believe. I like the title though. Naturally, I liked the man it fails to honor. I struggled with this piece — searching, pleading alone; all for FORM. Richard's Form. His language. His spirit. Of course I failed. Only three small changes occured, maybe four. It is not a poem. I am not a poet. But I adored the craftsman style of the art I wrote it for.

11

6th Thursday Morning - Feb 22?

Dear Paul,

I'm too tired and sleepy to proof this the way I ought to be done.
If I touch it —— you'll never get it on time. I'll seal
it tonight and mail it in the morning. Please!
When you have time - type me a carbon. I'd like to see
it again. Make ANY corrections you wish. I'm not egomaniac.
Here's hoping it's worth reading. I felt it all the way through—
writing directly on the top of my emotion. whew!

            Good Night

Watch my ; and , — first drafts. I'm sloppy.

I'll send you some newer things - more experimental. Facing race
and the American culture and all that sort of thing— in time.

Postscript

This poem should not have been published.
Strangely enough, it was not only published,
but read. I let the cup pass, and the weeks,
then I began to feel dishonest.
Is it really a poem, I asked –
and what is the poetry of?

I was living and dying and dreaming
in Harlem, at the time of my best failure.
I gave my aunt Lucille a copy to read
– I think it embarrassed her.
My mother shouted 'Oh! Conrad!'
My brother wasn't around, but I am sure
he would have called it as he felt, saw, heard –
assuming always that these senses functioned at the time.

I never found the borderline between prose and poetry.
Richard never found it either. It must not exist.
I did not sleep or eat for three days, after his sudden death.
His language took me on a journey.
His sincerity showed me how ignorant and ugly
and how beautiful I am.
His prophecy warned me that soon I would be dead
unless ...

He wrote the truth. The truth shall write about him.
It shall do him honor after you and I
have become blank pages.

His truth told me that the american negro
did not buy the biggest car, nor wear
the brightly colored ornaments, just to be seen or heard.
No – it was something altogether different,
and it involved our sanity –
for to be hated is not to be loved
by those who dare to hate.

We hate what we fear and do not understand.
We teach our children to hate.
Hate can become a moral.
Look at our streets, look into our average home.
Forget about your front-page heroes.
All the men are dead.
Forget about your century of progress.
All the men are dead –
and what is fairer to the dead than for the living
to be unalive?

13

Walk into an alley near a bar in an all
non-integrated neighborhood – and tell me
what you hear. If you have any culture don't
expect to believe what you see – and don't
give me that snow job about Lena Horne and the rest –
nice people!
but they *don't* live around here anymore.

I struggled with this piece, searching,
pleading alone: all for *form.*
Richard's form. His language. His spirit.
Of course I failed.
It is not a poem.
I am not a poet.
But I adored the craftsmanship
of the poet I wrote it for.

complained about Breman's unwanted editing of his poems. Perhaps wishing to play Pound to Rivers's Eliot, Breman drastically edited the piece originally called "Postscript to a Poem," which Breman published in both *Sixes and Sevens* and *The Wright Poems* under the title "Postscript." In the interview published in the Appendix of this book, Breman said that the original was a long rambling letter never intended for publication, implying that Breman transformed it into a publishable literary work. That does not appear to be an accurate representation of Rivers's intent as shown in the original version. The original is not only indisputably a literary work but one that indicates Rivers's aspirations to innovatively interrogate conceptual and conventional boundaries of the lyric poetry genre, in contrast with his usual critical reception. "Postscript to a Poem" is given a literary title rather than being presented by a customary address to a recipient as in a letter or even some epistolary poems. It is formally divided into four sections headed by Roman numerals, lineated, in stanzas, and filled with self-reflexive lines, including "I never found the borderline between prose and poetry" (line one, section II, stanza three). The poem is followed by a separate letter to Breman saying "Make any corrections you wish." It logically seems unlikely for Rivers to invite such editorial incursions in a document that he considered to be a letter. Breman created a radically different poem from the one that Rivers hand-wrote and which was subsequently published twice. Whether this permission extended to a full-scale overhaul can be debated. The poem appeared during Rivers's lifetime, suggesting that he found it acceptable, but we also recall his Statement that he would never let a white man write his life's story. Perhaps influenced by Atkins and Jordan, the original combines the creative and critical functions in a brilliantly self-conscious mode that evokes much later works like Charles Bernstein's *Artifice of Absorption*. My intent with Rivers, as with other neglected poets, is to stimulate interest in his writing and encourage further critical appreciation.

Written during the period of the Black Arts Movement, Atkins's poem "Spyrytual" (1966), exemplifies this motive of postmodern experimentalism grounded in the genre's roots. Contrary to misconceptions of stylistic homogeneity of the 1960s and 1970s, this poem also suggests the wide array of verse that was produced during this politically mobilized era. "Spyrytual" displays how foundational materials can be inventively repurposed as a living legacy for postmodern readers. This concrete poem is reminiscent of the international influences of Guillaume Apollinaire's Calligrammes – in particular, his poem "Il Pleut," which spatially and tyographically depicts the image of a heavy rainstorm (see Figure 5).

Spyrytual

Figure 5   "Spyrytual" by Russell Atkins

As suggested by Nielsen, one of Atkins's earliest and best critics, his inter-media and cross-genre body of cultural, musical, aesthetic, philosophical, creative, theoretical, and educational prose has been woefully lacking in serious scholarly attention in spite of its centrality to literary ideas. "Spyrytual" embodies Atkins's motive to perpetuate tradition and make incursions into the ways "knowledge" of the past is co-opted by dominant groups and educational practices, and must be deconstructed and rebuilt. Atkins is concerned to reclaim and reconfigure black cultural materials that have been later filtered through the national imaginary. He wrote in 1966:

> To begin a new history is a prodigious undertaking. A non-dominant group might have to assume the DEFINING OF KNOWLEDGE (what can or cannot or should or need be "known," and how much treated as such). It may have to create what it knows and know what it creates; and create what it learns and learn what it has created.[49]

[49] Russell Atkins, "The Invalidity of Dominant-Group 'Education' Forms for 'Progress' for Non-Dominant Ethnic Groups as Americans," *Free Lance* 7.2 (1963), pp. 19–32; pp. 31-2.

Nielsen describes Atkins's avant-garde techniques as "a black American's remastery of the signifying materials of American English."[50]

By changing the "I" in "spirituals" to "y" in "Spyrytual," Atkins extends the experiments of the historical avant-garde by defamiliarizing this word visually, auditorally, and semantically. In doing so, he liberates this product of slavery, releasing "spirit" and "spiritual" from a possible state as frozen signifiers into new realms of reanimated meanings. Instead of a rime with "ear" – and evocations of the oral tradition which birthed the slave songs or spirituals –the "y" (why?) repositions readers in a later era of technological advances. Oral and textual frames are mapped over each other and co-exist, as the past is thrust into the present. The first syllable can be broken into refreshed lexical units: "pyre," "spy," and "spire." "Pyre" guides the eye to see the word clusters in the poem's layout as piles of combustible agents at a funeral, lighting the fires that the poem's renewing rain has the power to extinguish. "Spy" – suggesting a political game of cat and mouse – implies the surreptitious role of the slave songs as subterfuge and hidden messages. "Spires," the architectural structures forming the pyramidal roofs of churches, cleverly evokes the religious dimension of slave songs. This postmodern poet, in a sense, is raising the roof as an integral participant in the continuous process of building on these folk products. The poem is structured as call-and-response, but one between the oral and textual domains, the past and the present. The call alludes to the slave song "Oh Didn't It Rain?," but the response echoes back from the textual world of the future. The sets of quotation marks, mimicking the appearance of raindrops, can be read visually, but have no oral or aural equivalents. The poem cannot be either wholly "read" or wholly "spoken"; rather, both actions are needed for its full comprehension in a brilliant cognitive blend of written and oral history.

The period from approximately 1960 to 1975 was highly political, openly dissident, and characterized by artistic self-determination and independence, ranging from issues of style to ownership to production to audience. New York, Chicago, DC, London, and Detroit were some of the dynamic social, political, and creative centers leading to a wealth of poetic production. Yet this era of broadsides and manifestos also generated certain kinds of aesthetic repression – for example, of stylistic divergence and the voices of women – alongside its political and creative productivity and progress. This period still afforded

[50] Ramey, *The Heritage Series of Black Poetry*, p. 68.

relatively few publication and review opportunities in mainstream venues for African American poets. Jones's resounding *Preface to a Twenty Volume Suicide Note* was published in 1961 by Eli and Ted Wilentz's Beat-oriented Corinth Books. In a two-year period, Major published *Symptoms & Madness* with Corinth (1971), two collections with black presses (*Private Line* in the Heritage Series in 1971 and *The Cotton Club* with Randall's Broadside Press in 1972), and a fourth collection under a mainstream imprint (*Swallow the Lake* with Wesleyan University Press, 1970). Several African American poets (Reed and Lorde as two important examples, in addition to Major) exhibited this high level of ingenuity, originality, and a nuanced approach to individual literary artistry during a time of increased ideological dogmatism. In addition to the Black Arts Movement as the aesthetic wing – so perceived – of the Black Power Movement, key issues of the era include the relationships of both of those movements to the Civil Rights Movement; to other literary/artistic movements and organizations including Umbra, Free Lance, and Dasein; and to questions of American nationalism/self-empowerment, and Pan-African internationalism, separatism, and diasporic consciousness. An important summary of this era that is now considered a classic is Kalamu ya Salaam's entry on the Black Arts Movement in the *Oxford Companion to African American Literature* (1997), which is available on the Modern American Poetry (MAPS) website.[51]

As this chapter has demonstrated, the twentieth century displayed more continuity from the first to the second so-called Renaissance than is often recognized. Little magazines and presses – many black-owned – rose to prominence during this era, notably the literary magazines of HBCUs and journals such as *Black World/Negro Digest*, *Journal of Black Poetry*, *Phylon*, *Umbra*, *Black Dialogue*, and *Soulbook*, along with the advent of black presses such as Broadside, Third World, Heritage, and Lotus. The poetry of protest created during the time of the Black Arts Movement of the 1960s and 1970s by writers such as Sonia Sanchez, Don L. Lee/Madhubuti, Nikki Giovanni, and Carolyn Rodgers radically shaped the political texture of America with lasting impact during a time of national turmoil. These poets, and this era, foregrounded even more emphatically two major historical themes and technical operations of African American poetry: its integral relationship with music and musicality, and its implicit goal to achieve social benefit. During this period

---

[51] www.english.illinois.edu/Maps/blackarts/historical.htm (last accessed August 19, 2018).

of the Civil Rights and Black Arts Movements, Sanchez was publishing love poems, LeRoi Jones became Amiri Baraka, and, under Hoyt Fuller, *Negro Digest* became *Black World* and then was discontinued. Jazz poetry intertwined with the Beat and Black Arts writers. The cross-sections and dialogues of this tumultuous time are less clear-cut than conventional representations may have it, allowing excellent opportunity to imagine a revised and more nuanced perspective as the foundation for the post-modern period to follow.

CHAPTER 5

Contemporary African American Poetry

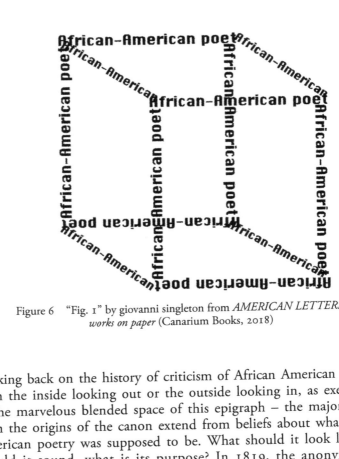

Figure 6 "Fig. 1" by giovanni singleton from *AMERICAN LETTERS: works on paper* (Canarium Books, 2018)

Looking back on the history of criticism of African American poetry – from the inside looking out or the outside looking in, as exemplified in the marvelous blended space of this epigraph – the major debates from the origins of the canon extend from beliefs about what African American poetry was supposed to be. What should it look like, how should it sound, what is its purpose? In 1819, the anonymous "A Wesleyan Methodist," later revealed to be John Watson, called slave songs "miserable as poetry, and senseless as matter, and most frequently sung by the illiterate blacks of the society" versus "the junction of our own discipline."[1] Watson, in his title and throughout his book, differentiates and criticizes African American poetry *as different* for its displays of physical activity and emotional expression, its "screaming, jumping up and down in the same place," versus "our own" content and modes of delivery.[2] In 1868, John Mason Brown wrote a letter to *Lippincott's Magazine* saying, "The religious songs of the negro slave were composed and communicated without the aid of writing, and were unmistakably marked in their construction."[3] In this case, the oral tradition was identified as the source of slave songs' *difference* and identity as a marked term.

As this book has established, the foundation of contemporary African American poetry and the African American poetry canon itself, are still the ever-durable and regenerative slave songs. Their manifestations of influence and brilliantly creative re-makings prove the strength of these roots. In the literature on slave songs from the earliest reviews, commentators have mentioned their anonymous and communal nature as an important part of their meaning. They have been consistently excluded from the canons of American and African American poetry, where individuality, originality, agency, self-determination, and ownership are viewed as premiums in literary production and cultural esteem. This focus on the slave songs' uncertain origins has resulted in an absence of serious literary treatment and recognition of their central place in the canon. Certainly, it is a causal factor that their creators were in fact not seen as "self-owned" or "self-possessed," which meant that these poems were invisible as art created by gifted autonomous individuals with subjectivity and personal agency. Slave songs often were dismissed as utilitarian rather than aesthetic when they were not associated solely with Christian faith. This idea that these foundational poems belonged to and represented a group has haunted the African American poetry tradition ever since. The emphasis on collaborative and untraceable authorship is part of the debate about whether African American poetry is truly "American" or something *different*, and truly the individuated expressions of self-determined subjective consciousnesses whose voices and ideas are integral to America.

---

[1] Watson, *Methodist Error Or, Friendly, Christian Advice*, p. 82.
[2] Watson, *Methodist Error Or, Friendly, Christian Advice*, p. 86.
[3] John Mason Brown, "Letter to *Lippincott's Magazine*, 1868," in Bernard Katz, ed., *The Social Implications of Early Negro Music in the United States* (New York: Arno Press and the *New York Times*, 1969), pp. 617–23.

By 1912, W. H. Thomas acknowledged the potential ("if") literariness of slave songs and considered that there could be "parallels" between African American poetry and "English literature." But he still addressed the former as a *different* body of writing that was not part of this separate tradition, and whose comparability was based on a much less advanced stage in English literary development: "If you consider these songs as the negro's literature, you will notice some striking parallels between its history and that of English literature. As all of you know, English literature for several centuries was little more than paraphrases of various parts of the Bible."[4] African American poetry was given a backhanded compliment by comparing it to a retrograde form of English literature, implicitly lauded for its mainline Christianity, and not attempting to judge it on its own terms.

Jumping ahead to 1969, we find *a different kind of difference* being applied when Jewel C. Latimore criticizes Russell Atkins in a *Negro Digest* review for sounding too white and not black enough. The influence of T. S. Eliot on Atkins's book *Heretofore* was called "unfortunate"; Atkins was accused of using "white intonated swearing," and taken to task for not showing enough concern in his "black-related" poems for "dealing with history as he should be about doing (blkartists are responsible to the blkcommunity)."[5] By these black critical standards, Atkins was *not different enough* from white culture and failed to fulfill a communitarian standard of blackness. Throughout the history of criticism, it has been challenging to measure the identity and quality of African American poetry without relying on a comparison to something that is not African American poetry.

Starting with slave songs, the African American experience – in its full diversity – has progressively developed a body of texts, figures, concepts, events, and experiences that serve as allusions and direct reference points. Atkins and Kearney, among many others, have followed in the footsteps of predecessors including Brown, Dunbar, Hayden, Hughes, Fenton Johnson, Tolson, Margaret Walker, and countless others to use folk materials to link current practices to African American origins. As we have seen, from the start of the African American literary tradition, there was a critical split – the repercussions of which are still felt today – between the diasporic "oral" literature and inscribed verse, including the explorations

---

[4] W. H. Thomas, *Some Current Folk-Songs of the Negro and their Economic Interpretation* (College Station, TX: The Folklore Society of Texas, 1912), p. 6.
[5] *Negro Digest*, September 1969, p. 95, by Johari Amini (Jewel C. Latimore).

of visuality and signing systems that have been pursued by Norman H. Pritchard, De Leon Harrison, Atkins, singleton, Kearney, Patton, and numerous others. In integrating these paths, which represent the same tradition, a practical and ideological schism is denied and repaired by figures such as Atkins, Reed, Mullen, Morris, Shockley, Kearney, Patton, and Baraka, among many others, who work in the interstices of oral and written language.

The critical situation of slave songs presents a fascinating early touch-stone for the dilemma of postmodern poetry – for centuries, it had been a given that lyric poetry represents the voice of the individual poet. Yet the dilemma of postmodernism is the imbrication of the language user in the system of language itself, and doubt about the possibility of a unitary lyric subject. We can appropriately look at African American poetry – whose very origins engage in debate about whether this writing represents a group or an individual – to be a precursor of this debate. From the early twentieth century to the advent of the twenty-first, slave songs are alluded to, appropriated, and directly cited in poetry with widely different goals and styles. The complexities of their role as the expression of an individual and universalized and anonymized voice of a group or society remain part of their power and critical interest.

In 1997, shortly after the publication of his *Black Chant: Languages of African-American Postmodernism*, Aldon Lynn Nielsen and I started on a project that was to take the better part of two decades: compiling a two-volume anthology set to access and preserve formally innovative poetry since World War II. It was the era of high theory and the compression of the canon. The first edition of the *Norton Anthology of African American Literature* had been published that year with great fanfare. While an immense milestone and an important contribution to teaching and scholarship, the selections unsurprisingly marched in stylistic step with the fundamentally conservative Norton anthologies of American literature and poetry. In the 1960s and 1970s, most of the poets that Nielsen discussed in *Black Chant* had writing, or at least selections of their writing, that was readily available in anthologies published by commercial presses. Readers could open *American Negro Poetry* edited by Arna Bontemps or *Natural Process* co-edited by Ted Wilentz and Tom Weatherly, both published by Hill and Wang, or Arnold Adoff's *The Poetry of Black America*, published by HarperCollins, and find poems by Oliver Pitcher, Walter Everette Hawkins, Atkins, Rivers, Margaret Danner, Pritchard, Harrison, Weatherly, and Elouise Loftin, most of whom gradually disappeared from collections over the next two decades.

Their writing by the 1990s was largely unknown and unavailable except in out-of-print books. Because there was little market or interest in poets who had dropped from sight, much of their more recent innovative poetry remained unpublished. In 2006, when Nielsen and I completed *Every Goodbye Ain't Gone*, the first volume of this project, covering the period roughly from World War II to the mid-1970s, very few of the thirty-seven "formally innovative" poets represented had a book in print. Among those thirty-seven, only a handful of figures were widely known among readers of contemporary poetry: among them, chiefly, Reed, Baraka, Tolson, Roberson, Major, and Kaufman. We had not set out to anthologize marginalized poets – only formally innovative poets – but marginalized and largely invisible is how it turned out by the 1990s.

In 1976, it was possible for Eugene B. Redmond to discuss virtually the entire roster of poets that became viewed in the 1980s and 1990s as "experimental," "innovative," or "avant-garde," during the period that coincided with the heyday of the definitionally experimental L=A=N=G=U=A=G=E Poetry. Though they were given no such ideological or aesthetic designation, these black experimentalists were incorporated in Redmond's critical history side by side with other poets who had come to be considered "conservative," "social realist," or neo-formalist. *Drumvoices*, published in the critical context of literary studies in the 1970s, is strikingly free of typologies of style. Redmond does not claim to espouse a theory or a poetics, yet *Drumvoices* does offer explicit critical evaluations and implicit judgments through its inclusions. One of the innumerable strengths of Redmond's book is its embrace of a multiplicity of definitions for what constitutes the genre of African American poetry. But the circumstances are circular: it was possible to be inclusive because exclusions based on style and theme were less likely to take place in that brief post-Black Arts halcyon moment.

It may be that we are moving back once again in the direction of breaking down labels and barriers of "conservative" or "experimental," or other delimiting categories. A startling transformation in the public and critical reception of this field has taken place, especially in the second decade of the twenty-first century. In about 2007, Nielsen and I started compiling the second volume of the anthology set, *What I Say*. The situation was similar to when we began gathering materials for volume 1. Because we were focusing on the period from about the mid-1970s to 2015, a few of the older figures had achieved stature, recognition, and success, and had books in print. Of the twenty-nine poets in this second volume, Mullen, Mackey, and Hunt were perhaps the best known and most widely published. By the time the volume was published in 2015, virtually all the contributors had books in print, and many, such as John Keene and Claudia Rankine, had earned major honors and awards. Other projects of recovery, in addition to these anthologies, also were taking place for some of the living poets in *Every Goodbye Ain't Gone*. An issue of *Jacket2* focuses on the work of Weatherly, edited by David Grundy, and two tribute volumes have been devoted to Atkins with more on the way, as two examples. Several of the earlier poets have resumed active writing projects, among them William J. Harris and A. B. Spellman, whose first book, *The Beautiful Days* (1964) was followed, after a hiatus of four decades, by the highly acclaimed *Things I Must Have Known* (2008), which earned wide admiration including an Honorable Mention from the Gustavus Myers Outstanding Book Award and nomination for an NAACP Image Award for Outstanding Literary Work in Poetry. Roberson continues to soar in stature and productivity, with commensurate recognition including an Academy of American Poets Fellowship (2017), PEN/Voelcker Award for Poetry (2016), and Shelley Memorial Award (2008).

From the 1980s onwards, African American postmodernism has reflected paths of (auto)biographical and persona poems; reclamations, reanimations, and tributes to events and figures in African American history and culture; influences of black music in compositional methods and themes, including the slave songs, blues, jazz, gospel, black church traditions, Motown, rhythm and blues, soul, and hip-hop; haiku and nature poems; use of poetic forms, including neo-realism, conventional forms such as sonnets, and development of new forms such as kwansabas and Golden Shovel poems; verbal jazz improvisation and influences of recent music; L=A=N=G=U=A=G=E Poetry-inspired textual innovations; inter-media conceptual projects; and auditorily inventive performance poetries. There has been an astronomical rise in prestigious honors and recognition not based on race or ethnicity earned by African American and African diaspora poets, as indicated by a representative and partial listing. The Pulitzer Prize in Poetry went to Rita Dove in 1987, Yusef Komunyakaa in 1994, Natasha Trethewey in 2007, Tracy K. Smith in 2012, Gregory Pardlo in 2015, and Tyehimba Jess in 2017. The Shelley Memorial Award of the Poetry Society of America was founded in 1930. It was not until 1976 that an African American poet received the award: Gwendolyn Brooks in 1976, followed by Etheridge Knight in 1985, Lucille Clifton in 1992, Angela Jackson in 2002, Yusef Komunyakaa in 2004, Roberson in 2008, Wanda Coleman in 2012, and Sonia Sanchez in 2016. The frequency of major poetry honors being bestowed on African American poets has rapidly increased in the late twentieth century and especially in the twenty-first.

In 1992, Derek Walcott received the Nobel Prize in Literature. MacArthur Fellowship recipients include Thylias Moss in 1996, Reed in 1998, Hayes in 2014, and Rankine in 2016. The National Book Award for Poetry went to Ai in 1996, Clifton in 2000, Mackey in 2006, Hayes in 2010, Nikky Finney in 2011, and Robin Coste Lewis in 2015. Victor Hernández Cruz was appointed the first Latino-African diasporic Chancellor of the Academy of American Poets; other black chancellors have included Dove, Komunyakaa, Mackey, Carl Phillips, Clifton, Alexander, Toi Derricotte, Hayes, Rankine, and Marilyn Nelson. African American poets are firmly installed in prestigious positions at academic institutions across the United States in quantities too great to enumerate, including Dove at the University of Virginia, C. S. Giscombe at University of California, Berkeley, Mackey at Duke University, and Mullen at UCLA to name only a few.

The artistic advances since approximately 1980 extend and build on many of the features discussed throughout this book and argue resolutely that progress and reclamation go hand in hand in this tradition. As we see African American poetry become increasingly influential nationally and internationally, a resounding case is made that this genre has fully articulated its own identity as a body of writing with distinctive features that are worthy of special attention and has shown itself to have the capability to evolve meaningfully. Music soars in the poetry of Harper; slave songs are ironically reformulated in Kearney's *The Black Automaton;* Shockley's *The New Black* is a volume of postmodern self-articulation coupled with close connection to a true family history in the ancient depths of plantation culture. Baraka's "The Changing Same" sets the tune for the way contemporary African American poetry connects to its past. We see an increasing concern with critical race theory and racial identity framed in a contemporary environment of racial mixing and so-called "post-racialism," and in conjunction with issues of American nationalism, ownership, migration, belonging, and identity. The ever-present role of African American music carries on from the start of the tradition, including the increasing synthesis of African beats with Latin inflections, the authentic American products of jazz and blues, the permanent inclusion of slave songs, the international phenomenon of hip-hop, and the omnipresent influences of these genres on African American poetry and poetics.

Many recent critical studies emphasize the continuing and evolving role of music in this tradition. Adam Bradley's *Book of Rhymes: The Poetics of Hip Hop* (2009, 2017) explicitly defines rap, rising in the 1970s, as part of the African American poetry tradition. Not only does he claim that rap can be considered critically in the same way as "old school poetry," but he also states that its earliest practitioners drew on the resources of all English lyric poetry traditions:

> [the] first generation fashioned an art form that draws not only from the legacy of Western verse but from the folk idioms of the African diaspora; the musical legacy of jazz, blues, and funk; and the creative capacities conditioned by the often harsh realities of people's everyday surroundings. The artists commandeered the English language, the forms of William Shakespeare and Emily Dickinson as well as those of Sonia Sanchez and Amiri Baraka, to serve their own expressive and imaginative purposes.[6]

Bradley is careful to identify rap as oral poetry and provides astute and illuminating discussion of the challenges of transcription. The same issues of transforming an inherently transmutable, performative, interactive, musical-linguistic form of oral expression into the fixed and static conventions of printed textuality apply just as readily to rap as to the slave songs.

In his marvelous volume *Afro-Blue: Improvisations in African American Poetry and Culture*, now regrettably out of print, Tony Bolden examines "blues poetics," which he associates with a wide range of modern poets such as Fenton Johnson, Helene Johnson, Cuney, Frank Marshall Davis, Walker, and Brooks. Bolden does a superb job of tracing the influence of blues as a motif in these precursor figures through the jazz orientation of Umbra-affiliated poets such as Hernton, Tom Dent, Reed, Henderson, and Askia M. Touré. Following the development of this path towards the present, Bolden identifies hip-hop as "a new phase of blues poetics," and explains how a group of poets starting in the 1990s built their work on the foundations of hip-hop culture, including Tony Medina, Ruth Forman, Kevin Powell, and Saul Williams. In examining some of the most recent examples, Bolden offers the concept of "epistrophy," taken from Thelonius Monk, which involves riffing, and employs the same mode of synthesis and collaging of diverse resources discussed by Bradley. According to Bolden, poets "like Yusef Komunyakaa in *Copacetic* (1984) and Harryette Mullen in *Muse and Drudge* (1995), resorted to epistrophy,

---

[6] Adam Bradley, *Book of Rhymes: The Poetics of Hip Hop*, 2nd edn. (New York: Basic Civitas Books, 2017), p. xvi.

fusing their poems with the imagery and rhythmic cadences of black song."[7] Again we return to the origins of this genre and tradition.

Bolden's study in innovation and funk established solid groundwork in an aesthetic of what we might think of as fully multi-modal collage. We see manifestations of radical citationality increase since the 1970s, expanding on seeds already present in the mid-twentieth century. A vivid demonstration appears in the relationship between poets in Nielsen and Ramey's two-volume anthology of formally innovative African American poetry from World War II to the present. In volume 1, *Every Goodbye Ain't Gone*, covering the period from the mid-1940s to the mid-1970s, we find examples of verbal play like those of Lloyd Addison (1931–2014). Addison embraces the need for paradoxical and contradictory multiple lexicons, registers, and vocabularies placed in rapidly cross-cut staccato juxtaposition as a necessary means to understand and represent information about the current world that he inhabits, which may remain a contingent and incomplete project of his poetics. His poem titled "All the things of which there are none" opens:

> Among all the things of which there are none
> I'll have a little bit of play widt/ with having
>   that one/ full body of knowledge
>
> Here with we will open buds
>   & scatter seeds far as are accountings[8]

Addison's exploratory undertaking is greatly expanded and developed by the next generations of poets in the second volume, *What I Say*, which covers the period from the mid-1970s to 2015, in the work of poets such as Will Alexander. His writing further encompasses a selectively free and open inclusion of conceptual, auditory, sonic, visual, lexical, phonological, and semantic realms, materials, and properties of idea and expression. Alexander's poem in parallel with Addison's earlier example more dominantly asserts the lyric "I" as the one who coalesces and inhabits this carefully orchestrated maelstrom. For example, his poem "Apprenticeship" embodies these alternating gestures of assertion and retreat as it opens with an epigraph from Mexican poet Octavio Paz's *Eagle or Sun?*: "between impulse and resistances / between advances and

---

[7] Tony Bolden, *Afro-Blue: Improvisations in African American Poetry and Culture* (Urbana: University of Illinois Press, 2004), p. 144.
[8] Lloyd Addison, "All the things of which there are none," in Nielsen and Ramey, eds., *Every Goodbye Ain't Gone*, p. 4.

retreats."[9] Exploring related terrain to Alexander, Paz himself describes the central purpose of his book: "above all, it is an exploration of the relations between language and the poet, reality and language, the poet and history." Alexander's poem opens:

> Here I am
> posing in a mirror of scratch paper sonnets
> sonnets as rare
> as a live Aegean rhino

The poem progresses through a series of postulates about what poetry is and what it means to be its apprentice. It closes:

> yes
> poetics
> its force
> jettisoned by "hypotaxis"
> by ... paratactic co-ordination
> & fire[10]

With the development of the Internet and ease of electronic communication in multiple modes, the international influence of African American poetry and its traditions continues as a topic of strengthening importance. This theme connects to developments in modernism through the massive strides in technological developments in the early decades of the twentieth century. Previously, the ability to record and distribute poetry by Dunbar and slave songs sung by the Fisk Jubilee Singers resulted in international prominence for African American cultural products. Those early developments relate to the recent world-shaking advances and their influence on poetic form, style, production, and reception, including such issues as the ease of dissemination and access afforded by technology. Examples include the inter-media poetry and sound environments of keith+mendi obadike, the graphic and textual innovations of singleton and Patton, the opera libretti of Kearney, the signifying and double voicing of Morris in performative dialogue with the film *Eyes Wide Shut* among other projects, the phenomenal impact of *Citizen* by Rankine which now has been produced as a successful play across the United States and assigned as university-wide reading, and the

---

[9] *Eagle or Sun? Poetry by Octavio Paz*, trans. and ed. Eliot Weinberger, New Directions, 1976, www .ndbooks.com/book/eagle-or-sun (last accessed August 28, 2018).
[10] "Apprenticeship," in Aldon Lynn Nielsen and Lauri Ramey, eds., *What I Say: Innovative Poetry by Black Writers in America* (Tuscaloosa: University of Alabama Press, 2015), p. 8.

impact of digitization and the Internet on diasporic dialogue and contact, including the spread of hip-hop internationally.

Another theme of increasing focus is the new openness to literary representations of gender and sexual diversity, which we see explored in the practices of poets such as Danez Smith, Ronaldo V. Wilson, Dawn Lundy Martin, and Jericho Brown. The continuing impact of Black Arts Movement concepts such as performance, the democratization of poetry, and art as political action are key themes as represented by figures including the Last Poets and Gil Scott-Heron, whose impacts stretched from the period discussed in Chapter 4 through to the present. Formal innovation and decentered self-positions of the poetic subject – or ironizing of the poetic speaker's role and identity – have been exemplified in African American poetry since the slave songs and Dunbar. These patterns continue – along with the prominent role of female poets – such as the formal innovator Harryette Mullen, who slyly announces herself to be as closely connected to Sappho as Sapphire. This is an auspicious moment to recognize the past and present of African American poetry and contextualize its dynamic future.

This chapter also calls for homage to be paid to those figures, some living and some deceased, who were productive in earlier eras, and who have been powerfully influential in ways that have not always been fully recognized and appreciated. Some of these figures are self-evident and some are surprising. Because they are still so actively productive, it may not be obvious how influential has been the writing of Roberson, Mackey, Hunt, Patton, and Mullen. Unfortunately, there are still countless African American writers fading from sight such as the brilliantly original poet and playwright Oliver Pitcher (born in 1923), author of the poetry collection *Dust of Silence*. Glenn Towery has been devoted to calling attention to Pitcher's theatre and performed his play "The One" in 1999 at the Inglewood Playhouse in Los Angeles.[11] Pitcher is one of many poets with a body of writing that desperately needs to be fully uncovered, researched, preserved, and shared. His work, which appears in Bontemps's *American Negro Poetry* and Adoff's *The Poetry of Black America*, used to be readily accessible, but has largely slipped from sight. Further examples of Pitcher's poems are found in Nielsen and Ramey's *Every Goodbye Ain't Gone*. His extravagant melding of surrealism,

---

[11] Oliver Pitcher, *The One (A Play)* (New York: Plume, 1986). There is a recording of the performance (May 30, 1999) on YouTube: www.youtube.com/watch?v=XMdxTB6t4vQ (last accessed 28 August 2018).

absurdism, word play, puns, and witty philosophical assessment evoke aspects of the poetics of Atkins, Will Alexander, and Fenton Johnson; Pitcher could and should readily be incorporated into the innovative legacy of this tradition. As an example, here is his poem "Raison d'Etre" posted on the African American Registry database. Note the glorious word play and punning in such usages as "unwareness," the kenning-like "sun-roses," the cognitive blend of "cynical comma over the madness," and brilliant packages of sonic-semantic effects combining the cohering property of internal rhyme with the disjuncture of oxymoron as in "rusty luster:"

Over the eye behind the moon's cloud
over you whose touch to a Stradavari heart shames
the chorale of angels over Mr. Eros
who tramples the sun-roses
and sits amid willow trees to weep
over the wood over the vibrant reds, blacks, luminous golds of decay
over the strength of silence and advantages of
unwareness
over the geyser in the toilet bowl
over the cynical comma over the madness
itself the occupational hazards of artist
over the catcher caught in his catcher's mitt
over oil and opal, blood and bone of
the earth
over the iron touch behind pink gloves
over retired civilizations sunken below levels
shimmering in rusty luster
over myself I wave the flag raison d'etre ...[12]

In spite of the positive new attention being paid to this field, there remain countless opportunities for preservation, research, and rediscovery of powerful and diverse voices in African American poetry, which marks both a tragedy and an invitation. From 1945 to 1975, a tradition of diverse and difficult African American poetry was formulated, though it may have been marginalized from general collections of contemporaneous verse, as well as some black poetry collections. We see the continuities of this tradition exemplified in every period, both earlier and later. The African American poetry tradition always has had more

---

[12] Oliver Pitcher, "Raison d'Etre," https://aaregistry.org/poem/raison-detre-by-oliver-pitcher/ (last accessed August 20, 2018).

continuity than has been commonly recognized. It has been and remains integrally innovative, which makes its progressions part of its continuity. Each period is linked to the past as it moves into the future, and we see it no less in the postmodern period than in the past in terms of theory and poetic production. An example of this direct connection is explicitly articulated in the essay collection *Afro-Pessimism: An Introduction* (2017) whose distinguished roster of contributors includes Saidiya Hartman and Hortense J. Spillers. The introduction of this book states that "Afro-Pessimism, in many ways, picks up the critiques started by black revolutionaries in the 1960s and 70s, elaborating their shortcomings and addressing their failures" (The Editors). From 1975 to the present, building on powerful precursors, this tradition has solidified and is moving forward.

Kearney, a younger generation inter-media experimentalist, also shows the continuing presence of the oral and folk traditions in contemporary avant-garde African American poetry. Kearney frequently incorporates folk materials in his writing, often positioning them, both rhetorically and spatially, as alternately familiar and precarious. An example of how Kearney has actively repurposed originary materials is his use of Stackolee as a composite of visual, conceptual, auditory, and culturally mnemonic emblems in his collection *Buck Studies* (2016). Similarly to Atkins, he problematizes water as a fraught symbol in African American history in his Floodsong series – which conflates Hurricane Katrina with black history – from *The Black Automaton*, a National Poetry Series Selection (2009). When he performs "Floodsong 2: Water Moccasin's Spiritual," Kearney sings the poem rather than reciting the words, and uses the traditional tune of the slave song on which he is signifying:

> wade in the water
> wade in the water, children
> wade in the water
> god's gon' trouble the water
> wade in the water
> wade in the water, children
> wade in the water
> god's gon' trouble the water
> wade in
> wade in
> wade in
>   trouble
>   in the water
>   the water, children

in the water
    the water children
in the water
     trouble the water
god's
         children
in the water
god's
         children
  gon'
in the water
  trouble
in the water
  trouble
in the water
  trouble
in the water
    water
    water
    water
god's gon

Water is essential to life, yet it is also the medium of the Middle Passage, in which Africans were transported to enslavement. Drowning at sea while in transit – due to illness, murder, or suicide – was the fate of untold numbers of captives. The slave song that forms the allusive frame of Kearney's poem is called "Wade in the Water" or "God's a-Gwineter Trouble the Water." It is a powerful anthem of retributive justice.

The reference[13] to the snake in the title foreshadows the presence of evil in this Edenic scene. Kearney's poem opens with a virtually classic evocation of the slave song's lyrics: "wade in the water / wade in the water, children / wade in the water / god's gon' trouble the water." The original slave song expresses abiding faith in God and in the mercy of God's parental power. In the Book of Exodus in the Old Testament, God drowned the Pharoah's army, and delivered the enslaved Hebrews to safety in the Promised Land. In a vision of identification with another enslaved population, the slave song expresses a belief in God's power to comparably intervene once again, and free the enslaved African Americans. After eight lines that echo the original slave song, Kearney's poem cannot manage to continue in that vein of optimism. The salvaged

---

[13] Douglas Kearney, *The Black Automaton* (Albany, NY: Fence Books, 2009), p. 60.

text begins to break down and stutter: "wade in / wade in / wade in," which sounds like a robotic instruction or a broken recording stuck on an ominous note in the message. Is this an invitation or a warning about wading in? Where is God? What has become of the central metaphor of God as the protective parent of children? The mid-section of this one-stanza poem breaks down even more as the original components keep going awry: "trouble / in the water" devolves further still into the pronouncement at the end: "god's gon'," with a lower case "g" for the deity, as Kearney continues to sing the slave song with its familiar tune in what has now become an ironic performance of signification on the original poem. "Gon'" in the slave song means "going to," which implies imminent or intended action. Here it transforms phonetically into the homonym "gone," meaning the absence of potential to perform a meaningful action, which is realized in Kearney's bleaker retelling for postmodern times. The presence of biblical and Judeo-Christian imagery continues to be repurposed by Kearney in *Buck Studies*. Through revisions of tradition by mechanized and emotional cross-mappings, he creates technologically sophisticated collage, bricolage, and linguistic portraiture.

Gregory Pardlo is an example of a more formally traditional poet than the more avant-garde Kearney. Yet Pardlo also uses slave songs very productively in his writing. These quite different poets' shared use of slave songs illustrates the point that it is a traditional feature of African American poetry to productively utilize foundational resources to generate new effects in varied styles of writing. Some of the most interesting and exciting verbal and cognitive effects in the poetry of Pardlo, who won the 2015 Pulitzer Prize, result from creative blends, where two or more disparate input spaces are brought into startling conjunction to reveal new meanings not found in either of the domains being compared. Important revelations about Pardlo's poetry and poetics – as well as African diasporic representations of space, time, and experience – may be discerned from these innovative metaphorical juxtapositions. Pardlo's poetry uses an exceptional array of forms and styles for varied purposes, including linear and sentimental personal narratives, extended philosophical meditations, ekphrastic poems and still lives, evocations of music, literary portraits and tributes, and folk materials and imagery, including slave songs and slave narratives. "What is the self?" is one of the central questions of Pardlo's poetics. He frequently uses conceptual integration, which is performed by creative blends, to both raise and try to answer that question. We find plentiful examples of polysemy, double-scope blending, counterfactuals, fictive motion, and compression, among other operations, which enable us to move from intimate to global realms, embodiment to abstraction, and within and outside time and space.

Pardlo's talent for producing creative blends often employs polysemy – playing with words that have multiple, and often quite different, meanings – as one of his most effective techniques to generate unstable planes of identity, location, and chronology. Creative blends are plentiful in Pardlo's two collections, where his assymetrical and disjunctive metaphors often use polysemy – itself a type of lexical trickster figure – which can require significant interpretive work to derive sense. An example of one of his creative blends drawing on polysemy is "conjuring away his essence like some bootleg golem," from the poem "Landscape with Intervention," the opening poem of his first collection, *Totem* (2007). We start with an African survival of ghostly spirits in the phrase "conjuring away his essence," which evokes the conjure man or witch doctor from macumba, Santeria, or voudun, who practices medicine using mystical spiritual rituals. It suggests the stealing away of one's identity (the essence of who one is) as well as causing the disappearance of potency and the power to inseminate or propagate, with "essence" in the sense of semen. The space of this African diasporic belief system is brought into conjunction with the time and place of Prohibition in early twentieth century American culture, when alcohol was made illegal and the term "bootleg" was popularized. The word "bootleg" plays on the polysemous character of the word "spirits" in its meaning as banned alcoholic beverages. A third space is brought into the creative blend through the incorporation of ancient Jewish mysticism. "Golem" is a mystical anthropomorphic figure, first named in the biblical Psalms, who is mythically created from an inanimate substance. So, to selectively cross-map the relevant features of the spaces, times, and inputs of the domains brought into conjunction, we can understand the blended space to refer to human fears of unsanctioned, otherworldly, forbidden, and potent forces operating in the interstices between embodied anthropomorphism and inanimate substances – the thin line between clay and flesh – and the terror of being deprived of the human spirit through unholy means. Exemplifying Du Boisian double consciousness and the play with voices and levels of meaning that are inherent throughout this tradition, Pardlo said in an interview, "I'm trying to lampoon academic language, but my little secret is that I actually speak that."[14]

---

[14] Alexandra Alter, "Gregory Pardlo, Pulitzer Prize Winner for Poetry, on his Sudden Fame," April 22, 2015, *New York Times*, www.nytimes.com/2015/04/23/books/gregory-pardlo-pulitzer-winner-for-poetry-on-his-sudden-fame.html (last accessed August 20, 2018).

In Pardlo's verse, polysemy enables us to move seamlessly between what we perceive as literal and figurative realms, which confirms the claims of Turner that there are not different cognitive processes involved in accessing these realms, though we may – through what he calls folk processes – perceive them as fundamentally different. According to Turner and Fauconnier, polysemy is "an essential manifestation of the flexibility, adaptability, and richness in meaning potential that lie at the very heart of what a language is and what it is for." Turner and Fauconnier claim that "most polysemy is invisible," which makes its recognition a subtle and effective tool to understand the cognitive complexity of Pardlo's poetry.[15]

By foregrounding this level of creativity which is omnipresent in language use, Pardlo ignites processes that allow us to alternately connect and disconnect time and space, stasis and movement, meaning and mystery, individualism and universalism, and other apparent dichotomies that are constantly melded and separated in the processes of cognition. Through this technique, readers are constantly kept off balance, stimulated, and challenged to produce a series of new meanings and insights which accrue special weight in an African diasporic context. The opening poems of both of his collections offer vivid examples of Pardlo's use of polysemy to initiate and destabilize the decoding process. For two extended examples of how this process takes place, we can turn to the word "role" in "Landscape with Intervention" (*Totem*) and the word "born" in "Written by Himself" (*Digest*).

"Role" is a spectacularly polysemous word with especially important associations in the fields of sociology and theatre. In sociological terms, it means one's purpose or function – the expected set of behaviors for a person's identity or status, the behavioral patterns that locate an individual in society, one's set of customary duties, and relational and familial positions. In theatrical terms, it denotes the distinction between an actor and the part or character being played. These definitions gain additional layers of meaning in a racialized context, where "to perform blackness" has both sociological and theatrical implications and associations. These understandings include the racial masking that accompanies double consciousness,

15 Gilles Fauconnier and Mark Turner, "Polysemy and Conceptual Blending," in Brigitte Nerlich, Vimala Herman, Zazie Todd, and David Clarke, eds., *Polysemy: Flexible Patterns of Meaning in Mind and Language* (Berlin and New York: Mouton de Gruyter, 2003), pp. 79–94: www.cogsci .ucsd.edu/~coulson/203/turner (last accessed August 28, 2018).

and the wearing or adopting of a mask to either foreground or hide blackness. Consider this excerpt from "Landscape with Intervention" in Pardlo's
strategic employment of multiple senses of the word "role" (my emphasis
in the bolded phrases):

> [...] Accordingly, among actors, fathers
> encouraged the mingling of identity and act by raising
>   their sons in **dedication**
>
> **to a single role** – the way craftsmen took their trade to be
> their name: carpenter, tailor, the ubiquitous
> smith – and stack eternal odds in their favor: that the Calvinist
> god's estimation of the man match the quality of that man's
> performance **in the role he'd been given**. Such piety doubling
> as social currency, suggesting an audience of more than
>   just One. The American
>
> actor, Thomas Dartmouth Rice, **developed a role** in the late
> 1820's which he dedicated his life to performing. He covered
> his white face in burnt cork and dubbed himself "Jim Crow".
> His influence was epidemic.[16]

The first use of "role" in this excerpt – "dedication to a single role" – is
sociological and abstract. It refers to an Aristotelian melding of action
and identity by positing the capability to choose and perform a specific
role in life to which one is dedicated. This process is genealogical and
cyclical, as each generation of fathers encourages the mingling of self and
performance (identity and act) by "raising their sons in dedication" to a
single role. In a Calvinist sense, the successful performance of this single
role defines the quality of a man.

The second use of "role" – "man's performance in the role he'd been
given" – is both sociological and theatrical. It suggests the passive receipt
of an assigned task or identity, and the virtue of fulfilling that role well,
in sociological and/or theatrical terms. In an African American context,
where this condition could readily define the expectations for a slave, the
double-voicing of this usage of "role" has ominous undertones, leading to
the third appearance of "role" in this excerpt.

The third use of "role" – "developed a role" – refers to a particular theatrical part, which in this case, encourages practices of institutional racism

---

[16] Gregory Pardlo, *Totem* (Philadelphia: The American Poetry Review, 2007), p. 3.

by promulgating the minstrelsy, burlesque of black physical appearance, racist stereotyping, and perpetuation of discrimination that were performed in the context of "Jim Crow." In the blended space, we therefore must cross-map racial, sociological, and theatrical roles to derive meaning. Filial obedience and respect are displayed by choosing a role in life to fulfill successfully. This use of "role" is juxtaposed with the historical conditions of racial discrimination that thrust generations of African Americans into performing the role of the slave, which denied their right to choose their own role in life.

We find a similar process in the opening poem of Pardlo's Pulitzer Prize winning second collection, *Digest*, which offers us at least fourteen different uses and senses of the phrase "I was born," and polysemous meanings of the word "born." In this single-stanza poem, the title alludes to the common subtitle for slave narratives, "Written by Himself." The insistently and acceptingly repeated phrase "I was born" creates a frame structure in opening and closing the poem, and weaves throughout the poem's body as a central motif that is both flexible and fixed, enjambed and end-stop. It evokes a conventional trope for the genre of autobiography, with special resonance for African American writing where the ability to tell one's own story was a hard-won right. "I was born" also evokes the revolutionary statement of Albery A. Whitman, "I was born in bondage – I was never a slave," and the opening of Sam Cooke's magnificent poem in song, "A Change is Gonna Come."

WRITTEN BY HIMSELF

I was born in minutes in a roadside kitchen a skillet
whispering my name. I was born to rainwater and lye;
I was born across the river where I
was borrowed with clothespins, a harrow tooth,
broadsides sewn in my shoes. I returned, though
it please you, through no fault of my own,
pockets filled with coffee grounds and eggshells.
I was born still and superstitious; I bore an unexpected burden.
I gave birth, I gave blessing, I gave rise to suspicion.
I was born abandoned outdoors in the heat-shaped air,
air drifting like spirits and old windows.
I was born a fraction and a cipher and a ledger entry;
I was an index of first lines when I was born.
I was born waist-deep stubborn in the water crying
          ain't I a woman and a brother I was born

to this hall of mirrors, this horror story I was
born with a prologue of references, pursued
by mosquitoes and thieves, I was born passing
off the problem of the twentieth century: I was born.
I read minds before I could read fishes and loaves;
I walked a piece of the way alone before I was born.[17]

As a few examples of Pardlo's skillful manipulation of the multiple senses of the word "born" and the phrase "I was born," the poem opens with "I was born in minutes" (line 1), which suggests the physical act of the speaker's own birth. In "I was born to rainwater and lye" (line 2), "born" refers to the life that awaited the speaker, where even the bathing practices were rough. "I was born across the river" (line 3) describes the geographical location of the speaker's place of birth. "I was born a fraction and a cipher and a ledger entry" (line 12) describes the speaker's birth as a slave in antebellum America by referring to the accounting documentation of slaves by their "owners." Line 15, indented to call particular attention to itself, juxtaposes a shift of gender in the speaker by alluding to Sojourner Truth ("ain't I a woman") and to the Black Power revolutionaries of the 1960s ("a brother I was born"). In that sense, we take this poem that is in some ways highly restricted to the perspective and voice of a first person lyric subject and universalize it to include (Walt) Whitmanian multitudes. The phrase "I was born" powerfully bookends lines throughout the poem, serving as the initiatory and concluding moments, the alpha and the omega. I was born: that is all. "I was born" appears both in enjambed and end-stop lines, sometimes in direct conjunction, to alternate dead-ends with poetic puns ("I was born passing / off the problem of the twentieth century: I was born"). "Born" transmutes into a series of alliterative terms to perpetuate the sense of interrelated cycles and inescapable systems: "borrowed," "birth," "broadsides," "blessing," and "burden." The examples of play with the concept of what it means to be born and to write one's story by oneself proliferate from line to line. As the poem develops, we make sense of the polysemy by recognizing that the speaker was born to a family legacy, a history of African American struggle, a place in American history, and an identity as a self-defining and self-articulating individual through the mechanism of language.

---

[17] Gregory Pardlo, *Digest* (New York: Four Way Books, 2015), p. 3.

Through his use of polysemy, what is Pardlo blending? He employs the creativity that is integral to language to produce poems that examine multiple possibilities, foreclose few, and open what is most painfully revealed. In the context of African diasporic and African American experience, geography, identity, and history, Pardlo's use of the words "role" and "born" provide resonant correspondence by evoking the phrases "the role one was born for" and "born for a role." Each phrase carries with it a burden and an opportunity; we are graced by the poetry of Pardlo to be faced with the terror and beauty of both.

The next generations of progressive and visionary African American poets also include Mendi Lewis Obadike, Dawn Lundy Martin, Will Alexander, Rankine, Ron Allen, Hunt, Keene, Kearney, Morris, Patton, Mullen, Giscombe, and Mackey. As white experimental writing has been mined for a century – since the time of T. S. Eliot, Hart Crane, Ezra Pound, and William Carlos Williams – or even a century earlier with the innovations of Emily Dickinson and Walt Whitman – it is clear that history has not evaluated poetry solely on the basis of style and quality, but also on the basis of who wrote it. African American poets associated with practices of stylistic innovation often show great inventiveness by drawing on a variety of formally innovative trends associated with the historical avant-gardes and blending them with African American references and racial signifiers. Their work contains numerous and varied references to writers, artists, musicians, activists, and political figures and events, both within and outside African American culture and traditions. They purposely incorporate and slyly signify on the dual levels of meaning-making encompassed in Du Bois's concept of double consciousness. Much of this writing explores the uses of unconventional forms: prose poems, collages, fragments, inter-media forms, and mixed forms. The poetry also displays other features that are normative in avant-garde practices from modernism to postmodernism: the absence, questioning, or decentering of unitary speaking subjects or identities; breakdowns of conventional genre boundaries and expectations; play with absurd or ironic juxtapositions taken from widely contrasting realms of information and language uses; contrasting discourses coming from inside and beyond African American reference points; intermingling of allusions, imagery and dictions from American and international high and low art and culture, and diverse fields of knowledge; use of the double entendre, punning, wit, humor, signifying, and parody; compositional styles reflecting cross-genre and cross-media artistic practices; and reliance on engaged readers to actively construct meaning from these challenging poems.

Studies of avant-garde practice, which typically concentrate on poets associated with the formal avant-garde movements at the turn of the twentieth century and the later movements seen to be influenced by them, have generally been viewed as white. Criticism has tended to exclude black poets, and to most often attribute experimentalism or independence to strangeness or incompetency, as we saw with slave songs. Here we have an area where the diasporic position coheres. A series of poets follow their independent paths throughout this genre where the original absence of an inherited tradition coupled with an insistence on forging one's own mode of expression have coincided to produce poetries of difference. That may consist of reacting against a mainstream that does not represent – or is even hostile to – one's race, or simply choosing not to define one's own artistic practice in the terms of the mainstream. Slave songs were both: the lyrics often attacked the mainstream, as we see in avant-gardes, and yet the form of presentation was likely to have been motivated primarily by adopting practices that were their own creations and inheritances. We see the presence of slave songs, references to themes and figures of special importance to a black population, and compositional features that inhere throughout the tradition in poets with radically different styles yet who could all be categorized as avant-garde or at least independent in vision and practice. That circumstance explains the tenacity of certain black literary inheritances where we can see a lineage from slave songs straight through the tradition to the present. What are the complications of mapping race over aesthetic practices conventionally associated with whiteness? Is it "avant-garde" for "minority" poets to produce poetry that is "different" or contrary to expectations for them based on cultural preconceptions and perceived inheritances?

Manifestations of avant-garde practice generally are regarded as formal and sociopolitical, and typically involve groups of artists with shared principles who often work in more than one medium or genre; synthesize disparate influences and techniques including "high" and "popular" culture; deliberately attempt to undermine or contradict formal markers of rigidified artistic structures and ruling ideologies; consider art to be a political and aesthetic instrument with direct agency; push art and society forward into new and unfamiliar terrain; employ technical features designed to unsettle and interrogate unitary voices of authority and totalizing narratives; explore formal modes such as open field, performative, and alternative poetics based on extra-semantic properties such as visuality and sound; question the nature and possibility of a non-problematical speaking subject; animate multiple voices in preference to a centralized stable narrator or persona; transcend boundaries of nationalism, draw on international influences, and maintain dialogue with artists in other nations and cultures; and frequently use collage, bricolage, fragmentation, and pastiche in order to create palimpsestic or dialogic texts revealing multiple frames of reference and mechanisms of interpretation.

By black diaspora, I refer to a population whose ancestral origins are in Africa, and which has dispersed throughout the globe by choice, force, or necessity through race slavery, economic or political circumstances, or other reasons relating to opportunity or survival. As we have seen in each chapter, poets of the black diaspora, including African American, often incorporate a variety of African survivals in their work. These features, selectively applied, may include directly addressing ancestors and spirit guides; foregrounding elements of orality and performance in written discourse with equal or greater stress than textuality; depicting the mind as able to travel freely from the body by supplanting the Western philosophical framework of Cartesian dualism with African concepts of body and mind; conveying a permeable boundary between the sacred and secular; operating within a sense of time that regards the future as a direct and immediate extension of the present with the past and present as dominant modes of consciousness; describing human relationships and connections as possible to maintain in states of absence including after death; building historical narratives to share and preserve communal memory; and stressing the integral importance of community for all individuals. Secondary characteristics that specifically reflect migratory experiences are such themes as the location and meaning of "home," racial discrimination, the effects of displacement, the ramifications of alienation, and a reflexive consciousness of the characteristics and functions of diasporic communities.

Paul Gilroy has described the aesthetics of black diasporic writing as something new, and composed in forms reflecting the history, aesthetics, ontology, and philosophy of a migratory population:

> The fractal patterns of cultural and political exchange and transformation that we try and specify through manifestly inadequate theoretical terms like creolization and syncretism indicate how both ethnicities and political cultures have been made anew in ways that are significant not simply for the peoples of the Caribbean but for Europe, for Africa, especially Liberia and Sierra Leone, and of course, for black America.[18]

---

[18] Paul Gilroy, *The Black Atlantic: Modernity and Double Consciousness* (Cambridge, MA: Harvard University Press, 1993), p. 15.

Based on Gilroy's assessment, fragmentary and synthetic practices should be expected and embraced as "typical" of black diasporic writing to question unitary speaking subjects and to provide voices from multiple input spaces to undermine hegemony, restriction, unanimity, and repression. But throughout the history of African American poetry, and in fact African diasporic writing in general, critics – if not practitioners – have relegated this genre to heavily circumscribed aesthetic, cultural, and critical spaces, which generally have been closely connected to preconceptions about the identities of their creators. Little enthusiasm has been afforded to formally innovative African diasporic literature, resulting in a canon of "esteemed" African American poetry that has tended to be relatively conservative.

This history of neglect includes the founding texts of the African American literary tradition that have been addressed as touchstones throughout this book: the highly original slave songs; the remarkable political satires and parodies of nineteenth century poets such as Whitfield and Simpson; and the intentional and often misunderstood double voicing of the first African American professional "Man of Letters," Dunbar. African American modernists like Tolson, Hayden, Lorde, and Fenton Johnson continue this tradition of innovation, which appeared as traces throughout the mid- to late twentieth century with avant-garde movements such as Free Lance, Dasein, and Umbra. It continues today with such innovators as singleton, Morris, Kearney, Patton, Mullen, Mackey, Keene, Tyrone Williams, Hunt, and many others.

We find the innovative practices and critical appreciations in essential records like *tripwire 5: Expanding the Repertoire: Continuity and Change*, co-edited by singleton and Renee Gladman. We find it in the exceptional number of African American poets' voices represented in *Best American Experimental Writing*, edited by Kearney. In that volume, even under the rubric of "experimental," we still find an astonishing range of styles and forms represented. It starts with Kearney's own collage as his editorial introduction, and progresses through the surreal stream-of-consciousness meditation of Ronaldo V. Wilson. Among the varied compilations of voices and ideas is the Fall 2015 Double Issue of *Obsidian* featuring verbal and visual experimentation. Kore Press, which has featured writing by women since 1993, has published a poetry collection titled *Letters to the Future: Black WOMEN/ Radical WRITING* (2018). This superb intergenerational anthology of black women writers includes a diverse array of artistic figures including Jayne Cortez, Wanda Coleman, LaTasha N. Nevada Diggs, Duriel E. Harris, Dawn Lundy Martin, Mullen, singleton, Shockley, Adrienne Kennedy, Adrian Piper, Harmony Holiday, Morris, Rankine, Deborah Richards, Kara Walker, Tonya Foster, Patton, Akilah Oliver, Tisa Bryant, M. NourbeSe Philip, Hunt, Clifton, and Sanchez. The Introduction by Hunt explains that the writers included may be stylistically diverse, but all are "committed to a radical practice of literary work" with an orientation towards envisioning possible black futures, where "The future is a slippery project."[19] While the poets are all black women, the construction of race is not conceived of as either stable or dogmatic, and presumably, neither is the performance of sex or gender.

The critical literature has widely regarded "diasporic" and "avant-garde" writings as unrelated to each other: there are extensive studies of the innovators of modernism and postmodernism, but surprisingly little attention has been paid to the long legacy of black experimentalism. Literary criticism typically has regarded "black" and "avant-garde" writing as unrelated, even antithetical, bodies. Formally exploratory poetics is considered "normative" for white avant-garde poets who are interested in decentering and re-conceptualizing identity, examining literary connections across metaphysical boundaries with others who have engaged in experimental practices, transcending the restrictions of genre and form, and interrogating language as a system of discourse. Why have African American poets working in similar terrain not had comparable attention and impact? The goal of destabilizing or interrogating boundaries, and the power that derives from a position of providing critique to the cultural center, is mentioned by many African American poets whose writing is associated with stylistic innovation. Until the end of the twentieth century, too few of these figures received deserved attention in their lifetimes and achieved lasting posterity by entering the canon. Without that seal of approval, their writing may inevitably enter the margins of the genre and be prevented from influencing its character, values, and direction.

Kwesi Owusu refers to a group as "avant-garde" if it has been marginalized by the dominant culture and is driven to remake the center by entering it. Such avant-gardists, according to Owusu, reject the occupation of a fixed and externally assigned role on the social and historical periphery. Instead, they insist on inserting their previously disregarded voices and perspectives into the narrative of the mainstream as the necessary and recuperated missing and essential elements. Artists of the

[19] Erica Hunt and Dawn Lundy Martin, eds. *Letters to the Future: Black WOMEN/Radical WRITING* (Tucson: Kore Press, 2018), p. 12.

historical avant-gardes of modernism and their intentional contemporary successors generally have displayed an ethos of group oppositionality and rejection of the principles of the aesthetic and cultural status quo. They typically have adopted postures of alienation by choice or conscience and pointed out fundamental flaws in the values and practices of the center while embracing positions on the margins. Avant-gardes – when separated from the concept of diaspora – represent resistance, refusal, and redirection when the center is seen to have gone awry. They have served as the gadfly whose strength and point of view come from a stance of critical distance on the periphery.

Owusu builds on this definition by proposing a diasporic avant-garde whose "newness" derives from demanding representation in a narrative that is otherwise incomplete, misrepresented, or distorted. This "new" diasporic avant-garde is characterized by its determination to reject a former position of marginality to take pride of place in the center of society, politics, culture, and communication. Consistent with the stylistic markers of the historical avant-garde, "experimentalism" is identified by Owusu as the formal mechanism used to achieve "a new revisionism" by artistic means. As Abiola Irele points out, orality is the *traditional* feature that distinguishes African literature as "different" and significant in relation to conventional Western textuality: "The centrality of orality to the African imagination, the original dimension it confers on African forms of expression, has provided the principal means for demonstrating not merely the distinctive character of African literary genres but also their comparative interest."[20]

For the poets of the historical avant-garde, orality and performance signify a transgressive attack on their own cultural values and traditions rather than a reinforcement of them. These techniques represent aesthetic and political strategies that are anti-textual, anti-elitist, anti-linear, anti-hierarchical, anti-static, and anti-semantic. By privileging sound, spontaneity, and audience participation, orality and performance are effective in leading society forward in a new direction by aggressively attacking unexamined or unchallenged continuities of meaning, control, order, hierarchy, and preservation. For African diasporic poets, African-inspired orality also represents a way to communicate change, forge individual and community identity, disrupt the dominant narrative, work across strict boundaries of medium and genre, represent a minority

[20] Irele, *The African Imagination*, p. xv.

viewpoint, overcome domination and isolation through group tactics, draw on syncretic practices and influences that cross national boundaries, explode unitary concepts of literary transmission as solely text-based, expand notions of authority as to who may serve as the speaking subject in an esteemed work of art, and infuse a work of art with a sociopolitical agenda. Here we have an example of an area of practice where the diasporic heritage of African American poets has historically provided the inspiration for them to create styles and forms that enabled them to adjust to their forcibly adopted homeland of America, at the origins of this genre, and should allow them to be recognized as innovators.

Gilroy's description shows how some major manifestations of the historical avant-garde are relevant to black diasporic writers, including the use of fragmentation and collage, a cross-genre or cross-media aesthetic practice, and the production and reception of art that transcends boundaries of nationalism. Similarly, Bill Ashcroft, Gareth Griffiths, and Helen Tiffin write that individuals who have migrated from their places of origin, either by choice or by force, are likely to bear a residual resistance to totalizing narratives of wholeness and unanimity: "The development of diasporic cultures necessarily questions essentialist models, interrogating the ideology of a unified, 'natural' cultural norm, one that underpins the centre/margin model of colonialist discourse."[21] Following Gilroy and Ashcroft et al., it would be reasonable to expect the fragmentary and synthetic practices that characterize the historical avant-garde to appear in black diasporic writing. Readers should expect to find numerous examples of poems in experimental forms that question unitary speaking subjects deriving from multiple inputs intended to undermine hegemony, restriction, unanimity, and repression. The solid theoretical foundations established by scholars such as Gilroy, Ashcroft, Owusu, Stuart Hall, and others for the term "avant-garde" should lead readers to expect that there is a substantial body of past and contemporary avant-garde African American poetry.

This imagined formally inventive poetry would be expected to be neither traditionally American nor a naïve vision of African return. It would be an imaginative mélange of deconstructed, composite, and alternative ways of conceiving and conveying a range of identities and experiences. Readers should expect the contemporary condition of African American poetry to be well represented by recursive iterations composed

[21] Bill Ashcroft, Gareth Griffiths, and Helen Tiffin, *Key Concepts in Post-Colonial Studies* (London: Routledge, 1998), p. 70.

of broken fragments juxtaposed to accrue and reveal new meaning. Irele has coined[22] a term to describe the generative force behind such potential new creations – "the African Imagination." This force should be expected to be the source of dynamic new poetry conveying diverse but recognizable continuities, including emphasis on the oral tradition. For Owusu, the designation "avant-garde" means a re-inscription of national identity by absorbing black artists into its imaginary. With this new position being described as forward-looking, and less burdened by past exclusions, the question is whether black poets have been wrongly expected to reduce their diasporic and racial identification to achieve increased national status and the designation of "avant-garde." These "avant-gardists" insisted on assuming a social role of their own choosing and by their own means, on the basis that their voices and experiences were and are essential to presenting a whole national narrative.

Dove raised the concern: "We all understand the dangers of being put into one little box."[23] From its origins, African American poetry has been more diverse and innovative than is commonly realized. In the past and present, a persistent bind for this genre has been the criterion of "authenticity," which has relegated it to narrow stereotypes of how African American poetry should look, sound, and operate. The period from the end of World War II to the contemporary period has been an explosive time of poetic experimentation that extends the innovations of modernism into the twenty-first century. This expanding body of new poetic styles equally builds on the genre's origins. Rather than signaling a departure or new direction, such exploratory and diverse practices are based on long-present trends, goals, and characteristics. These developments are an invitation to re-examine the canon, to speculate on why such dynamic, even difficult, writing has been systematically excluded, and to redraw the picture for a more accurate and richer view of the full range of African American poetry. Exposure to overlooked, under-appreciated, and forgotten voices produces a radically transformed perspective of the scope of recent African American poetry. When examined through the prospect of innovation, a hidden canon is revealed, putting to rest those stereotypes that African American poetry is autobiographical, vernacular, unitary, and exclusively about the theme of oppression. Its legacy of bold challenge to the status quo is a defining trait. This body of writing, whose

---

[22] See Irele, *The African Imagination*, pp. xiv–xv.
[23] Rita Dove, Joanne V. Gabbin, Producer, 2015. Furious Flower III DVD. Episode 1, California Newsreel.

founding texts are among the most original ever produced in America, proves that tradition and innovation are not mutually exclusive.

In the second decade of the twenty-first century, especially, very productive attention has been paid to African American stylistic experimentalists. Examples of some of the superb scholarship – including several key sources produced by poet-critics – are *A Transnational Poetics* by Jahan Ramazani, *Renegade Poetics: Black Aesthetics and Formal Innovation in African American Poetry* by Shockley, *Discrepant Engagement: Dissonance, Cross-Culturality, and Experimental Writing* and *The Paracritical Hinge: Essays, Talks, Notes, Interviews* by Mackey, *In the Break: The Aesthetics of the Black Radical Tradition* by Moten, *The Cracks Between What We Are and What We Are Supposed to Be* by Mullen, *Integral Music* by Nielsen, *The Practice of Diaspora* by Brent Hayes Edwards, and *Freedom Time: The Poetics and Politics of Black Experimental Writing* by Anthony Reed. Elizabeth Alexander's 2011 Hopwood Lecture "New Ideas About Black Experimental Poetry"[24] operates on a perspective of experimentalism as doing something new and unexpected for who you are or within your perceived tradition. In this sense, she argues for the experimentalism of Hayden's documentary interleaving in "Middle Passage" and Brooks's use of the sonnet form.

Now that there has been a small surge of interest in some of what Giscombe prefers to call "difficult" poetry that has been pushed out and ignored, we may ask this question: if this diverse body of poetry were more available and better known, how might it change the African American poetry canon – and even the canons of American and Anglophone poetry? Coupled with its stylistic diversity, many African American poems address a body of recurring themes, figures, events, and experiences that still provide cohesion as a canon. This lineage of direct references and allusions reveals an African American literary identity that is inextricably connected to the imaginary of America – including themes, people, and events that have had to fight to rise to the surface of mainstream national consciousness, beginning with slavery and progressing through the fight for human rights. Poetic tributes to African American literary precursors and role models offer an alternative pantheon to those usually revered in the Anglo-American tradition. This poetry provides a line of sight on to the figures and events that have had lasting impact on African Americans. This implied narrative may be part

[24] Available at https://lsa.umich.edu/content/dam/hopwood-assets/documents/Hopwood%20 Lectures/HopwoodLecture-2011_AlexanderE.pdf (last accessed August 26, 2018).

of American and world history, but its function and impact have special weight and meaning in the context of the African American experience.

Some of the most formally progressive and innovative late modern and contemporary African American poetry serves as a repository to name, honor, perpetuate, and preserve the major figures, influences, events, products, and experiences of African American history. The Middle Passage is the central theme of Clifton's "Slaveship," Hayden's "Middle Passage," and Kearney's "Swimchant for Nigger Mer-folk (An Aquaboogie Set in Lapis)." Literary figures are the focus of poems such as "Search for Robert Hayden" by Kyle Dargan, "The Death of William Edward Burghardt Du Bois by African Moonlight and Forgotten Shores" by Rivers, "Paul Laurence Dunbar" and "A Letter from Phillis Wheatley" by Hayden, "Booker T and W. E. B." by Randall, "For Etheridge Knight" by Lamont Steptoe, "Paul Laurence Dunbar in the Tenderloin" by Reed, and "The Rhetoric of Langston Hughes" by Danner. Countless poems are dedicated to figures and movements referring to the African American musical tradition. Examples of such poems include "Photo of Miles Davis at Lennies-on-the-Turnpike, 1968" by Cornelius Eady, "On Listening to the Spirituals" by Lance Jeffers, "I've Got a Home in that Rock" by Patterson, "Cross Over the River" by Sam Cornish, "To Satch (Louis Armstrong)" by Samuel Allen, "'Homage to Paul Robeson" by Hayden, "Paul Robeson" by Brooks, "Yardbird's Skull (For Charlie Parker)" by Dodson, "John Coltrane" by Spellman, *leadbelly* by Tyehimba Jess, and "Here is Where Coltrane Is," "Last Affair: Bessie's Blues Song," "Dear John, Dear Coltrane," and "A Dance for Ma Rainey" by Al Young, and "To James Brown" and "Don't Explain: A Ballad Played by Dexter Gordon" by Michael S. Harper.

To trace the history of musically influenced poetry, two highly recommended resources by musicologists are *The Power of Black Music: Interpreting Its History from Africa to the United States* by Samuel A. Floyd, Jr. (1995) and *The Music of Black Americans* by Eileen Southern, 3rd edition (1997). For an exhaustive listing of the explosion in scholarship on jazz poetry, an invaluable resource is "A Bibliography of Jazz Poetry Criticism" by Brent Hayes Edwards and John F. Szwed.[25] In literary studies, *The Muse is Music: Jazz Poetry from the Harlem Renaissance to Spoken Word* by Meta DuEwa Jones is an outstanding text. This title in The New Black Studies Series received an Honorable Mention for

[25] Brent Hayes Edwards and John F. Szwed, "A Bibliography of Jazz Poetry Criticism," *Callaloo* 25, No. 1 (Winter 2002), pp. 338–46.

the Modern Language Association's W. S. Scarborough Prize. With a jumping off point at roughly the same chronological moment as Jon Woodson's *Anthems, Sonnets, and Chants*, Jones similarly fulfills one of the prime functions of criticism: to reveal topics of interest and lay the groundwork for further study. Jones's book is divided into two sections, with two sweeping and well-developed chapters in each. The first section, "Riff, Remembrance and Revision," consists of "Listening to What the Ear Demands: Langston Hughes on the (Jazz) Record" and "Jazz Prosody: The Gendered Contours of the Post-Soul Coltrane Moment." Section two, titled "New Traditions, New Translations," contains "Opening the Canary's Cage: Sex, Gender, and the Jazz Body" and "A Cave Canem Continuum or a Dark Room Renaissance? From Jazz Improvisation to Hip-Hop Stylization in Contemporary Black Poetry." These titles indicate the creativity and broad reach of the chapters as well as the profound impact of poetry collectives like Cave Canem and Dark Room. She opens with a virtuoso Introduction articulating her senses and uses of key terms such as the body, race, "tradition," and gender. The Introduction also offers a scintillating analysis of the history of recordings of Dunbar's "When Malindy Sings," a moment of origin for the modern and contemporary African American poetry which followed. From these roots, we progress through a dazzling array of topics (the "Coltrane poem" as the poetic relative of a musical standard, the female body as performer, persona, and producer) to an Epilogue, "The Muse is Music: Collaboration and Improvisation in Jazz Poetics." Jones's knowledge and passion for jazz and for poetry infuse this book and allow her to move with impressive range through nearly a century of African American poetic production. Some of her main topics are poetry's employment of jazz prosody, the impact of recorded music on poetry, the gendered "jazz body," styles associated with "jazz improvisation," "hiphop stylization" as well as black poetry collectives and organizations, and finally, collaboration and improvisation. She covers a remarkable array of topics from the roots of poetry and jazz to the state-of-the art in contemporary practices. In the Epilogue, she breaks down and preserves a unique collaborative performance by Komunyakaa, Mackey, and baritone saxophonist Hamiet Bluiett in 2000. This closing section, along with the finest systematic analysis that I have read of the deceptively complex practices of Tracie Morris, highlights another particular strength of this critic: her ability to sketch vivid pragmatic details and elevate them to the level of sophisticated theory. The scope of this text and the quality of execution of its ambitious range are stunning, as Jones builds with skill on one of the foundational tropes of African American poetry: its relationship with music.

Hernton is an example of a major poet – along with figures such as Harper, singleton, Jess, and Spellman – who draws easily on jazz and blues influences as subject and style in their writing. Two of his poems that certainly belong in the canon respectively perpetuate and re-envision the traditions of jazz ("Fall Down") and blues ("D Blues") in their allusive reference points, musical motion, repetitive patterns, sonic echoes, visual/rhythmic form, and concepts:

> FALL DOWN
> In memory of Eric Dolphy
>
> All men are locked in their cells.
> Though we quake
> In the fist of the body
> Keys rattle, set us free.
> I remember and wonder why?
> In fall, in summer; times we had
> Will be no more. Journeys have
> Their end.
> I remember, and wonder why?
> In the sacred suffering of lung
> Spine and groin,
> You cease, fly away
> To what? To autumn, to
> Winter, to brown leaves, to
> Wind where no lark sings; yet
> Through dominion of air, jaw and fire
> I remember!
> Eric Dolphy, you swung
> A beautiful axe. You lived a clean
> Life. You were young
> Then
> You
> Died.
>   *
> D BLUES
>
> D blues
> What you woke up wit
> Dhis mourning
> What you toss and turn
> All night in your bed wit
> Nothing, no
> One in your arms Nobody.

Dats
What D blues
Is.[26]

Examples of late modern and contemporary poems about the most revered activists and cultural and political figures are "Hattie McDaniel Arrives at the Coconut Grove" by Dove, "Making Stars with Jacob Lawrence" by Myronn Hardy, "Sally Hemings to Thomas Jefferson" by Cyrus Cassells, "Robeson at Rutgers" by Elizabeth Alexander, "Nat Turner" by Samuel Allen, "Frederick Douglass," "The Ballad of Nat Turner," and "El-Hajj Malik El-Shabazz (Malcolm X)" by Hayden, "Medgar Evers" and "Malcolm X" by Brooks, "Malcolm's Blues" by Harper, "Malcolm Spoke / who listened?" and "Possibilities: Remembering Malcolm X" by Madhubuti, "Saint Malcolm" by Johari Amini, "Malcolm X – An Autobiography" and "The Summer After Malcolm" by Neal, "For Malcolm: After Mecca" by Gerald W. Barrax, "Portrait of Malcolm X" by Knight, "Harriet Tubman" by Samuel Allen, "Harriet Tubman" by Margaret Walker, "Death of Dr. King" and "Harriet Tubman" by Sam Cornish, "For Malcolm X" by Julia Fields, "Assassination" by Don L. Lee (Madhubuti) on the murder of Martin Luther King, Jr., "The Last Quatrain of the Ballad of Emmett Till" by Brooks, "In Memoriam: Martin Luther King, Jr." by June Jordan, "The Funeral of Martin Luther King, Jr." by Nikki Giovanni, "Emmett Till" by James A. Emanuel, "After MLK" by Addison, and "Elegy (for MOVE and Philadelphia)" and "Malcolm" by Sanchez. The concepts of lineage, heritage, family, and home – as well as Africa, as an imagined ancestral homeland – are resonant themes for this diasporic population that was unnaturally separated from its roots. Late modern and contemporary examples are "Heritage" by Gwendolyn Bennett, "Far from Africa: Four Poems" by Danner, "The Idea of Ancestry" by Knight, "African Dream" by Kaufman, "Legacy: My South" by Randall, and "For My People" by Walker.

African American poetry has always been looked on to express the key issues of contemporary politics, serve as a vehicle of political action, and reach a vast black audience, calling for art as a means to effect social change, and using stylized representations of black speech as an aestheticized simulacrum of poetic diction. There has been recognition of the influence of slave songs as cultural artefacts and rallying cries for

---

[26] "Fall Down: In Memory of Eric Dolphy," in Adoff, ed., *The Poetry of Black America*, pp. 243–4.

freedom, but not appreciation for their determinative role as a foundational body of lyric poetry. The continuing influence of slave songs on African American poetry since the 1980s remains a fruitful topic that is drastically underexplored – especially their role in breaking down perceptions of African American poetry as homogeneous, aesthetically conservative, and the product of diasporic rather than avant-garde influences. Slave songs are bold in structure, tone, function, and concept – by refusing to be reduced to the voice of the individual or the voice of a people, they have shown us how both are mutually entailed in explaining the impact of such powerful, personal, and universal poetry. They are the unacknowledged bedrock of the African American poetry tradition.

Was it seen as easier in earlier periods – for various reasons – to delineate, define, and analyze cultural products by African Americans? Is it a greater challenge to frame and evaluate this genre from the contemporary vantage point as it relates to its past, especially as the quantity and diversity of poetry by African Americans proliferates? It is more necessary than ever to open concepts of the field to new additions and discoveries that require the re-conceptualization of African American poetry. Surely the changes in researching and teaching of literary studies and the practices of theory and criticism demand such reconsideration. There appears to be a current upswing in public and scholarly interest in the field of African American poetry and its study. Though ethnic studies departments are under siege at many American universities, the study of African American and other "minority" writing and culture is fully entrenched in higher education. One explanation offered for a possible surge of attention is that African American poetry has become more mainstream partly as a result of the prominence and acceptance of rap as lyric poetry. There are other indicators that African American poetry has become established as culturally central. In 2009, Elizabeth Alexander was invited to write and read an occasional poem, "Praise Song for the Day," at the first inauguration of President Barack Obama, the United States' first President to self-identify as an African American, and tellingly, has now written her well-known essay on experimentalism in African American poetry. In 1993, Maya Angelou previously had been invited to read her poem, "On the Pulse of Morning," for the first inauguration of President Bill Clinton. Three comparatively young African American women, Natasha Trethewey, Rita Dove, and Tracy K. Smith have served as Poet Laureate of the United States.

The loss of notable figures – Cortez, Coleman, Baraka, and Maya Angelou – has suggested for many people that an era led by powerful voices is ending, spurring a moment of critical retrospection. With Angelou's death (May 2014), Americans joined together in lauding and mourning a beloved icon, whose passing generated national news coverage virtually at state hero level. Angelou's funeral was broadcast live and featured former President Bill Clinton and then-First Lady Michelle Obama as speakers, in addition to Oprah Winfrey. The death of oft-perceived "firebrand" Baraka (January 2014) also generated a national outpouring of emotion bordering on shock that he would contribute no bold new poetry and perspectives to future political and cultural dialogue. In addition to news coverage in all major outlets, 3,000 people attended the four-hour funeral service for Baraka, which was broadcast live and featured actor Danny Glover as the officiator and the Rev. Jesse Jackson as a speaker. A host of prominent African American poets read their work and offered tributes, including Sanchez, who read a poem written for Baraka by Angelou.

Of fifteen prestigious national positions as Chancellors of the Academy of American Poets, several of them have been held by African American women – Toi Derricotte, Marilyn Nelson, and Rankine – an unimaginable situation in the not too distant past. Additional focus on African American poetry may be attributed to the third (and perhaps final) Furious Flower Conference at James Madison University directed by Joanne V. Gabbin in September 2014. This historic series of three conferences on African American poetry, held every ten years since 1994, has been called "black poetry planet" by Nikky Finney. In a March 2014 interview, former Poet Laureate Trethewey said that participating in Furious Flower was worth "every word I've written since then." The 2014 conference – whose theme was to examine the present and future of African American poetry and to honor its past – was dedicated to Dove, and recognized "the achievements of literary trailblazers Toi Derricotte, Michael Harper, Yusef Komunyakaa, Marilyn Nelson, Ishmael Reed, and Quincy Troupe with Lifetime Achievement Awards."[27] Tributes to Baraka, Angelou, and others who had passed were added to the proceedings. Since the event, Harper, who was too ill to attend, has also passed away.

This brief overview offers context for the development of recent scholarship on African American poetry, which displays some shared research interests and themes: increased attention to formally diverse and

[27] www.jmu.edu/furiousflower/2014-conference.shtml#sthash.20fDjFCT.dpuf (last accessed June 26, 2014).

innovative poetry, poetry as a medium of sociopolitical and individual agency, new and interdisciplinary directions in scholarship, the legacy and influence of precursors, the need to reclaim underappreciated African American poetry of the past, the rise and impact of digital humanities, the prominent role of women, and the relationship between music and African American poetry. Coupled with its stylistic diversity, much contemporary African American poetry addresses a body of recurring themes, figures, events, and experiences that still define its cohesion.

From approximately the mid-1980s onwards, African American poetry has reflected trends of neo-realism, verbal jazz improvisation, L=A=N=G=U=A=G=E Poetry-inspired textual innovation, and hip-hop-inflected performance poetries. With the full-blown emergence of performance poetry, spoken word, rap, and poetry slams, performance and orality reached a pinnacle of importance in the 1980s and became organically re-connected to the genre. Organizations such as the Black Took Collective, Cave Canem, Carolina African American Writers Collective, and Dark Room Collective have provided support and training, and produced some of today's most prominent young African American poets. Master of Fine Arts programs in creative writing have become more aesthetically and culturally receptive to the presence and artistic goals of African American poets.

This is an auspicious moment for African American poetry to be recognized as an indispensable contribution to the American and Anglophone canon. African American poetry has maintained its traditional role by articulating both individual and communal concerns; using music, language, and performance to convey resistance; and creating unity and self-determined expression. It also has expanded in a wide array of styles and forms. A constant in African American poetry has been a belief that art can produce social change and challenge. African American poetry holds an inextricable role in reflecting and defining American identity, in addition to its ability to inspire world poetry and serve as a source of literary and cultural inspiration. The years of African American poetry since the middle of the twentieth century are the extension of a sophisticated, bold, and brilliantly avant-garde legacy. The future will most beneficially incorporate the full range of African American poetry in all its stylistic, formal, thematic, and conceptual manifestations – including the most "different" – to properly delineate the magnitude of this body of verse. The genre's diversity is now truly staggering; yet it retains a strong and recognizable core of character, concerns, values, and manifestations carried along by a gifted cadre of unique and indispensable poetic voices.

Interview with Paul Breman

Note from Lauri Ramey

This compilation results from many conversations with Paul Breman in his London home from 1999 to 2004. The final editing, which is an accurate reflection of our dialogue, was performed by Breman. Meticulous and insistent in his tastes on visual presentation, Breman also designed the interview's format. As seen in the Heritage Series, book design was of great interest to him, and he put in substantial effort to find a design and format that he believed suited and served the concept of his series with its distinctive Fritz Stoepman Bauhaus-style image and typography, portrait covers, substantial white space to allow poems to breathe and stretch, elegant heavy stock in muted tones of pale green, ivory, and grey, and an overall impression that conveyed contemporary cleanness with a timelessness that would not become dated. That he succeeded is evidenced by collectors of these volumes throughout the world, and other important publications that were inspired by this series, most notably the brilliant series of *nocturnes (re)view of the literary arts*, run and edited by poet giovanni singleton.

Rosey Pool

LR: You knew Rosey Pool (is that how you pronounce it?) – did she explain how she got into black poetry?

PB: It's pronounced "pole" in Dutch. We are, or were, both Dutch – I met her in Amsterdam in 1948, just before I finished high school. She was the first person I ever came across who knew there was such a thing as black poetry – well, Negro poetry, then. She opened up a lot of roads to material, and to people. I never knew how she had become interested – probably some identification with the oppressed. She had been underground for most of the war, in Holland, because she was Jewish – she knew what an oppressed minority was, what it felt like. She said that she started collecting black literature before the war – it is possible, but I don't know, and I rather doubt it. You were never quite sure of the truth with Rosey; she was a great poser.

LR: Eugene B. Redmond describes you as her assistant, in *Drumvoices*.

PB: I never read that, although it is probably somewhere on the shelves – I still have my whole collection, frozen in time at about 1973 when I stopped publishing, stopped collecting, stopped reading. Twenty-five years is enough for any hobby – time to change. Anyway, no, I was never Rosey's assistant. She moved to London only about a year after we met. The only thing we ever did together was a bilingual anthology of black poetry – English opposite Dutch translations. That happened years later, in 1958, my own last year in Amsterdam, when Ro was laid up there for a long while, after a traffic accident. A Dutch publisher had asked her to do such an anthology, but there was no money in it, so she suggested we combine what translations we already had, to see if we could flesh the skeleton out with some new work, filling the gaps. My first translations, of Langston and W. E. B. Du Bois, had appeared in a literary magazine when I was still at school – I used to be quite proud of that. Only the translations were lousy.

Robert Hayden

LR: How did you first make contact with Robert Hayden?

PB: Through Rosey Pool, who had the pamphlets he and Myron O'Higgins published privately at Fisk. Rosey and Bob were both converted Baha'i – I don't know whether that brought them into contact with each other or whether it was poetry that did it. I think I wrote to Hayden around '54, after reading (and copying) the pamphlets. "Dear Mr Hayden" and all that – he wrote back something about "no formal introduction being necessary" between people interested in the same things. I liked his work enormously, even then, and tried in vain to get anybody on our side of the water to take an interest and publish it. Eventually it dawned on me that if I was halfway serious about it, I had better print it myself. We corresponded about that first book, *A Ballad of Remembrance*, from early 1959 – but it didn't appear until the spring of '62. It had a difficult gestation period.

I will tell you the goriest story of my life. When I started work on what became the Penguin anthology [*You Better Believe It*] I went through a lot of other anthologies and things like that, things I knew but had never worked through systematically. One of the books I checked through from page 1 for the first time was Hayden's *Kaleidoscope*. When I turned the title-page I found a blank page just saying "for Paul Breman." I had never

highly. Anyway, it was only much later that I came as far as the Loop in Chicago – I think I had been coming to Chicago for more than ten years before I ever went downtown, but one of the first things you noticed then about the Loop is that it changed color after six – the white shoppers and office workers leave, the black cleaners, janitors and small-timers take over. Spooky.

I even met Don Lee on that first trip, a nice young man working at Margaret Burroughs's. He had just done his first pamphlet of poetry. He sent me a copy, later, with dedication and all. Probably haunts him, if he remembers. Dudley told me that when Don saw his entry in *You Better Believe It* he didn't stop swearing for a full five minutes.

Motivation

LR: You mention Madhubuti's dislike of you, and Redmond also talks about that feeling of suspicion, that in the end he felt he did not know why you were doing these things – they did not understand your motivation.

PB: Neither did I – it was just one of those things that happen. Having discovered the poetic discipline of the blues I felt certain that at another level members of the same group would have written what we call formal poetry. So I started looking for that, and everybody I asked sort of said "huh?"' and that makes you go on. Had I found a whole sheaf of stuff straightaway I would probably have said, oh good – and left it at that. But I kept looking, and before long I was writing to people and word got around that there was this idiot on the other side of the water, a white idiot at that, who wanted to know what nobody in America wanted to know. So I started getting unpublished material and letters from people saying "I can't find anybody here; is there anyone on your side who does ..."

When I started publishing you could not give the stuff away on either side of the Atlantic. Even when the whole readings thing started, even then poetry sales were so pathetically small that poets flogged a few copies wherever they read. A living it isn't. Neither is publishing poetry. Could you make a living out of printing twenty-seven books in thirteen years?

LR: So why did you do it?

PB: Because I felt like it – something academics find hard to understand. We all have hobbies, and this was mine for a long time. And because it was just a hobby I could also stop it. In the end it was getting to be a hassle and it was costing too much money, so what the hell, go and do something else a bit less strenuous. More or less since then I have been collecting books on military architecture printed in Venice. It made a nice change, but whether Redmond can fit it into his agenda of acceptable motivations I shudder to think.

Dudley Randall

LR: What about Dudley Randall?

PB: Dudley I must have met on my first visit to Detroit, in 1966. He was
      already running Broadside. I think we had been aware of each other's
      parallel activity. We got on well; I visited Dudley whenever I was in
      Detroit, about every other year. I upset him once by making a remark
      about his drum kit – he was very serious about his drumming. When I
      started Heritage up again he became my American distributor, which
      saved the whole operation. I printed 500 copies of each new title and
      Dudley took half of that. It took a lot of pressure off. It was quite brave of
      Dudley to do this then, but he also realized that our lists complemented
      each other rather well.
          Eventually he asked me to do a volume of his in the series. He wrote,
      "I would be quite pleased if you could do this because I cannot possibly
      publish this under Broadside" – it was a set of straight love poems, with no
      political content, no black content, no nothing that was fashionable, no
      nothing that Broadside stood for. Doing it under Broadside was asking for
      trouble – from the same club that did not like Hayden, for instance. We
      were quite amused by the idea that the two of us were running the oldest
      black presses in existence at the time.
          Then Broadside went more or less belly-up – for which I have always
      largely blamed Gwen Brooks. I believe she talked Dudley into rather
      grandiose ideas for the Broadside anniversary; they spent too much, did
      too expensive an anniversary production and I think that is where the
      whole thing started to implode, with Broadside getting into terrible
      financial difficulty. Stupid, seeing how careful Dudley had been for many
      years, keeping his job at the university, running his tapes off as and when
      on an office machine, and spacing his publishing according to means and
      opportunity. Of course I am talking as an interested party, because the
      demise of Broadside also meant the end of Heritage. Dudley couldn't
      bring himself to warn or even tell me, so the last four Heritage titles went
      into the débâcle and my publishing venture was seriously broke.
          Eventually it seems Broadside was built up again by people who were
      complete idiots, as far as I have ever been aware. I had a long letter from
      them, asking if they could do new editions of some of the Heritage books –
      they should have known I didn't have the rights in any of them. I wrote
      back saying that as I had never been paid for the last four, perhaps we
      should talk money first. Never heard from them again – don't know
      whether they made it or not. Small presses are like that. Heritage never
      paid anybody – except the printers, obviously.

LR: The authors were never paid?

PB: Nobody. Everybody knew that they weren't going to be paid – those books
      lost money anyway. Which is why there was a long gap between the first

four, which were too ambitious in production and cost too much. They didn't sell; I knew sod-all about publishing, less about distribution. There might have been a market in the States, although I doubt even that in 1962, but anyway I had no access. So I ran out of money, and it was only after my first trip to the States, in 1966, when I met lots of people from *Sixes*, the anthology I had done, that I started thinking about revising the format and doing something a bit more modest. That's when I started portrait covers and smaller books. There were still people in need of being recognized, published – even if there was not much of a public to read them.

Sixes and Sevens

LR: How did the anthology come about?

PB: When I started working on the Hayden book it occurred to me that publishing just one book was an act of utter madness – so I compounded the madness by thinking of doing an anthology of interesting but unpublished poets. I had been in touch with a number of younger people, and I had a lot of unpublished stuff that was actually good as it had already been through somebody else's sieve, either Langston Hughes or Harold Jackman or a couple of others. Langston, for instance, had years earlier sent me a batch of Ray Durem's poems, with a note saying "an interesting, I think, poet but, unfortunately, I cannot do anything with it" – far too political for the early sixties, quite apart from the fact that Ray did not even make a nice picture because he looked completely white. As an outsider I could use what Langston could not.

The whole idea of the Heritage series was to publish people who were new. A very few of the authors had done the odd pamphlet – Hayden a couple of private pieces which were virtually unobtainable even then, Conrad Rivers one mimeographed booklet. The only one who had really something published was Audre Lorde; her first book was done by Diane di Prima in the years that Heritage looked as if it had run out of the steam called money. Audre was in *Sixes* before that, of course. We were very close for a long while. Right at the end of Heritage there was Sam Allen, who had been published quite extensively, but in Europe, under the very un-American and pre-black banner of *négritude* and under a different name, Paul Vesey. Getting some of his work out under the title of *Paul Vesey's Ledger* suited a rather wry sense of humor in both of us.

LR: Is it because of this search for new talent that you rarely repeated authors in the series?

PB: Actually I did repeat two, but yes, the whole idea was to publish people who were beginning, and also those who had long had a reputation through anthologies and such but who had never had a book of their own out – Arna Bontemps, Waring Cuney. Arna had been very helpful from the start, from well before the start. He and Alberta visited us in London, and when my younger son was born they sent him a nice silver trinket – can't remember quite what. I do remember Harold Jackman sending a musical mobile which hung for years over the kid's bed. I am still in touch with Alberta; she has everlasting life, still in the same house in Nashville.

With Waring I suppose I was cheating, because I had edited a huge book of his in Holland, but that was done in 175 copies for a bibliophile society so it doesn't count. And the two I repeated were Hayden, as I mentioned earlier, and Conrad Kent Rivers. We had been very fond of Connie and it was devastating when he died an incredibly stupid death just before his first book came out. He saw the proofs and all, but never the book itself. He had been working on various poems dealing with the "to make a poet black and bid him sing" theme, mostly in the form of letters to or musings about Richard Wright. I wanted those out; I thought they would make a very good platform for discussion in schools, for opening up ideas. The book was called *The Wright Poems*; it never went anywhere. I didn't know anybody who could have put it into a curriculum. Still think it would be worth it. If anybody remembers Richard Wright.

LR: Can you please tell me about Allen Polite? You mentioned him once before.

PB: Allen came out of the New York "beat" scene. He is in *Sixes and Sevens*; we met in London several times in the very early sixties. He settled in Sweden for most of his later life, married, kept writing but never publishing. It was impossible to get anything out of him, except in conversation – he was great company. He died several years ago, and his widow is very actively promoting his leftover work, of which there is quite a lot, paintings and drawings as well as poetry and prose. She can afford to, does not want anything out of it but finds it important, so she builds monument after monument. I did a small pamphlet of Allen's, in this annual afterlife of Heritage I started some years ago, to amuse myself. It was nice to devise yet another format, an eight-page fold-out which I send out as New Year's cards to a handful of friends.

Other Authors

LR: Are the contributors to Heritage among those friends?

PB: Sure, several – although there are others I published whom I have never met, hardly even spoken to. Ishmael Reed, for instance, I have once spoken to for two minutes on the telephone, only because Ron Fair was staying with me, they were mates, and Ron passed the phone to me when he had Ish on. We had nothing to say to each other then, and have kept it that way. But his manuscript was the only one that ever rolled into my letterbox ready-made and irresistible.

LR: How had he found you? Through the other Heritage editions?

PB: I think either Ron or Clarence Major had told him about the series, probably shown him one or two, and he just went and sent a tailor-made manuscript. One look at it and I said "yeah, great" and sent it off to the printers. Quite nice to have something like that once in a while. What you get very tired of is 90-page typescripts of deathless poetry by eighteen-year olds. Quite honestly I would find it hard to think of anybody who has written 90 pages of deathless poetry in a lifetime, let alone at eighteen. It is all very important and it will usually save the world. All right, we're all like that when we're eighteen, but we don't all take it that seriously. And you run out of ways of nicely saying "well, I think there are four or five things in there that you might work on for a good while and then they might become something." Poetry, even.

About once a quarter I still get a large buff envelope sent to an old address which I left in 1971 but which happens to be just down the road; the same people still live there and they drop it in to me. When I get one like that I know it's from another unpublished black poet. It's very sad. By the time someone is desperate enough to send stuff here on the off chance – it may not be any good, a lot of people have probably already said so, but all the same.

LR: Who are the poets that you did meet or develop a relationship with? Did you know Russell Atkins?

PB: Yes, and still do. We just did a pamphlet together, for his seventieth birthday. I cannot remember how we first made contact. It is possible that Casper Jordan, who ran the long-lived *Free Lance* magazine with Russell, told me to get in touch – he was certainly the one who suggested Conrad Kent Rivers; *Free Lance* had just done Conrad's first small pamphlet. It could also be that I originally wrote to Russell because I had seen his work and liked it. He was quite proud of being the youngest in the revised edition of the Hughes and Bontemps anthology. I went to see him in Cleveland in '66.

The Archive

LR: I hope you have kept all the correspondence and such that went on over the years.

PB: If I had, this house would be fuller than it is already. No, I never keep correspondence, these days don't even make copies of my own letters. I did when Heritage was active, and there was a lot of stuff – letters, notes, drafts, proofs, whatever. But around 1970 I needed money real bad, so I organized and listed all the Heritage material, and tried to sell it. A dealer I knew in Los Angeles eventually took it because he had managed to find a buyer. I found out much later and by chance that it was the Harsh Research Collection in Chicago, which is housed in the Carter Woodson branch of the public library, on lovely South Halsted. It's all there, in neat little boxes. I also found out that the Harsh had forked out twice what I got – they're quite proud of it, because they seldom buy anything: they're used to having stuff given to them because now that the black studies boom is over, the market is back to zero.

Bibliography

Addison, Lloyd. *The Aura & The Umbra*. London: Paul Breman, 1970. Volume 8 in the Heritage Series.

Adoff, Arnold, ed. *I am the Darker Brother: An Anthology of Modern Poems by African Americans*. New York: Simon Pulse Edition, 2002.

The Poetry of Black America: Anthology of the 20th Century. New York: HarperCollins, 1973.

Alexander, Elizabeth. "New Ideas About Black Experimental Poetry." Hopwood Lecture 2011. Accessed at https://lsa.umich.edu/content/dam/hopwood-assets/documents/Hopwood%20Lectures/HopwoodLecture-2011_AlexanderE.pdf

Allen, William Francis, Charles Pickard Ware, and Lucy McKim Garrison, eds. *Slave Songs of the United States*. New Bedford: Applewood Books. Reprint, n.d. Originally published 1867.

Andrews, William L., Frances Smith Foster, and Trudier Harris, eds. *The Oxford Companion to African American Literature*. New York and Oxford: Oxford University Press, 1997.

Armstrong, Julie Buckner, ed. *The Cambridge Companion to American Civil Rights Literature*. Cambridge: Cambridge University Press, 2015.

Atkins, Russell. *Heretofore*. London: Paul Breman, 1968. Volume 7 in the Heritage Series.

Spyrytual. Cleveland: 7 Flowers Press, 1966.

7 @ 70. Heritage Pamphlet 4. London: Paul Breman, 1996.

Baker, Houston A., Jr. *Afro-American Poetics: Revisions of Harlem and the Black Aesthetic*. Madison, WI: University of Wisconsin Press, 1988.

Modernism and the Harlem Renaissance. Chicago: University of Chicago Press, 1989.

Baraka, Amiri. *The Autobiography of LeRoi Jones/Amiri Baraka*. New York: Freundlich Brooks, 1984.

Transbluesency: Selected Poems 1961–1995. New York: Marsilio Publishers, 1995.

Baraka, Amiri and Larry Neal. *Black Fire: An Anthology of Afro-American Writing*. Baltimore: Black Classic Press, 2007.

Barksdale, Richard and Keneth Kinnamon, eds. *Black Writers of America*. Upper Saddle River, NJ: Prentice Hall, 1972.

Barton, William E. *Old Plantation Hymns: A Collection of Hitherto Unpublished Melodies of the Slave and the Freeman, With Historical and Descriptive Notes.* 1899. Reprint, New York: AMS, 1972.

Benston, Kimberly W. *Performing Blackness: Enactments of African-American Modernism.* New York and London: Routledge, 2000.

Bennett, Paula Bernat. "Rewriting Dunbar." In Barbara McCaskill and Caroline Gebhard, eds. *Post-Bellum, Pre-Harlem: African American Literature and Culture, 1877–1919.* New York and London: New York University Press, 2006. 146–61.

Bernstein, Charles. *Artifice of Absorption.* Philadelphia: Singing Horse Press, 1987.

Bérubé, Michael. "Masks, Margins, and African American Modernism: Melvin Tolson's *Harlem Gallery*." *PMLA* 105, No. 1. Fall 1990. 57–69.

Bolden, Tony. *Afro-Blue: Improvisations in African American Poetry and Culture.* Urbana: University of Illinois Press, 2004.

Bontemps, Arna. *Personals.* London: Paul Breman, October 1963. Reprinted London 1973. Volume 4 in the Heritage Series.

Bontemps, Arna, ed. *American Negro Poetry.* New York: Hill and Wang, 1963.

Bontemps, Arna, with Langston Hughes, eds. "Spirituals." In Alex Preminger, ed. *Princeton Encyclopedia of Poetry and Poetics.* Princeton, NJ: Princeton University Press, 1974. 807.

Boyd, Melba Joyce. *Wrestling with the Muse: Dudley Randall and the Broadside Press.* New York: Columbia University Press, 2004.

Bradley, Adam. *Book of Rhymes: The Poetics of Hip Hop.* 2nd edition. New York: Basic Civitas Books, 2017.

Brawley, Benjamin. *Early Negro American Writers.* Chapel Hill: University of North Carolina Press, 1937.

The Negro in Literature and Art in the United States. Reprint. San Bernardino, CA, May 06, 2016. ISBN 9781500579722. Orig. New York: Duffield & Co., 1918.

Paul Laurence Dunbar: Poet of his People. Chapel Hill: University of North Carolina Press, 1936.

Braxton, Joanne M., ed. *The Collected Poetry of Paul Laurence Dunbar.* Charlottesville and London: University of Virginia Press, 1993.

Braxton, Joanne M., and Lauri Ramey. "Paul Laurence Dunbar." In Richardson, ed. *The Cambridge Companion to American Poets,* 136–143.

Breman, Paul, ed. *Sixes and Sevens.* London: Paul Breman, August 1962. Volume 2 in the Heritage Series.

You Better Believe It: Black Verse in English. Middlesex: Penguin, 1973.

Bremer, Fredrika. *The Homes of the New World: Impressions of America.* Trans. Mary Howitt, Vol. 1. New York: Harper & Brothers, 1853.

Brooks, Gwendolyn. *The Essential Gwendolyn Brooks,* ed. Elizabeth Alexander. New York: The Library of America. Literary Classics Project. 2005.

Brooks, Tim. *Lost Sounds: Blacks and the Birth of the Recording Industry, 1890–1919.* Urbana and Chicago: University of Illinois Press, 2004.

Brown, Fahamisha Patricia. *Performing the Word: African American Poetry as Vernacular Culture*. New Brunswick, NJ: Rutgers University Press, 1999.

Brown, Sterling A. *Negro Poetry and Drama and The Negro in American Fiction*. New York: Atheneum, 1972.

Brown, Sterling A., Arthur P. Davis, and Ulysses Lee, eds. *The Negro Caravan*. New York: Arno Press and *The New York Times*, 1970.

Brown, William Wells. *The Black Man: His Antecedents, His Genius, and His Achievements*. 2nd edn. New York and Boston: Thomas Hamilton, R. F. Wallcott, 1862.

Brown, William Wells, compiler. *The Anti-Slavery Harp: A Collection of Songs for Anti-Slavery Meetings*. Boston: Bella Marsh, 1848.

Burnim, Mellonee V., and Portia K. Maultsby, eds. *African American Music: An Introduction*. New York: Routledge, 2006.

Campbell, Alfred Gibbs. *Poems*. Newark, NJ: Advertiser Printing House, 1883.

"Song of the Decanter." *Alcohol, Temperance & Prohibition*. Brown Digital Repository. Brown University Library. https://repository.library.brown.edu/studio/item/bdr:30096/

Carretta, Vincent. *Phillis Wheatley: Biography of a Genius in Bondage*. Athens and London: University of Georgia Press, 2011.

Census, US, 1860. www2.census.gov/prod2/decennial/documents/1860a-02.pdf

Christy, E. P. *Christy's Plantation Melodies: Originator of Ethiopian Minstrelsy and the First to Harmonize Negro Melodies*. Philadelphia: Fisher & Brother, 1851.

Coleman, Will. *Tribal Talk: Black Theology, Hermeneutics and African/American Ways of "Telling the Story."* University Park, PA: The Pennsylvania State University Press, 2000.

Cook, Will Mercer Papers, Will Marion Cook Collection, Correspondence A–D File, Moorland-Spingarn Research Center, Howard University. "Paul Laurence Dunbar Up to and beyond Clorindy."

Coombs, Orde, ed., *We Speak as Liberators: Young Black Poets*. New York: Dodd Mead, 1970.

Cruz, Jon. *Culture on the Margins: The Black Spiritual and the Rise of American Cultural Interpretation*. Princeton: Princeton University Press, 1999.

Cullen, Countee, ed. *Caroling Dusk: An Anthology of Verse by Black Poets of the Twenties*. [1927]. New York: Citadel Press, 1993.

Cuney, William Waring, *Puzzles*, ed. and trans. Paul Breman. Utrecht: De Roos, 1960.

Sometimes I Wonder. London: Paul Breman, 1995. Heritage Pamphlet 3.

Storefront Church. London: Paul Breman, 1973. Volume 23 in the Heritage Series.

Cushway, Philip, and Michael Warr, eds. *Of Poetry & Protest: From Emmett Till to Trayvon Martin*. New York: W. W. Norton, 2016.

Davis, Arthur P., and Michael W. Peplow, eds. *The New Negro Renaissance: An Anthology*. New York: Holt, Rinehart and Winston, 1975.

Davis, Arthur P., and J. Saunders Redding, eds. *Cavalcade: Negro American Writing from 1760 to the Present.* Boston: Houghton Mifflin, 1971.

Davis, Arthur P., J. Saunders Redding, and Joyce Ann Joyce, eds. *The New Cavalcade: African American Writing from 1760 to the Present*, Vol. 1. Washington, DC: Howard University Press, 1991.

Selected African American Writing from 1760 to 1910. New York: Bantam, 1991.

DeSimone, Erika, and Fidel Louis, eds. *Voices Beyond Bondage: An Anthology of Verse by African Americans of the 19th Century.* Montgomery: NewSouth Books, 2014.

Dett, R. Nathaniel. *Religious Folk-Songs of the Negro: As Sung at Hampton Institute.* Hampton: Hampton Institute Press, 1927.

Dickson-Carr, Darryl. *Spoofing the Modern: Satire in the Harlem Renaissance.* Columbia: University of South Carolina Press, 2015.

Douglass, Frederick. *Narrative of the Life of Frederick Douglass, An American Slave, Written by Himself.* [1845]. Norton Critical Edition, edited by William L. Andrews, and William S. Feely. New York: W. W. Norton, 1997.

Du Bois, W. E. B. *The Souls of Black Folk.* [1903]. Reprint Boston: Bedford, 1997.

Dunbar, Paul Laurence. *The Collected Poetry of Paul Laurence Dunbar*, ed. with an introduction by Joanne M. Braxton. Charlottesville, VA: University of Virginia Press, 1993.

Dungy, Camille, ed. *Black Nature: Four Centuries of African American Nature Poetry.* Athens, GA: University of Georgia Press, 2009.

Durem, Ray. *Take No Prisoners.* London: Paul Breman, 1971. Volume 17 in the Heritage Series.

Editors, The. *Afro-Pessimism: An Introduction.* Minneapolis: racked & dispatched, 2017. Rackedanddispatched.noblogs.org

Edwards, Brent Hayes. *Epistrophies: Jazz and the Literary Imagination.* Cambridge: Harvard University Press, 2017.

The Practice of Diaspora: Literature, Translation, and the Rise of Black Internationalism. Cambridge, MA: Harvard University Press, 2003.

Edwards, Brent Hayes, and John F. Szwed. "A Bibliography of Jazz Poetry Criticism." *Callaloo* 25, No. 1. Winter, 2002. 338–46.

Elam, Harry J., Jr. "We Wear the Mask: Performance, Social Dramas, and Race." In Hazel Rose Markus and Paula M. L. Moya, eds. *Doing Race: 21 Essays for the 21st Century.* New York and London: Norton, 2010. 545–61.

Empson, William. *Seven Types of Ambiguity: A Study of Its Effects in English Verse.* Reprint. New York: Meridian, 1957.

Epstein, Dena J. *Sinful Tunes and Spirituals: Black Folk Music to the Civil War.* Urbana: University of Illinois Press, 1977.

Equiano, Olaudah. *The Interesting Narrative of the Life of Olaudah Equiano, or Gustavus Vassa, the African. Written by Himself*, Vol. 1. 1789. Electronic Edition. http://abolition.nypl.org/content/docs/text/life_of_equiano.pdf

Everett, Susanne. *History of Slavery*. Edison, NJ: Chartwell Books, 1996.

Fair, Ron. *Excerpts*. London: Paul Breman, 1975. Volume 26 in the Heritage Series.

Fenner, Thomas P., Frederic G. Rathbun, and Miss Bessie Cleaveland, arrangers. *Cabin and Plantation Songs as Sung by the Hampton Students*. [1901]. 3rd edn. New York: AMS Books Edition, 1977.

Ferguson, Jeffrey B. *The Harlem Renaissance: A Brief History with Documents*. Boston: Bedford/St. Martin's, 2008.

Ferguson, Margaret, Mary Jo Salter, and Jon Stallworthy, eds. *The Norton Anthology of Poetry*. 5th edn. New York: W. W. Norton and Co., 2005.

Fisk University Jubilee Singers. "Volume 1." *Fisk Jubilee Singers, Volume 1, 1909–1911*. Prod. Johnny Parth. Vienna: Document Records, 1997.

"Volume 3." *Fisk Jubilee Singers, Volume 3, 1924–1940*. Prod. Johnny Parth. Vienna: Document Records, 1997.

Floyd, Samuel A., Jr. *The Power of Black Music: Interpreting Its History from Africa to the United States*. New York: Oxford University Press, 1995.

Foster, Frances Smith. *A Brighter Coming Day: A Frances Ellen Watkins Harper Reader*. New York: The Feminist Press at CUNY, 1993.

Gabbin, Joanne V., ed. *The Furious Flowering of African American Poetry*. Charlottesville: University Press of Virginia, 1999.

Gancie, Rosalie. "Notes on Welborn Victor Jenkins." *Flashpoint*, Spring 2015, Web Issue 17. www.flashpointmag.com/Welborn_Victor_Jenkins_main.htm

Garabedian, Steven. "Reds, Whites, and the Blues: Lawrence Gellert, 'Negro Songs of Protest' and the Left-Wing Folk Song Revival of the 1930s and 1940s." *American Quarterly* 57, No. 1. 2005. 179–206.

Garner, Eric. "African American Women's Poetry in the 'Christian Recorder,' 1855–1865: A Bio-Bibliography With Sample Poems." *African American Review* 40, No. 4. Winter, 2006. 813–31. www.jstor.org/stable/40033755

Gates, Henry Louis, Jr. *The Classic Slave Narratives*. New York: Mentor/Penguin, 1987.

"Foreword: In Her Own Write." In Maria W. Stewart, Jarena Lee, Julia A. J. Foote, and Virginia W. Broughton, *Spiritual Narratives*. New York and Oxford: Oxford University Press, 1988.

"Introduction: 'Tell Me, Sir, … What Is "Black" Literature?'" *PMLA: Special Topic: African and African American Literature* 105, No. 1. January 1990. 11–22.

"The Master's Pieces: On Canon Formation and the African-American Tradition." *The South Atlantic Quarterly* 89, No. 1. Winter 1990. 89–111.

Gates, Henry Louis, Jr., and Valerie Smith, gen. eds. *The Norton Anthology of African American Literature*, Vols. 1 and 2. 3rd edn. New York: Norton, 2014.

Genovese, Eugene D. *Roll, Jordan, Roll: The World the Slaves Made*. New York: Vintage, 1976.

Gerzina, Gretchen Holbrook. *Mr. and Mrs. Prince: How an Extraordinary Eighteenth-Century Family Moved Out of Slavery and Into Legend.* New York: Amistad/HarperCollins, 2009.

Gilroy, Paul. *The Black Atlantic: Modernity and Double Consciousness.* Cambridge, MA: Harvard University Press, 1993.

Gilyard, Keith. "The Bible and African American Poetry." In Vincent L. Wimbush, ed. *African Americans and the Bible.* New York and London: Continuum, 2001. 205–20.

Gladman, Renee, and giovanni singleton, eds. "Expanding the Repertoire: Continuity and Change in African American Writing." *Tripwire: a Journal of Poetics,* Issue 5, Fall 2001.

Gomez, Michael A. *Reversing Sail: A History of the African Diaspora.* Cambridge: Cambridge University Press, 2005.

Graham, Maryemma, ed. *Complete Poems of Frances E. W. Harper.* New York and Oxford: Oxford University Press, 1988.

Graham, Maryemma, and Jerry W. Ward, Jr., eds. *The Cambridge History of African American Literature.* Cambridge: Cambridge University Press, 2011.

Harper, Michael S., and Anthony Walton, eds. *Every Shut Eye Ain't Asleep: An Anthology of Poetry by African Americans Since 1945.* Boston and New York: Little Brown, 1994.

The Vintage Book of African American Poetry. New York: Vintage Books, 2000.

Harris, Duriel E., ed. *Obsidian: Literature and Arts in the African Diaspora.* Fall 2015. 41.1/41.2.

Hartman, Saidiya V. *Scenes of Subjection: Terror, Slavery, and Self-Making in Nineteenth Century America.* New York: Oxford University Press, 1997.

Hatfield, Edwin F., compiler. *Freedom's Lyre: or, Psalms, Hymns and Sacred Songs, for the Slave and his Friends.* New York: S. W. Benedict publishers, 1840.

Hawkins, Walter Everette. *Chords and Discords.* Washington, DC: The Murray Brothers Press, 1909.

Hayden, Robert. *A Ballad of Remembrance.* London: Paul Breman, April 1962. Volume 1 in the Heritage Series.

Collected Poems, ed. Frederick Glaysher. Centenary Edition. New York and London: Liveright Publishing Corp., 2013.

The Night-Blooming Cereus. London: Paul Breman, 1972. Volume 20 in the Heritage Series.

Henderson, Stephen. *Understanding the New Black Poetry: Black Speech and Black Music as Poetic References.* New York: William Morrow, 1973.

Hernton, Calvin C. *The Coming of Chronos to the House of Nightsong: An Epical Narrative of the South.* New York: Interim Books, 1964.

Medicine Man: Collected Poems. New York: Reed, Cannon, and Johnson, 1976.

The Red Crab Gang and Black River Poems. Berkeley, CA: Ishmael Reed Publishing Co., 1999.

Sex and Racism in America. Garden City, New York: Doubleday, 1965.

The Sexual Mountain and Black Women Writers: Adventures in Sex, Literature, and Real Life. New York: Anchor Press, 1987.

Higginson, Thomas Wentworth. *Army Life in a Black Regiment and Other Writings*. [1870]. New York: Penguin, 1997.

Hill, Patricia Liggins, gen. ed., *Call & Response: The Riverside Anthology of the African American Literary Tradition*. Boston: Houghton Mifflin Co., 1998.

Hine, Darlene Clark, and John McCluskey, Jr. *The Black Chicago Renaissance*. Urbana: University of Illinois Press, 2012.

Hogan, Moses, ed. *The Oxford Book of Spirituals*. Oxford: Oxford University Press, 2002.

Horne, Frank. *Haverstraw*. London: Paul Breman, 1963. Volume 3 in the Heritage Series.

Horton, George Moses. *Naked Genius*. Greensboro, NC: The Chapel Hill Historical Society, 1982.

Hughes, Langston, ed. *Negro Poets, USA*. Bloomington, IN: Indiana University Press, 1964.

Hughes, Langston, and Arna Bontemps, eds. *The Poetry of the Negro 1746–1949*. Garden City, New York: Doubleday, 1949. Revised edn, *The Poetry of the Negro 1746–1970*. Garden City, New York: Doubleday, 1970.

Hunt, Erica, and Dawn Lundy Martin, eds. *Letters to the Future: Black WOMEN/Radical WRITING*. Tucson: Kore Press, 2018.

Hutchinson, George, ed. *The Cambridge Companion to the Harlem Renaissance*. Cambridge: Cambridge University Press, 2007.

Irele, F. Abiola. *The African Imagination: Literature in Africa and the Black Diaspora*. Oxford: Oxford University Press, 2001.

Jenkins, Welborn Victor. *The "Incident" at Monroe*. Atlanta, GA: United Negro Youth of America, 1948. Accessed at www.flashpointmag.com/Incident_at_Monroe/Incident_at_Monroe/content/_6552831735_large.html

Johnson, Fenton. *A Little Dreaming*. Chicago: Peterson Linotyping Company, 1913.

The Daily Grind, ed. Arna Bontemps. Intended as Volume 4 of the Heritage Series. Unpublished.

The Daily Grind. London: Paul Breman, 1994. Heritage Pamphlet 2.

For the Highest Good. Chicago: *Favorite Magazine*, 1920.

Songs of the Soil. New York: Press of Trachtenberg Co., 1916.

Tales of Darkest America. Chicago: *Favorite Magazine*, 1920.

Visions of the Dusk. New York: F.J., 1915.

Johnson, James Weldon. *Complete Poems*. New York: Penguin, 2000.

Johnson, James Weldon, ed. *The Book of American Negro Poetry*. New York: Harcourt, Brace and Co., 1922.

Johnson, James Weldon, and J. Rosamond Johnson, eds. *The Books of American Negro Spirituals*. [1925 (Vol. 1), 1926 (Vol. 2)]. New York: Da Capo Press Edition, 1969.

Jones, LeRoi. *Blues People: The Negro Experience in White America and the Music that Developed from It.* New York: William Morrow, 1963.

Jones, Meta DuEwa. *The Muse Is Music: Jazz Poetry from the Harlem Renaissance to Spoken Word.* Urbana: University of Illinois Press, 2011.

Jordan, June, ed. *Soulscript: A Collection of African American Poetry.* New York: Harlem Moon/Broadway Books, Random House, 1970.

Katz, Bernard, and Jonathan Katz. *Black Woman: A Fictionalized Biography of Lucy Terry Prince.* New York: Knopf Books for Young Readers, 1973.

Kearney, Douglas. *The Black Automaton.* Albany, NY: Fence Books, 2009.

Buck Studies. Albany, New York: Fence Books, 2016.

Fear, Some. Los Angeles: Red Hen Press, 2006.

Mess And Mess And Mess And Mess And. Las Cruces, NM: Noemi Press, 2015.

Patter. Pasadena, CA: Red Hen Press, 2014.

Someone Took They Tongues: 3 Operas. Boulder, CO: Subito Press, 2015.

Kearney, Douglas, ed. *BAX 2015: Best Experimental Writing.* Middletown, CT: Wesleyan University Press, 2015.

Kerlin, Robert Thomas. *Negro Poets and their Poems.* [1923]. 3rd edn. Washington, DC: The Associated Publishers, Inc. 1935.

Kinnamon, Keneth. "Anthologies of African-American Literature from 1845 to 1994." *Callaloo* 20, No. 2. Spring, 1997. 461–81. www.jstor.org/stable/3299277.

Krehbiel, Henry Edward. *Afro-American Folksongs: A Study in Racial and National Music.* [1913]. New York: Frederick Ungar Publishing Co., 1962.

Lee, Valerie, ed. *The Prentice Hall Anthology of African American Women's Literature.* Upper Saddle River, NJ: Pearson Prentice Hall, 2006.

Leonard, Keith D. *Fettered Genius: The African American Bardic Poet from Slavery to Civil Rights.* Charlottesville: University of Virginia Press, 2006.

Levine, Lawrence. *Black Culture and Black Consciousness: Afro-American Folk Thought From Slavery to Freedom.* Oxford: Oxford University Press, 1978.

Levine, Robert S., and Ivy G. Wilson, eds. *The Works of James M. Whitfield: America and Other Writings by a Nineteenth Century African American Poet.* Chapel Hill: University of North Carolina Press, 2011.

Lewis, David Levering, ed. *The Portable Harlem Renaissance Reader.* New York: Penguin, 1994.

When Harlem Was In Vogue. New York: Penguin, 1997.

Locke, Alain, ed. *The New Negro.* [1925]. Reprint, New York: Atheneum, 1968.

The Pamphlet Poets: Four Negro Poets. New York: Simon and Schuster, 1927.

Lomax, Alan, and Raoul Abdul, eds. *3000 Years of Black Poetry.* Greenwich, CT: Fawcett, 1970.

Lorde, Audre. *Cables to Rage.* London: Paul Breman, 1970. Volume 9 in the Heritage Series.

The First Cities. New York: The Poets Press, Inc., 1968.

Lovell, John, Jr. *Black Song: The Forge and the Flame: The Story of How the Spiritual Got Hammered Out.* New York: Macmillan, 1972.

Mackey, Nathaniel. *Discrepant Engagement: Dissonance, Cross-Culturality, and Experimental Writing*. Tuscaloosa, AL and London: University of Alabama Press, 2000.

The Paracritical Hinge: Essays, Talks, Notes, Interviews. Iowa City: University of Iowa Press, 2018.

Major, Clarence. *Configurations, 1958–1998: New and Selected Poems*. Port Townsend, WA: Copper Canyon Press, 1998.

Necessary Distance: Essays and Criticism. St. Paul: Coffee House Press, 2001.

Private Line. London: Paul Breman, 1971. Volume 15 in the Heritage Series.

Swallow the Lake. Middletown, CT: Wesleyan University Press, 1970.

Symptoms & Madness. New York: Corinth Books, 1971.

Major, Clarence, ed. *The Garden Thrives: Twentieth Century African-American Poetry*. New York: Harper Perennial, 1996.

The New Black Poetry. New York: International Publishers, 1970.

Marable, Manning, and Leith Mullings, eds. *Let Nobody Turn Us Around: Voices of Resistance, Reform, and Renewal*. Lanham: Rowman & Littlefield, 2000.

Marcoux, Jean-Philippe. *Jazz Griots: Music as History in the 1960s African American Poem*. Lanham, MD: Lexington Books, 2012.

Marsh, J. B. T. *The Story of the Jubilee Singers; with their Songs*. 4th edn. London: Hodder and Stoughton, 1875.

McCaskill, Barbara, and Caroline Gebhard, eds. *Post-Bellum, Pre-Harlem: African American Literature and Culture, 1877–1919*. New York: New York University Press, 2006.

Miller, Adam David, ed. *Dices or Black Bones: Black Voices of the Seventies*. Boston: Houghton Mifflin, 1970.

Miller, R. Baxter, ed. *Black American Poets Between Worlds, 1940–1960*. Knoxville: University of Tennessee Press, 1986.

Mitchell, Angelyn, ed. *Within the Circle: An Anthology of African American Literary Criticism from the Harlem Renaissance to the Present*. Durham, NC and London: Duke University Press, 1994.

Mitchell, Angelyn, and Danille K. Taylor, eds. *The Cambridge Companion to African American Women's Literature*. Cambridge: Cambridge University Press, 2009.

Mitchell, Verner D., ed. *This Waiting for Love: Helene Johnson: Poet of the Harlem Renaissance*. Amherst: University of Massachusetts Press, 2000.

Moore, Lenard D., ed. and intro. *One Window's Light: A Collection of Haiku*. Greensboro, NC: Unicorn Press, 2018.

Moten, Fred. *In the Break: The Aesthetics of the Radical Black Tradition*. Minneapolis: University of Minnesota Press, 2003.

Mullen, Harryette. *The Cracks Between What We Are and What We Are Supposed to Be*. Tuscaloosa, AL and London: University of Alabama Press, 2012.

Sleeping with the Dictionary. Berkeley, Los Angeles, London: University of California Press, 2002.

S*PeRM**K*T. Philadelphia: Singing Horse Press, 1992.

Tree Tall Woman. Galveston: Energy Earth Communications, 1981.

Mustapha, Mukhtarr. *Thorns and Thistles*. London: Paul Breman, 1971. Volume 16 in the Heritage Series.

Napier, Winston, ed. *African American Literary Theory: A Reader*. New York and London: New York University Press, 2000.

Nielsen, Aldon Lynn. *Black Chant: Languages of African-American Postmodernism*. Cambridge: Cambridge University Press, 1997.

Integral Music: Languages of African-American Innovation. Tuscaloosa: University of Alabama Press, 2004.

Nielsen, Aldon Lynn, and Lauri Ramey, eds. *Every Goodbye Ain't Gone: An Anthology of Innovative Poetry by African Americans*. Tuscaloosa: University of Alabama Press, 2006.

What I Say: Innovative Poetry by Black Writers in America. Tuscaloosa: University of Alabama Press, 2015.

Noland, Carrie, and Barrett Watten, eds. *Diasporic Avant-Gardes: Experimental Poetics and Cultural Displacement*. New York: Palgrave Macmillan, 2009.

Odum, Howard W., and Guy B. Johnson. *The Negro and His Songs: A Study of Typical Negro Songs in the South*. Chapel Hill: University of North Carolina Press, 1925.

Negro Workday Songs. Chapel Hill: University of North Carolina Press, 1926.

Ortner, Johanna. "Lost no More: Recovering Frances Ellen Watkins Harper's Forest Leaves." *Common-Place* 15, No. 4. Summer 2015. http://commonplace.org/book/lost-no-more-recovering-frances-ellen-watkins-harpers-forest-leaves/

Oyewole, Abiodun, and Umar Bin Hassan with Kim Green. *On a Mission: Selected Poems and a History of the Last Poets*. New York: Henry Holt and Co., 1996.

Pardlo, Gregory. *Digest*. New York: Four Way Books, 2014.

Totem. Philadelphia: The American Poetry Review, 2007.

Patton, Venetria K., and Maureen Honey, eds. *Double-Take: A Revisionist Harlem Renaissance Anthology*. New Brunswick, NJ: Rutgers University Press, 2001.

Patterson, Anita. *Race, American Literature and Transnational Modernisms*. Cambridge: Cambridge University Press, 2011.

Patterson, Orlando. *Slavery and Social Death: A Comparative Study*. Cambridge, MA: Harvard University Press, 1982.

Pike, Rev. Gustavus D. *The Singing Campaign for Ten Thousand Pounds: Jubilee Singers in Great Britain*. Rev. edn. New York: American Missionary Association, 1875.

Polite, Allen. *Looka Here, Now! and Other Poems from the Fifties*. Stockholm: Helene Polite, 1997.

Magic Words. London: Paul Breman, 1997. Heritage Pamphlet 5.

Poems. Stockholm: Helene Polite, 1996.

Ramazani, Jahan. *A Transnational Poetics*. Chicago and London: University of Chicago Press, 2009.

Rambsy, Howard II. *The Black Arts Enterprise and the Production of African American Poetry*. Ann Arbor: University of Michigan Press, 2013.

Ramey, Lauri. *The Heritage Series of Black Poetry: A Research Compendium.* London: Routledge, 2008.

Slave Songs and the Birth of African American Poetry. New York: Palgrave Macmillan, 2010.

Rampersad, Arnold. *The Life of Langston Hughes: Volume I: 1902–1941, I, Too, Sing America. Book 1.* Oxford: Oxford University Press, 2002.

The Life of Langston Hughes: Volume II: 1941–1967, I Dream a World. Oxford: Oxford University Press, 2002.

Rampersad, Arnold, ed. *The Oxford Anthology of African-American Poetry.* Oxford: Oxford University Press, 2006.

Randall, Dudley. *Love You.* London: Paul Breman, 1970. Volume 10 in the Heritage Series.

Randall, Dudley, ed. *The Black Poets.* New York: Bantam, 1971.

Rediker, Marcus. *The Slave Ship: A Human History.* New York: Penguin Books, 2007.

Redding, J. Saunders. *To Make a Poet Black.* Ithaca: Cornell University Press, 1988.

Redmond, Eugene B. *Drumvoices: The Mission of Afro-American Poetry: A Critical History.* New York: Anchor Books/Doubleday, 1976.

Redmond, Eugene B., ed. *Drumvoices: A Confluence of Literary, Cultural & Visual Arts.* Volume 17, 2011–12.

Reed, Anthony. *Freedom Time: The Poetics and Politics of Black Experimental Writing.* Baltimore: Johns Hopkins University Press, 2014.

Reed, Ishmael. *catechism of d neoamerican hoodoo church.* London: Paul Breman, 1968, 1969, 1970. Volume 11 in the Heritage Series.

Richardson, Mark, ed. *The Cambridge Companion to American Poets.* Cambridge: Cambridge University Press, 2015.

Rivers, Conrad Kent. *Dusk at Selma.* Cleveland: Free Lance, 1965.

Perchance to Dream, Othello. Wilberforce, OH: Wilberforce University, 1959.

These Black Bodies and this Sunburnt Face. Cleveland: Free Lance, 1962.

The Still Voice of Harlem. London: Paul Breman, 1968. Volume 5 in the Heritage Series.

The Wright Poems, introduced by Ronald Fair. London: Paul Breman, 1972. Volume 18 in the Heritage Series.

Rowell, Charles Henry, ed. *Angles of Ascent: A Norton Anthology of Contemporary African American Poetry.* New York and London: W. W. Norton and Co., 2013.

Sanders, Mark A., "African American Folk Roots and Harlem Renaissance Poetry." In Hutchinson, ed., *The Cambridge Companion to the Harlem Renaissance*, pp. 96–111.

Seward, Theo. F. *Jubilee Songs: As Sung by the Jubilee Singers of Fisk University (Nashville, Tenn.), under the auspices of the American Missionary Association.* New York: Biglow & Main, 1872.

Sherman, Joan R., ed. *African-American Poetry: An Anthology, 1773–1927.* Mineola, NY: Dover, 1997.

African-American Poetry of the Nineteenth Century: An Anthology. Urbana: University of Illinois Press, 1992.

Invisible Poets: Afro-Americans of the Nineteenth Century. Urbana: University of Illinois Press, 1974.

Shields, John C. *Phillis Wheatley's Poetics of Liberation*. Knoxville: University of Tennessee Press, 2008.

Shockley, Evie. *The Gorgon Goddess*. Durham, NC: Carolina Wren Press, 2001.

The New Black. Middletown, CT: Wesleyan University Press, 2011.

Renegade Poetics: Black Aesthetics and Formal Innovation in African American Poetry. Iowa City: University of Iowa Press, 2011.

Simpson, Joshua McCarter. *The Emancipation Car, being an Original Composition of Anti-Slavery Ballads, composed exclusively for the Under Ground Rail Road*. Zanesville, OH: Sullivan and Brown, 1874.

Original Anti-Slavery Songs. Zanesville, OH: Printed for the Author, 1852.

singleton, giovanni. *AMERICAN LETTERS: Works on Paper*. Marfa, TX: Canarium Books, 2018.

Ascension. Denver: Counterpath, 2012.

singleton, giovanni, ed. *nocturnes 1 (re) view of the literary arts*. Fall, 2001.

nocturnes 2 (re)view of the literary arts. Fall, 2002.

nocturnes 3 (re)view of the literary arts. Spring, 2004.

nocturnes 4 (re)view of the literary arts. Fall, 2005.

Smethurst, James, ed. *The New Red Negro: The Literary Left and African American Poetry, 1930–1946*. New York: Oxford University Press, 1999.

Smith, Barbara Herrnstein. "Contingencies of Value." In Robert von Hallberg, ed. *Canons*. Chicago and London: University of Chicago Press, 1984.

Smith, Rochelle, and Sharon L. Jones, eds. *The Prentice Hall Anthology of African American Literature*. Upper Saddle River, NJ: Prentice Hall, 2000. 5–39.

Smythe, Augustine T. et al. *The Carolina Low-Country*. New York: The Macmillan Co., 1931.

Southern, Eileen. *The Music of Black Americans: A History*. 3rd edn. New York: Norton, 1997.

Southern, Eileen, ed. *Readings in Black American Music*. 2nd edn. New York: Norton. 1983.

Spellman, A. B. *The Beautiful Days*. New York: The Poet's Press, 1965.

Things I Must Have Known. Minneapolis: Coffee House, 2008.

Spencer, Eleanor, ed. *American Poetry Since 1945*. London: Palgrave, 2017.

Stuckey, Sterling. *Slave Culture: Nationalist Theory and the Foundations of Black America*. New York: Oxford University Press, 1987.

Taylor, Rev. Marshall W., D.D. *Plantation Melodies*. Cincinnati: Marshall W. Taylor and W. C. Echols, Publishers, 1882.

The New Negro Forget-Me-Not Songster. Cincinnati: University Press James. No date.

Thomas, Lorenzo. *Extraordinary Measures: Afrocentric Modernism and Twentieth-Century American Poetry*. Tuscaloosa and London: University of Alabama Press, 2000.

Thomas, W. H. *Some Current Folk-Songs of the Negro and their Economic Interpretation*. College Station, TX: The Folklore Society of TX, 1912.

Thompson, Gordon E., ed. *Black Music, Black Poetry: Blues and Jazz's Impact on African American Versification*. Farnham, Surrey and Burlington, VT: Ashgate, 2014.

Thompson, Katrina Dyonne. *Ring Shout, Wheel About: The Racial Politics of Music and Dance in North American Slavery*. Urbana: University of Illinois Press, 2014.

Thurman, Howard. *Deep River and the Negro Spiritual Speaks of Life and Death* [1945]. Richmond: Friends United, 1975.

Turner, Mark, ed. *The Artful Mind: Cognitive Science and the Riddle of Human Creativity*. Oxford: Oxford University Press, 2006.

The Literary Mind: The Origins of Thought and Language. Oxford: Oxford University Press, 1998.

US History Online Textbook. ushistory.org. The Harlem Renaissance. 2017. www.ushistory.org/us/46e.asp.

von Hallberg, Robert, ed. *Canons*. Chicago: University of Chicago Press, 1984.

Wagner, Jean. *Black Poets of the United States: From Paul Laurence Dunbar to Langston Hughes*, tr. Kenneth Douglas. Urbana and Chicago: University of Illinois Press, 1973.

Ward, Andrew. *Dark Midnight When I Rise: The Story of the Fisk Jubilee Singers: How Black Music Changed America and the World*. New York: Amistad/HarperCollins, 2001.

Ward, Jerry W., Jr., ed. *Trouble the Water: 250 Years of African-American Poetry*. New York: Penguin, 1997.

Ward, Jerry W., Jr., and Maryemma Graham, eds. *Margaret Walker and Gwendolyn Brooks: A Special Issue. Journal of Ethnic American Literature*. Issue 7, 2017.

Warren, Kenneth W. *What Was African American Literature?* Cambridge, MA: Harvard University Press, 2011.

Watkins, James. *Narrative of the Life of James Watkins, Formerly a "Chattel" in Maryland, US; Containing an Account of His Escape from Slavery, Together with an Appeal on Behalf of Three Millions of Such "Pieces of Property," Still Held Under the Standard of the Eagle*. Bolton: Kenyon and Abbatt, Printers, Market Street, 1852. A facsimile edition of the original is made available by University of North Carolina at: http://docsouth.unc.edu/neh/watkin52/watkin52.html

Poems, Original and Selected. Manchester: Abel Heywood, n.d., 1859?

Watson, John F. (A Wesleyan Methodist). *Methodist Error Or, Friendly, Christian Advice, to those Methodists, who indulge in extravagant emotions and bodily exercises*. Trenton: D. & E. Fenton, 1819.

Watson, Steven. *The Harlem Renaissance: Hub of African-American Culture, 1920–1930*. New York: Pantheon Books, 1995.

Wilentz, Ted, and Tom Weatherly, eds. *Natural Process: An Anthology of New Black Poetry*. New York: Hill and Wang, 1970.

Wilson, Ivy G. *At the Dawn of Dusk: Selected Poetry and Prose of Albery Allson Whitman*. Lebanon, NH: Northeastern University Press, 2009.

Wimbush, Vincent, ed. *African Americans and the Bible: Sacred Texts and Social Textures*. New York: Continuum, 2001.

Woodson, Jon. *Anthems, Sonnets, and Chants: Recovering the African American Poetry of the 1930s*. Columbus: The Ohio State University Press, 2011.

"Anti-Lynching Poems in the 1930s." *Flashpoint*, Spring 2015, Web Issue 17. www.flashpointmag.com/Woodson_Anti_Lynching_Poems_in_the_1930s .htm

Woodson, Jon, ed. and intro. *Cries in the Wilderness: African American Poetry of the 1930s*. Unpublished anthology.

Work, John W. *American Negro Songs: 230 Folk Songs and Spirituals, Religious and Secular*. Mineola: Dover, 1998.

Yu, Timothy. *Race and the Avant-Garde: Experimental and Asian American Poetry Since 1965*. Stanford, CA: Stanford University Press, 2009.

Index

CPSIA information can be obtained
at www.ICGtesting.com
Printed in the USA
BVHW080507111121
621277BV00012B/205